DATE D

The Opening of
the Canadian West

DOUGLAS HILL

The Opening
of the Canadian West

Where Strong Men Gathered

THE JOHN DAY COMPANY
NEW YORK

For GAILA and MICHAEL

her home, his heritage

FIRST AMERICAN EDITION 1967

Library of Congress Catalogue Card Number: 67-14611
PRINTED IN THE UNITED STATES OF AMERICA

Contents

Illustrations

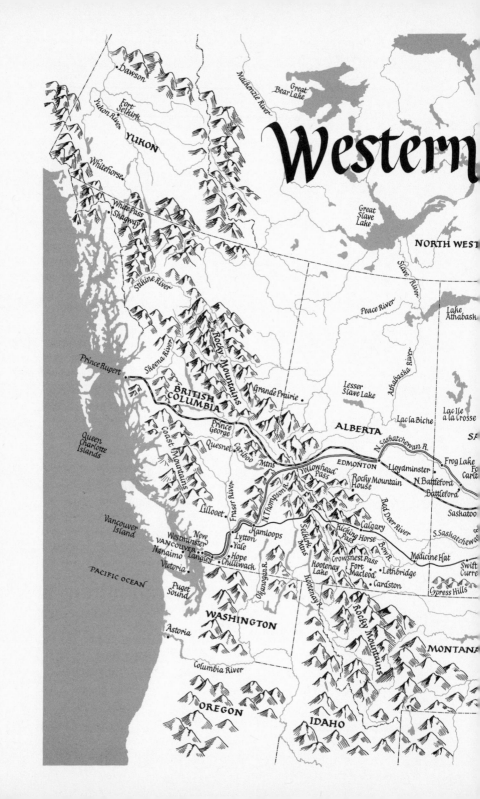

Dawson

Yukon River

fort
Selkirk

YUKON

Whitehorse

White Pass
Skagway

Stikine River

Mackenzie River

Great
Bear
Lake

Western

Great
Slave
Lake

NORTH WEST

Slave River

Peace River

Lake
Athabask

Prince Rupert

Skeena River

Rocky Mountains

BRITISH
COLUMBIA

Grande Prairie

Lesser
Slave Lake

Athabaska River

Lac la Biche

Lac Ile
a la Crosse

SA

ALBERTA

N. Saskatchewan R.

Queen
Charlotte
Islands

Coast Mountains

Prince
George

Quesnel

Cariboo
Mtns

EDMONTON

Lloydminster

Frog Lake

Fo
Cart

N. Battleford

Battleford

Saskato

Yellowhead
Pass

Rocky Mountain
House

Fraser River

Lillooet

N. Thompson R.

Red Deer River

S.Saskatchew

Vancouver
Island

New
Westminster
VANCOUVER
Nanaimo
Langley

Lytton
Yale
Hope
Chilliwack

Kamloops

Selkirk
Mtns

Kicking Horse
Pass

Calgary

Bow R.

Medicine Hat

Swift
Curre

Victoria

Okanagan R.

Crowsnest Pass

Kootenay
Lake

Fort
Macleod

Lethbridge

Cardston

S.Saskatchewan

PACIFIC OCEAN

Puget
Sound

Kootenay R.

Cypress Hills

Astoria

WASHINGTON

Rocky Mountains

MONTANA

Columbia River

OREGON

IDAHO

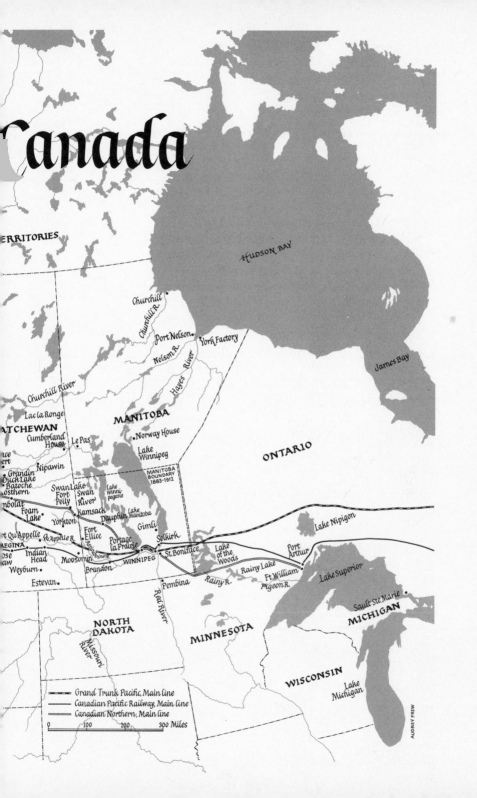

Canada

TERRITORIES

HUDSON BAY

James Bay

Churchill
Churchill R.
Port Nelson
Nelson R.
York Factory
Hayes River

Churchill River

Lac la Ronge

ATCHEWAN
Cumberland House
Le Pas

MANITOBA

Norway House

Lake Winnipeg

ONTARIO

ce
rt
Grandin
Duck Lake
Batoche
osthern
Nipawin

mbolt
Foam Lake
Yorkton
Swan Lake
Fort Pelly
Swan River
Lake winni-pegosis
Kamsack
Dauphin
Lake Manitoba

MANITOBA BOUNDARY 1883-1912

rt Qu'Appelle
REGINA
se
aw
Indian Head
Weyburn
Qu'Appelle R.
Moosomin
Brandon
Fort Ellice
Assiniboine R.
Portage la Prairie
WINNIPEG
Gimli
Selkirk
St. Boniface
Lake of the Woods

Lake Nipigon

Port Arthur

Estevan

Pembina
Red River
Rainy R.
Rainy Lake
Ft William
Pigeon R.

Lake Superior

Sault Ste Marie

MICHIGAN

NORTH DAKOTA
Missouri River

MINNESOTA

WISCONSIN
Lake Michigan

Lake Nipigon

--- Grand Trunk Pacific, Main line
—— Canadian Pacific Railway, Main line
—— Canadian Northern, Main line

0   100   200   300 Miles

AUDREY FREW

Preface

When a young fur trader called Henry Kelsey travelled south-west from Hudson Bay in 1690, he emerged from several hundred miles of treacherous rivers and forest into the immensity of the open prairie, and became the first white man to see Canada's western interior. He could only guess at its actual extent, yet dimly realized that a vast territory lay at the disposal of a relatively few wandering bands of Indians. To Kelsey, the west was a wilderness and an emptiness.

The description remained accurate for nearly two hundred years. From the Great Lakes to the Pacific, the country lay empty when Britain sent Captain Palliser to look at it in 1857, and even when Canada sent Sandford Fleming across it in 1872. Although, previously, explorers and fur traders had traversed the west year after year in increasing numbers, their flimsy camps and scattered posts had made no more impact on the emptiness than anthills on a mountain.

At the time of Canada's Confederation in 1867, two small settlements on the outermost fringes of that virgin wilderness marked its only advances towards civilization. Yet, merely thirty-eight years after that crucial date, the virgin had become something of a matron – the wild lands had been mostly domesticated, the emptiness occupied. Settlers were pouring in by many routes; the spaces between people were rapidly narrowing.

Those years, then, contain the opening of the Canadian west, when its lands were made available for settlement. But it must be understood that, in contrast to the winning of America's west, the settlers in Canada did not themselves do the job of opening. It had been begun by the fur traders who reluctantly planted a few – a very few – seeds of colonization during their 200-year reign. And, after 1867, the job had been carried on by other individuals and agencies – railway builders and revolutionaries, missionaries and gold miners and mounted police – who entered the west before the homesteaders and pioneers, to clear the way. The Canadian west was won *before* it was overrun.

I have chosen to avoid voluminous reference to sources, but the bibliography will indicate how heavily I have leaned on a host of Canadian historians. Here, more direct acknowledgements must be made. To Canada Council, for a generous research grant. To Dr W. Kaye Lamb, Dominion Archivist, and the patient and helpful staff of the Public Archives library, Ottawa. To Miss M. R. Murray and her staff of the Shortt Library of Canadiana, at the University of Saskatchewan – and to the staff of that university's general library as well. To Mr D. Bocking, Assistant Archivist of Saskatchewan, and Mr L. Rodwell, Archival Assistant. And to the staff of the Reading Room of the British Museum, London. Also, I am grateful to many individuals for suggestions and assistance: especially to Mr George Shepherd, curator of the Western Development Museum, Saskatoon; Mr and Mrs D. S. Spafford, of Saskatoon; Mr and Mrs R. Robinson, of Saskatoon; Mr W. Johnson, of New Westminster; and my mother, Mrs C. A. Hill, of Portage la Prairie. Finally – to avoid interrupting an ancient tradition in prefaces of this sort – I must thank my wife for her painstaking help with the research and her perceptive criticism of the writing.

London   D.H.
1967

1

Fortunes in Furs

Europeans first penetrated the Canadian west in search of a fur-bearing rodent called the beaver, a gentle and proverbially industrious water dweller and eater of trees. The penetration took place in the second half of the seventeenth century. Earlier, a fur trade of sorts had grown up in the eastern centres of New France, following a development in men's fashions in Europe. Hatters had discovered that a beaver pelt, without its long guard-hairs, makes perfect felt: and the beaver hat was born. It became the rage, creating a fur fever that was to reach proportions rivalling a gold rush. The traders of France and New France, and the forest Indians of the St Lawrence valley, profited vastly from the little animal which was Canada's first commercial export (and later, appropriately, a national emblem). But soon the beaver's natural abundance, over-harvested, dwindled, and the flagging trade was further disrupted by tribal war among the Indians. The need for new and peaceful regions that were equally plentiful in beaver sent footloose Frenchmen deeper into the wilds, and shifted the focus of the fur trade to the *pays d'en haut*, the great northwest.[1]

The men who carried the fur fever into the unknown lands were, of course, the 'great explorers' whose achievements occupy a disproportionate space in Canadian school histories. Nor do the schoolchildren find a great deal of emphasis on the fact that – while some explorers went to seek the mythical Northwest Passage, and others simply to look at new horizons – most set out on their heroic voyages of discovery for a sound commercial

[1] At this time the term 'northwest' referred to the immediate forest area that drains into Hudson Bay – northwest of the St Lawrence and New France. Later the term (used colloquially) took in the whole of Canada's west. But see note on page 4.

purpose: to find untapped sources of furs. For this reason, in 1661, two remarkable fur traders, explorers and *coureurs de bois*,[1] Radisson and Groseilliers, departed from New France for the Great Lakes, and by so doing inaugurated the western fur trade.

Radisson's account of their journey is secretive and vague enough to leave room for controversy. It is possible (though many doubt it) that they reached the sea at the lower curve of Hudson Bay. It is possible, but again often doubted, that they travelled far enough northwestward from Lake Superior to enter what is now Manitoba. Whether or not they were the first men west, they undeniably showed that canoe routes existed in that direction. They also established trade relations with the Woods Crees, whom Radisson called 'the best huntsmen of all America'.[2] With Cree help, the two explorers were able to return bearing an unusually fine cargo of pelts. But New France's ungrateful officials bled away their profits with a series of duties and taxes, and – more unforgivably – showed no interest in opening up the Bay region for trade. France herself was also cool towards the idea; and Radisson and Groseilliers lacked the capital to launch such an enterprise alone. In a mood of some despondency, they came into contact with English traders from the New England colonies, who listened to their tales of northwestern riches and hastily whisked them to London.

There the English snatched the opportunity that France had missed. Charles II and his government favoured colonial expansion, and favoured even more the prospect of fortunes in furs. Soon a group of businessmen outfitted an exploratory trip to the Bay, led by Groseilliers. (A companion ship, with Radisson aboard, was forced back by bad weather.) Upon landing, they built a fort which they called Charles on a river which they called Rupert,[3] and claimed the land for England. Groseilliers, as interpreter and principal trader, gathered from

[1] *sic*.

[2] The Woods (or Swampy) Crees and their cousins, the mounted buffalo-hunting Plains Crees, formed the most numerous tribe of the western interior. With their allies, the Assiniboines, they ruled most of Manitoba and Saskatchewan, wandering their territory in small, nomadic bands, following the migratory game on which they depended.

[3] On the southeast shore of James Bay, the southernmost extension of Hudson Bay.

local Indians a huge cargo of furs, and the ship returned in triumph. The cargo convinced the businessmen: they rushed to form a trading company to exploit the new territory, and in 1670 the king granted them a Royal Charter under the name of the Company of Adventurers of England Trading into Hudson Bay. Since none of the adventurers actually went adventuring, the title was soon shortened to the Hudson's Bay Company – which in turn became simply 'the Company' or 'H.B.C.'.

The Charter ensured that England and the Crown would benefit from the acquisition of new territory without having to finance its development. The Company received full title to the new area, named Rupert's Land (after the king's cousin, Prince Rupert, first governor of H.B.C.[1]). But those who drew up the document could have had no idea of how much was being given away:

> . . . all those seas, straits, bays, rivers, lakes, creeks, and sounds in whatsoever latitude they shall be, that lie within the entrance of the straits commonly called Hudson Straits, together with all the lands and territories upon the countries, coasts and confines of the seas, bays, lakes, rivers, creeks and sounds aforesaid, which are not already possessed by or granted to any of our subjects, or possessed by the subjects of any other Christian Prince or State. . . .

At the time, no one in England could have conceived of the size of the country (few can today) drained by the giant rivers that flow into the Bay. Yet the Charter did not stop there. H.B.C. also monopolized trading rights (as opposed to outright ownership) in

> all havens, bays, creeks, rivers, lakes and seas into which they shall find entrance or passage by water or land out of the territories . . . aforesaid; and to and with all the natives and people . . . and to and with all other nations inhabiting any of the coasts adjacent to the said territories . . . which are not already possessed as aforesaid. . . .

By these terms, because later explorers would show that

[1] The head of the Company was a 'governor' – rather than a chairman, president or whatever – because H.B.C. had been granted ownership of land, not merely trading rights. The land it owned was a titular colony, and colonies needed governors.

most of the northwest[1] could be traversed by linking waterways, the Hudson's Bay Company ruled alone over western Canada (though not for long).

Within one year of the Company's arrival in the west, the first of a series of competitors launched the first of a succession of trade wars. From 1671 to 1821, H.B.C. remained on the defensive against overpowering rivals, clinging to its few secure positions, trying to ignore the aggressors in hopes that they would go away – as in fact all of them were eventually to do. But before they went, they (and H.B.C., with the stimulus of competition) would have made the first semi-permanent scratches on the pristine surface of the wilderness. Almost in spite of itself, the fur trade gave civilization its earliest footholds in the west.

On the heels of the English came the French, belatedly realizing the value of Radisson's and Groseilliers' achievement, and seeing the danger of the English presence on the Bay. The Indians of the interior – who had formerly brought furs to the Indian middlemen of the St Lawrence (the Iroquois, Hurons and others) – could now trade directly with H.B.C. So, in the winter of 1671, to examine the opposition, a group from New France – including a tough old Jesuit named Albanel – visited the Bay, ostensibly as explorers and missionaries. They found Charles Fort empty, for the H.B.C. men had not yet begun to winter on the Bay; whereupon Albanel nailed up the fleur-de-lis and claimed the lands for France. (This act would later become a French weapon in the diplomatic quarrels that paralleled the rivalry in the forests.) Almost as an afterthought, Albanel baptized a few Indians, while the others did a brisk trade in furs.

[1] To forestall possible confusion: H.B.C. defined 'Rupert's Land' as the area draining into the Bay, and the 'northwest' as the rest of the wilderness – prairies, mountains, Pacific coast, etc. To H.B.C.'s rivals, rejecting the charter's validity, the whole country from the Lakes to the Pacific was the 'northwest'. In the nineteenth century the former usage faded (except in official documents and formal statements), and the latter became the colloquial and more common usage. Still later, after 1871, when both Manitoba and British Columbia had become provinces, the remaining lands (i.e. what now forms Alberta, Saskatchewan, the Yukon and the far north) were termed the 'Northwest Territories' – or, again, simply the northwest.

4

Following this curtain-raiser, the French moved in force into the forests south of the Bay to begin the long and destructive trade war. From simply enticing Indians away from H.B.C. (which busied itself setting up new coastal forts), the French gradually extended the conflict to direct harassment and armed forays. Always, action on the Bay took place against the background of European international politics: one French raid in particular shows the kind of intrigue that coloured these years of rivalry and war.

Some independent traders from New England, reconnoitring the northern forests, landed in 1682 at Nelson River – a valuable site for a post, coveted by both France and England. Soon a French party arrived, including Radisson and Groseilliers, who had tired of England and had defected back to their countrymen. The English arrived a late third, and when they did arrive they lost both ship and provisions in a wreck, and had to depend on the gallant Radisson for survival through the winter. In spring, Radisson imprisoned them, then captured the New England post and imprisoned its inmates as well, carrying them all off to Quebec. But at this time the French proved unwilling to provoke England, so the prisoners were released, and an envoy sent to London to placate English tempers. The envoy was Radisson. And shortly afterwards this irrepressible turncoat was back on the Bay, leading (once again) an *English* expedition – which proceeded to attack and capture the French post on the Nelson set up by Radisson, and to take its occupants as prisoners to London.

So for some years the rivalry continued as it had begun, the English huddled on the coast where the navy could protect them, the French roaming the forest waiting for chances to raid the coast. During the next few years H.B.C. built yet more posts, including Port Nelson at the strategic point mentioned above, and York Fort (or York Factory), which would be H.B.C.'s coastal headquarters for many years. The French had their bases – or way-stations – on the Great Lakes. So far the competition had been restricted mostly to south of the Bay: the real west had scarcely been touched. Then in 1690 H.B.C. bestirred itself in an effort to counteract French influence over the inland Indians. It sent Henry Kelsey into the interior, to instruct the Indians in the joys of the beaver trade and the merits of H.B.C.

5

But this step towards expansion nearly came too late for the Company. The French were pressing hard, in terms of both raiding and trading, and pressed harder when war broke out in Europe in 1702. The English retained their fingerholds in Canada only by virtue of good luck and the Royal Navy. Both sides were threatened financially by the rivalry, at a time of a fluctuating fur market; both were probably relieved when the War of the Spanish Succession ended and the Treaty of Utrecht in 1713 included an assertion of England's clear title to Hudson Bay. The French promptly abandoned the coast to H.B.C. and directed their attentions towards the interior, where the English could not hope to compete.

As yet few H.B.C. men knew how to travel in the interior: how to build and handle canoes, how to live off the land. But the traders from New France, *voyageurs* and *coureurs de bois*, had learned the Indians' skills on water and in the forest. H.B.C. was also hampered by its rigid 'Standards of Trade' – rules (devised by London businessmen who had never seen the fur forests) setting out what quantities of what goods could be exchanged for what quantities of furs. (Application of the Standards demanded a firm, condescending paternalism which formed the general H.B.C. attitude to the Indians.) Thus the English sat on the coast, waiting for the Indians to come to them, never altering their inflexible rates of exchange, while the French went to the source, took the furs for themselves, and provided gifts and special offers to encourage trade. Among these special offers was the rawest of brandy, which created the first Indian firewater addicts. Against salesmanship of this kind the English might never have traded with a single Indian had not H.B.C. been able to offer goods of slightly higher quality than the French, especially in cloth, ironware and Brazil tobacco.

One can only admire the singlemindedness with which H.B.C. refused to profit by the opposition's successful example, at least in terms of inland operations. Even when a few H.B.C. men followed in Kelsey's footsteps (though not so far), their object was to bring Indians to the Bay, never to trade on the spot. To H.B.C., expansion meant only new coastal forts, such as Churchill, built far in the north to bring in the Indians of the sub-arctic barrens. While this establishment was being constructed in 1731, the French were sweeping deep into the interior, establishing a chain of posts that would link Montreal with the heart of the prairies.

These first semi-permanent disruptions of the wilderness were caused by that incomparable French explorer, fur trader and soldier, Sieur de la Vérendrye. With his sons and nephew, La Vérendrye moved westward from Lake Superior in the 1730s, depositing posts at Rainy River and Lake of the Woods, then farther west, at Fort Rouge (today the site of Winnipeg) and Fort la Reine (near present-day Portage la Prairie). In the early 1740s the Vérendryes travelled southwest: the sons explored a wide area that touched the Little Missouri and Cheyenne rivers, then swung north in 1749 to reach the Saskatchewan river. Meanwhile other French explorers added links to the chain, such as the Chevalier de la Corne, who built a post bearing his name on the Saskatchewan. Along this relay route, tons of furs were funnelled to the St Lawrence. And once again the worried Englishmen bestirred themselves.

In 1744 H.B.C., which had by then acquired a few more experienced woodsmen, built Henley House, its first inland post. (Since it was just 150 miles up the Albany river, it barely deserved to be so called.) H.B.C. also sent another Kelsey-like explorer deep into the interior: Anthony Henday (sometimes spelled Hendry), whose journey took him southwest to the prairies and then west to what is now the Red Deer region of Alberta. There he spent some time with the Blackfoot,[1] fierce mounted buffalo[2] hunters who knew nothing of canoes and cared little for furs or white men. After joining a buffalo hunt (Henday is thought to have been the first white man to ride in this wild, suicidal slaughter, which remained a pivot of plains life well into the nineteenth century), he took a long-distance

---

[1] Properly the Blackfoot Confederacy, containing three tribes – Blood, Piegan and Blackfoot. Less numerous than the Crees, the Blackfoot made up in warlike ferocity what they lacked in manpower. They held their rich buffalo country (southern Alberta) against all comers: the Crees, the Snake and Sioux from the south, and the Kootenays from beyond the Rockies who slipped through mountain passes to hunt in Blackfoot territory. Incidentally, though many writers pluralize them as Black*feet*, their name in their own language is 'Siksika' – which is a singular collective noun. So in this book the plural of Blackfoot will be Blackfoot.

[2] This huge, shaggy bovine is properly called *bison*. But no westerners, except the stuffiest of schoolteachers, have ever called it anything but buffalo.

7

look at the Rocky Mountains and returned to the Bay. There he told of the Indians he had met, of the gigantic buffalo herds, each taking days to pass a given point, of rich grasslands suitable for agricultural settlement. But his employers paid him little attention. Though he also reported that the French inland trade seemed extensive and profitable, H.B.C. saw no way of extending its operations. For, once again, war had broken out in Europe – the Seven Years' War – and it was echoed in the fur trade by renewed violence.

As before, however, H.B.C. managed to hold on to its coastal possessions in the face of sporadic French attacks, from sea and land. Finally the focus of the war in North America shifted east, to culminate in 1759 on the Plains of Abraham. When the smoke cleared and the Treaty of Paris was signed in 1763, the French agreed to cede Canada (though there was a bad moment when England nearly took the Caribbean sugar island of Guadaloupe instead). The Hudson's Bay Company, having stubbornly remained in the picture for nearly a century, in spite of fierce opposition and its own hidebound caution, had ridden to victory on General Wolfe's coat-tails and now found itself miraculously the unchallenged ruler of the northwest.

No reversal of policy accompanied the renewal of H.B.C. monopoly. Company men still ventured inland occasionally (with the help of French *voyageurs*, former rivals now become invaluable employees), but the real purpose of these journeys was to induce more Indians to make the arduous and dangerous trip to the Bay. Without competition, the English relaxed. They did not bother to rebuild Henley House, destroyed in the war; and they ignored the inland chain of French posts, allowing them to remain unoccupied and crumbling. Even so they grew fat on furs.

But, predictably, the lull could not last. It might have been even more short-lived had not the great chief of the Ottawa Indians, Pontiac, led an alliance of eastern tribes into the most terrible Indian war the British colonies had ever seen. (The Indians had been disturbed by the sudden accession to power of the English, against whom the French had constantly poisoned their minds.) During the rising, in 1763, Indians attacked the main jumping-off place for westward travellers, Michilimackinac (on Lake Michigan), massacred the inhabitants, and so cut all lines of east-west communication. But soon Pontiac's dream of regaining Indian sovereignty came to an end with his defeat at Bushy Run, and the paths from the St Lawrence to the west were eventually cleared again. To H.B.C.'s dismay, they immediately began to carry some heavy traffic.

Where the fur traders of New France left off, businessmen and adventurers from the newly formed colony of Canada began. These were men with experience of trading around the Lakes or on the Hudson river – men who knew how empty the northwest was, and how ineffectual H.B.C. had been in keeping interlopers out of Rupert's Land. Some of the new interlopers came from the British colonies of New England, as did Alexander Henry,[1] who had been at Michilimackinac during the Indian massacre (he had been saved by an Indian whose blood brother he was), and who became one of the first lone-wolf traders to trespass on H.B.C. territory. The men who followed were French, Scots or English fortune hunters, working out of Montreal on their own capital or with backing from Montreal firms. Usually they were called Canadians, to distinguish them from the English of H.B.C. But to the Company, awakening from its 'sleep by the frozen sea'[2] to find its lands full of enemies again, they were sneeringly known as 'Pedlars'.

But contempt was no substitute for competitiveness. Suddenly the Pedlars seemed to be everywhere, and H.B.C.'s share of the trade dwindled. The heroic efforts of a few H.B.C. men, trekking inland to persuade Indians to visit the Bay, saved the English trade from vanishing entirely, aided by the fact that the newcomers did not present a united front to shut out the Company, but tended instead to compete strenuously and violently with one another. Even so, the Pedlars undeniably became, very quickly, what they and their inheritors always liked to call themselves: the Lords of the Lakes and Forests. When H.B.C. sent Matthew Cocking inland in 1772 he got a short answer from the Indians. The fur-gatherers enjoyed being vied for: they made it clear to Cocking that if H.B.C. wanted furs H.B.C. – like the Pedlars – could come and get them.

Cocking's report forced the Company into taking a radical

[1] Called the Elder, to distinguish him from his nephew who bore the same name into the annals of the fur trade.

[2] The phrase of an eighteenth-century ex-employee and violent critic of H.B.C., Joseph Robson.

9

decision with which, for some time, it had been toying: to build a truly inland post. A sturdy explorer named Samuel Hearne (who at great risk had opened up the northerly Coppermine region) journeyed to the North Saskatchewan river, where he oversaw the beginnings, in 1774, of Cumberland House, the oldest permanent settlement in the western interior. Then, of course, it was not a settlement, not even a fort – just a trading post, a small building made of rough-cut logs with a leaky plank roof. But it was a positive step for the Company.

The Pedlars, generally, ignored it. Indeed, they ignored H.B.C. for years. One inland post in all those trackless miles offered no threat. Their main worry concerned the internecine rivalry that was hotting up as more independent traders came into the west, quarrelling and fighting, forming and breaking alliances with each other, expanding the range of the fur trade into the farther reaches of the forest. In the process they were undermining the long-term stability and security of the trade: for their violent, free-for-all scramble for furs began to alienate the Indians, without whom there could be no trade.

The Indian had suffered, one way or another, from the inception of the fur trade. Initially he had exchanged furs, which he took for granted, for what seemed to him incalculable wealth: guns and powder and shot, knives and axes and metal utensils, cloth and trinkets and tobacco. These wonders, once he had mastered them, made life easier for him – especially the weapons. With guns, the Crees (the first western Indians to contact the whites) became even finer hunters and also invincible fighters. They widened their territory immensely, even at the expense of the powerful Blackfoot – until, of course, the Blackfoot also acquired guns. But there was a drawback. Using white men's implements, the Indian lost with startling speed his knowledge of survival in the old ways. He became entirely dependent for his living on the white man and European goods.

At first the dependence was mutual: the Indians taught the trader the ways of the wilderness, guided him, hunted for him. But eventually the Europeans learned and adapted, leaving the Indian with nothing on which to base his self-possession save the fact that he killed the beaver and produced the furs. Without the constant rivalry between fur traders, the Indian's dependence would have been exploited even more shamefully than it was. In any case, that dependence prevented the Indian from fully enjoying the seller's market that developed when the rivalry reached its heights.

As the fur trade expanded in the second half of the eighteenth century, no Indian tribes escaped this dependence. And no Indians escaped another ugly aspect of the fur fever: the trading of liquor for furs. Alcohol was entirely new to the Indians, and they were given no chance to develop a means of adjusting to it, or controlling its dire effect on them. Not that the effect differed from the effect on whites: Indians became drunk in exactly the same way as anyone else, and enjoyed it just as much.[1] But the traders soon found that drunken Indians were uncontrollable, unpredictable, dangerous. Occasional bloody clashes, in the past, between French traders and brandy-driven Indians seemed to prove the point: drink could turn reasonably friendly natives into belligerent, murderous savages. (No one seemed to reflect on the fact that drink has this effect on more or less everyone at some time. Certainly many Pedlars had no further to go towards savagery than the Indians.)

At any rate, whether or not the belief in the deadliness of drunken Indians was justified, it existed. More readily justifiable was the belief that an addiction to alcohol degraded the Indians. Like any drunk, the addicted Indian abandoned his usual way of life; he hung around trading posts begging drink, failed to provide for his family or do anything save occasionally trap a few beaver to trade for a bottle. Historians of H.B.C. assure us that for a long time the Company refused to counten-ance the use of liquor – at least, its extensive use – in trade. One can see why: as has been mentioned, the Indians first developed a taste for brandy from the French, and in England brandy was hard to come by. Also, H.B.C.'s permanent posts acquired Indian camps around them, because the English used the Indians as hunters, guides, labourers. So H.B.C. naturally preferred to keep its wild neighbours as sober – and peaceful – as possible. The French had had more brandy, were more mobile and less nervous – in spite of the fact that French traders, not H.B.C., had suffered attacks from Indians wanting goods and drink and having no furs to trade.

[1] Interestingly, some entire Indian tribes – including the Chipewyans – remained indifferent to the delights of drink. But, generally speaking, the Crees – and later the Blackfoot – succumbed wholeheartedly.

Closely connected with the problem of drink was that of sex. Few traders of any group refused an opportunity to take an Indian woman to cook, sew and drudge for him and keep his bed warm in winter. (Anthony Henday might not have succeeded in his journey without his Indian helpmate, who not only did most of the work but acted as a go-between with Indians whom they met on the way.) H.B.C. tried only to control, not suppress, this practice: clearly such attachments were a source of stability in a harsh land where few other comforts were available. But H.B.C. usually insisted that its employees formed their attachments with regard for proper Indian procedure – which generally meant outright purchase, accompanied by such formal ceremonies as pipe-smoking with the male head of the woman's family. Some traders married – in British terms – Indian women; at the other extreme, a man might buy the 'use' of a woman for a night or two. The going price at one time was a pint of brandy.

For a long time the principal results of these interracial relations proved favourable: trading relations remained amicable when the whites at a trading post were related by 'marriage' to local Indians, and the half-caste offspring of the unions served usefully as liaisons between the races and also as expert traders in their own right. (More will be said about these children of the fur trade in later chapters.) But the concord between the Indians and the relatively disciplined H.B.C. men sharply contrasted with the atmosphere generated by the more volatile freebooters among the Pedlars. The temperamental difference was striking. After a few unhappy experiences, the Company came to choose its employees for stability, reliability and stamina: the majority came from the dour and hardy fishermen of the Orkney Isles. The Pedlars, who were no one's employees, and who had in most cases been raised on the frontier of eastern Canada among the rugged *voyageurs* and pioneers of the St Lawrence backwoods, had as much stamina and hardihood as any man; but they were not noted for stability and caution. They went west to make a lot of money as quickly as possible, and to have a high and wild time doing so. They introduced the Indians to rum, importing it in a highly condensed form as 'high wines', watering it down and deluging the Indians with it. They took Indian women whenever and however they chose, with no regard for ceremony. They cheated the Indians, bullied them, threatened them to keep them away from rivals. Meanwhile H.B.C. intensified the problem by fighting firewater with firewater: rum was readily available in Britain, and many Indians would accept nothing else in trade. As the pressures increased, Indian leaders grew to hate the traders and the degradation that was being visited upon their people. Soon the hatred began to show itself violently.

Isolated incidents of Indian attacks on whites in the forest – ranging from sneak thievery to armed robbery to murder – had been reported and rumoured from the first days of the Pedlar invasion, but in the 1770s the reports became more frequent, and more authentic. The word spread across the west that Pedlars were being killed in the bush (at least seven died, definitely, in the winter of 1776). The Pedlars went out prepared for trouble – and often precipitated it, as in the following notorious incident. At a Pedlar camp in the Eagle Hills (Saskatchewan) a trader grew tired of being pestered by an Indian for more rum. He gave the Indian a drink heavily dosed with laudanum – no doubt intending merely to put the Indian to sleep. But he had not bothered to take care with the dosage, and the Indian died. The Pedlars left the area hastily, but the dead man's fellows caught up with them later: a Pedlar and several of their employees were killed in the fight.

As the situation worsened the Pedlars began to fear, at any moment in the late 1770s, an all-out Indian rising. The fear sparked a reappraisal: it filtered through to the rowdy traders that the imminent explosion in the west had been created by their no-holds-barred rivalry. So, for mutual protection and continuing profits, the Pedlars formed their first major 'co-partnership', as they called it.

They would form other, more important unions later; the first lasted only a short time, largely because the threat that justified it faded away. The Indians did not rise. They were deterred by another gift brought by the white man, one to be set beside guns and drink: disease. An epidemic of smallpox broke out in 1781, and spread westward like a prairie fire, carried by Indians who fled into the wilds to escape it. There was no escape. Whole bands were wiped out completely; no western tribe remained unscathed. And when the epidemic had run its course it had slaughtered about one-third of the total Indian population of the prairie provinces.

Strangely, few whites were affected. The smallpox must have taken a very mild form – a fact that heightens the tragedy of the Indians. Thus the whites could and did move among the Indians at the worst of the epidemic. To their credit, some H.B.C. men and Pedlars devoted themselves to helping in whatever ways they could: tending the sick, hunting for them, burying the dead and burning infected clothing. For others, on both sides, it was business as usual: if there were no Indians left alive in a camp to trade, these businessmen removed beaver robes from the corpses.

But then business had persisted throughout the days of Indian hostilities. The Pedlars had continued to increase their numbers, and their posts were scattered across the west, tying the fur lands up in a neat bundle. Then in 1778 the Pedlar Peter Pond, a morose lone wolf from Connecticut, fought his way alone into the north, reaching the almost virgin Athabasca region and opening up the richest fur country of all. It was a doubly important step. Pond's travels and crude but accurate maps showed the way for later explorers, and hinted at a likely route to the western sea: not a mythical Northwest Passage for ships, but a canoe route by which the Pedlars could establish themselves – as they were later to do – on the Pacific.

And all the while H.B.C. plodded cautiously on, not making its shareholders rich, yet not going bankrupt. Some Indians still came' to trade: their anger was not directed at the English, and they needed the heavy goods brought by H.B.C. ships. (The Pedlars' fast canoes preferred lighter wares, like rum.) Cumberland House traded steadily; so did Hudson House, built in 1779 farther west on the North Saskatchewan. The value of these posts became clear when new trouble arose on the Bay. Peter Pond's Athabasca achievement began to divert northern Indians, and the coastal trade suffered. Worse, H.B.C. prestige and finances were rocked by a ricochet from the American Revolution. An intrepid French captain (whose country had finally allied itself with the American colonies) sailed into the Bay and wrecked York Fort and Churchill. The inland posts had to subsidize repairs. But H.B.C. luck held: it obtained a badly needed breathing space from a disturbance among the Pedlars.

The smallpox had scattered the Indians, making Pedlar fur-gathering more arduous (remember that their supply lines stretched 2,000 miles back to Montreal). Also, the general co-partnership had split up in a flurry of wrangling, undoubtedly provoked by a murder in the north – in which Peter Pond was reportedly involved. The evidence was thin and circumstantial, but Pond was a moody, violent man whose reputation lent credence to the rumour. At any rate, the renewed rivalry did not last long. With the riches of Athabasca waiting for them, the Pedlars were unwilling to repeat old errors. In 1784 they came together in another common concern. This time they acquired a new name: the North-West Company. The Pedlars had become Northwesters.

The alliance was a trading partnership, with the shares divided among Montreal backers and the 'wintering partners' – the men who annually challenged the western bush and its fierce winters. But the shares were not divided evenly, and the fledgling company made the mistake of giving only one share to Peter Pond (who, whatever his nature, deserved better as the pathfinder to Athabasca) and entirely excluding a trader named Peter Pangman. The latter, a restless and independent woodsman who had gone on trading for himself while a member of the previous co-partnership, resented this exclusion. In Montreal he persuaded a firm to back him in a separate venture. And he was joined, in the west, by a young man named Alexander Mackenzie, who was so infected with the western restlessness as to be nicknamed 'Perpetual Motion', and who was to take second place to no man as an explorer and fur trader.

Pangman's group, wasting no time, sent one John Ross to Athabasca to build near Pond and drain off some of his trade. Mackenzie went to trade in what is now northern Manitoba. Pangman concerned himself with the heartland, on the Saskatchewan river. There he engaged in the familiar manœuvring of the fur trade, building near rival posts to undercut their monopoly of an area. The manœuvring could lead to outrageous extremes. In 1784 an independent trader named McKay (there were still a few such loners in the west, mostly ignored by the larger groups) built a post on an island in the North Saskatchewan river. H.B.C. followed him, building Manchester House on the same island. Within weeks the Northwesters set up a third post there. Then Peter Pangman arrived to build a post. And finally, to top it all, out of nowhere came a French-Canadian independent named Champagne, who provided the fifth post on the overcrowded island. When Indian canoes approached the island, the whole crowd of traders would rush down to the water's edge, jostling and scuffling, calling out the advantages of their separate posts. The Indians must have been as confused as tourists in an Arab bazaar.

Inevitably the Pangman–Northwester conflict led to rough harassment, then to bloodshed. Also inevitably, perhaps, the climax of the violence involved Peter Pond. In Athabasca, Pond and his men clashed with John Ross: the brawl became a gunfight, and Ross was killed. Whether Pond himself pulled the deadly trigger has been doubted, but some responsibility was surely his. The killing drove him from the fur country, and also (once again) sobered the competitors, who resolved to end these ruinous rivalries once and for all. In 1787 the Pangman–Mackenzie group amalgamated with the North-westers under the all-inclusive name of the North-West Company.

For the rest of their separate existence the Northwesters were the most powerful organization in the west – and, for many writers since, the most glamorous and picturesque. From Simon McTavish, the 'Marquis', who ruled the business side in Montreal, to the larger-than-life wintering partners – Mackenzie, Pangman, the Frobisher brothers, and more – they formed a Hollywood epic come true. Even so, their rule was not unchallenged. The N.W.C. met – or collided with – three sets of organized competitors in the years following 1787: a new company of Canadians out of Montreal; a group from the U.S.A., whose challenge came on the Pacific coast; and the Hudson's Bay Company. Though these conflicts overlapped one another in time, for clarity's sake they will be described separately.

The Treaty of Versailles, in 1783, gave the new U.S.A. sovereignty over the forest lands *south*west of the Great Lakes, where a number of British and Canadian trading concerns had been harvesting furs for years. Under U.S. pressure the tres-passers packed up and left, heading northwest to look for pickings at the N.W.C.'s feast. Mostly they arrived in small groups, or as individuals, and presented the Northwesters with no threat. The N.W.C. had hired thugs, 'bullies', to protect their dominance, and usually the independents could be frightened off by the threat of violence – or by its reality, in which the bullies smashed the canoes of the interlopers, destroyed their goods, frightened Indians away from them, and beat up the men themselves.

After some years of this the new Canadian traders imitated Northwester practice, and combined into a partnership (in 1800), which they named the XY Company. (The North-West Company marked its bales of furs 'NW', so the new rivals chose two other letters.) At its head was Alexander Mackenzie, whose previous adventures make an epic in themselves.

After the North-West Company had been launched Mackenzie had moved into Athabasca, planning to follow up certain tales of routes to the sea that he had had from Peter Pond. In 1789 he had found and followed the magnificent river that was named after him, to reach the Arctic Ocean. Shortly afterwards he clawed his way through the Rockies, by means of the Peace River and other waterways, down to the coast to become, in 1793, the first man to reach the northern Pacific coast overland. Now the farthest reaches of the west were within the ambit of N.W.C. and Montreal; and the next year Mackenzie returned to that city, convinced that the Northwesters' future lay in the far west and the far north, and that vastly shorter supply routes would be essential. To obtain them, he advocated a radical step: union with H.B.C., in order to get access to the Bay. But Simon McTavish strongly opposed any such ideas, and constant clashes with the old Marquis soon drove Mackenzie out to seek less conservative air. He found it with the XY Company, and brought his knowledge and experience to bear in the war with the Northwesters.

Once again – for it seemed that no fur traders of any group could profit by past mistakes – the pattern of rivalry took shape. The XYs kept pace with N.W.C. in the familiar posts-beside-posts race, and also in terms of violence, hiring their own bullies, and terrorizing a few Indians. In one case, Alexander Henry the Younger,[1] a Northwester, talked an Indian out of trading with an XY man. The latter's response, apparently the most common reaction to such a situation, was to try

[1] See note on page 9.

17

to urge and bribe the Indian to kill Henry. (The Indian didn't.) Eventually fights and beatings became part of the day's work, with shootings and violent deaths fairly unremarkable occurrences. Then the Indians joined in, since the atmosphere of untrammelled violence always harmed them more than anyone. As in the 1770s, traders were attacked and killed and posts destroyed on both sides – not in any great numbers, but enough to give the two factions pause. As before, they woke up to their (and their profits') danger, and found an answer in amalgamation. (The way had been smoothed for Mackenzie's return to the N.W.C. fold by McTavish's death.) In 1805 the XY Company vanished and its men became Northwesters.

In the meantime, far to the west, a more complex competition had begun, in which more than swashbuckling and violence would be needed if the Northwesters were to win beyond the Rockies. There the rivals were Americans, and American big business at that; international politics became involved, as a controversy grew up over the ownership of recently explored wilderness.

By the late 1790s Northwester routes to the northern Rockies, and to the Peace River and Athabasca regions, had been completed, and a major way-station erected in 1794, called Fort Augustus. (H.B.C. built Edmonton House next to it: the two posts and their successors formed the foundations of the present city of Edmonton, Alberta.) Farther west at the mountains' foot, Rocky Mountain House went up in 1799. From there, in the wake of Mackenzie, the Northwesters moved across the Rockies and south towards the valley of the Columbia river, in a never-ending search for untouched sources of beaver.

Simon Fraser, first, from Rocky Mountain House in 1807, travelled by means of lesser waterways to the river that bears his name – but believed he had reached the Columbia. So, in spite of Fraser's tortuous struggle against torrents and rapids on his way down that terrible waterway, the Northwesters were no nearer to being established in the heartland of what is today British Columbia. And now their approach became a race with U.S. traders who also coveted the Columbia river, that wide and navigable route to the Pacific from the transmontane forests.

Since the American Revolution, relations between British

North America and the U.S.A. had grown openly strained. The Americans resented Britain's continuing and (to them) oppressive presence north of them. (They had, indeed, staged an abortive invasion of Canada during the revolution.) In turn, the boundary settlement in the Treaty of Versailles angered the Canadians. The new boundary ran westward from Lake Superior (at the Pigeon river) roughly along the 49th parallel as far as the Mississippi. At the time, of course, the western frontier of U.S. settlement began at the Ohio river: it was unnecessary, then, to worry about precisely where the International Boundary would be drawn in the deep west. Canada did worry about the line's beginning on the Lake, which robbed the northwest fur trade of its two major depots, Michilimackinac and Grand Portage, and which made the southwest fur forests American. Then in 1794 'Jay's Treaty' (named after the U.S. Chief Justice who negotiated it) gave each side free access to the principal water routes of the fur trade, whether U.S. or Canadian. The Americans were again irate: the natural outlet of these routes had always been Montreal, which restored Canadian domination over the whole trade, south and north. Canadian traders who had previously worked the southwest smugly formed the Michilimackinac Company and moved back into the Mississippi valley. The Americans complained, and competed, and in 1808 – despite all treaties – were goaded into attacking and capturing some Canadian boats. The Canadians, foreseeing future violence, backed off and (as has been seen) set out for the northwest. The few who stayed were eventually swallowed up by a firm that made its appearance in 1811, called the American Fur Company.

It was the brainchild of that archetypal tycoon John Jacob Astor, and it shortly had a firm grip on the Mississippi and was stretching out tentacles towards the Columbia. American overland expeditions – especially that of Lewis and Clark in 1804-5 – had opened a route to the Pacific, along which Astor rushed his men, having hastily formed a Pacific Fur Company. In the north the Canadians had placed their entry in the race as well: David Thompson, surveyor and explorer, after whom Fraser had earlier named the Fraser river's great tributary.

Various hesitations delayed Thompson, and the Americans reached the Columbia first. They established themselves in the forests of the present states of Washington and Oregon, building a scattering of posts as well as their headquarters, Astoria. True to the old pattern, the Northwesters came along and built as well, rejecting the American claim to the region. Competition hovered on the threshold of violence. And over it all the question remained: would the Columbia valley be British or American?

As the rivalry deepened, the U.S.A. precipitated a good many crises by declaring itself – in 1812 – an ally of Napoleon. (America had grown enraged by a series of British infringements of maritime rights, national honour, and similar delicate matters.) The war of 1812 was fought mainly in the east, so has little bearing on this narrative; but it had its side effects on the Pacific. When the war was announced the Northwesters (through their powerful organization in London) petitioned Britain for a gunboat's protection. A ship duly arrived, but by then the Northwesters had already used its coming as a threat to lever the Americans out of the Columbia. The Americans managed to save face by selling, not surrendering, Astoria and the other posts, and left the N.W.C. to be lords of the Pacific lakes and forests as well. (The *title* to the region remained open for years, however, and later formed the nucleus of the noisy Anglo–American wrangle called the Oregon question, during which the seeds of British Columbia were sown. But see Chapter 3.) Now the Northwesters' hands were freed, and it could concentrate on its last remaining enemy.

Throughout the other struggles the N.W.C. had remained conscious of H.B.C., but unworried by it – even though H.B.C., following a policy of action, had built posts across the west, shadowing the Northwesters almost everywhere they went. H.B.C. did not cross the Rockies, but it had tried – during the height of the N.W.C. war against the XYs – to invade the Athabasca region. Unfortunately, in the heat of war the Northwesters had refined their competitive methods, and a relatively simple array of harassment and terrorism soon sent the H.B.C. men stumbling southwards again. The N.W.C. had tried to follow up its advantage by seeking, in London, to break the H.B.C. hold on its only advantage: the short route to Hudson's Bay.

Alexander Mackenzie, now Sir Alexander and the uncrowned king of the Northwesters, began manœuvring for a royal charter, which he hoped would give the N.W.C. a trading monopoly on the Pacific and also would give it prestige enough to shake down the old H.B.C. charter, and open up rights of access to the Bay. But the government hedged. Impatient, Mackenzie turned to the stock market, setting out to gain control of H.B.C. through buying shares. (His purchasing agent in these transactions was a young earl named Selkirk.) But the takeover bid failed. So, in 1805, did the attempt to *buy* rights of access from H.B.C.

The Northwesters fell back on more reliable methods. They began another rule of terror in the bush – H.B.C. posts harassed and fired upon, its men assaulted, its furs stolen, its boats wrecked, its few loyal Indians driven off. The older company was to be forced into a position where it had to negotiate a peace, on Northwester terms, or go under. The process was inexorable. H.B.C. had to fortify and extensively man its posts, which ate into profits and dividends, while it took out drastically reduced quantities of furs. Inevitably, stock market prices reflected its dwindling fortunes: and in 1808 Mackenzie began again to buy shares, reaching for control.

But he was forestalled. The man who stopped him was his purchasing agent, Lord Selkirk, whose arrival as an eleventh-hour saviour begins a new, climactic chapter in this story. It brought about the last and worst battle in the wars of the fur trade, and it also brought about the true beginning of settlement in the west.

2

The First Western Settlers

For its first 150 years of operation, the Hudson's Bay Company had viewed the subject of western settlement with indifference bordering on passive opposition. As has been seen, Rupert's Land was officially an English colony in the terms of the Charter of 1670: so H.B.C. had been created, on paper, as a colonizing agency, not just a trading company. But the Charter – in which privileges far outweighed obligations – did not *require* H.B.C. to colonize, and it was unwilling to pursue any unnecessary enterprise. At first, to be sure, H.B.C. believed – from the appearance of the Bay's bleak coast – that the whole of Rupert's Land would be inhospitable to settlement. (Many responsible people held this belief even as late as 1867.) So the Charter's settlement aspects became a neglected formality, and the existence of Rupert's Land was justified by trade. Late in the 1670s a faction within H.B.C., led by Lord Shaftesbury (a convinced empire builder), pressed the Company to live up to the Charter's implications regarding settlement. The Company was briefly split over the issue, but soon a trade faction led by James Hayes triumphed, and thoughts of settlement again faded in H.B.C. minds.

Many western trading posts, of course, were permanent establishments – made more so as the traders settled down with Indian women. Where it was possible, agriculture was encouraged at H.B.C. posts, though on a small scale, only to provide some change in diet for the men. Thus some groundwork was laid for these posts' transition, much later, into outright settlements.

In the eighteenth century, as in the seventeenth, no real concern for colonization appeared in the fur trade. Nor was there any real need. Britain was not overcrowded, so emigration was not necessary, and for those who wanted to emigrate the wholly habitable American colonies were available. H.B.C.'s most vehement eighteenth-century critic, Arthur Dobbs, who tried to break the Company's monopoly in the 1730s, attacked its non-policy regarding settlement: but to Dobbs H.B.C.'s failure to penetrate inland and, especially, to search for a Northwest Passage were more serious sins of omission. When Dobbs's challenge to the Charter failed, colonization in Rupert's Land once again became a dead issue and remained buried for nearly 100 years – that is, until the advent of Lord Selkirk.

Early in his young manhood, Thomas Douglas, fifth Earl of Selkirk, had acquired certain liberal and humanitarian leanings, though they were tempered by his inherited Scots aristocratic conservatism. This liberality, together with the ideas and proposals that grew out of it, allows his biographers to present him as a high-minded philanthropist. His aristocratic position permitted his enemies to see him as a selfish laird intent only on aggrandizing the Douglas name and fortune. He was, of course, a measure of both: liberal enough to be aware of the people's sufferings in the backwaters of Great Britain at the turn of the century and humanitarian enough to want to do something about it; canny enough to seek a way that would do the job and also pay for itself. The way was to be colonization.

The first Selkirk colonial scheme grew from the Irish troubles of the late 1790s – the aftermath of the rebellion in Ireland which had been so harshly crushed by the British. Selkirk dreamed of Irish Catholic colonies giving these unhappy people a new life and religious freedom – and which, incidentally, might remove the most turbulent Irishmen from dangerous proximity to Britain. He had just the place in mind: the Red River valley in Rupert's Land, which he had read about in Sir Alexander Mackenzie's *Voyages*.

The Colonial Office, however, squelched his dream. It felt that the Irish were too intractable to be successful colonists, and that the Hudson's Bay Company held title to the Red River region, which should be left to it. Also, the cold war in Europe following the Peace of Amiens led to a feeling in Britain that likely recruits for the army should not be wasted on colonies. But, in spite of this refusal, Selkirk did not abandon his vision. He adapted it, thinking now in terms of

Highlanders rather than the Irish, and of elsewhere in British North America.

Indeed, the Highland Scots needed someone to think of them. These were the days of the Highland Clearances, no less infamous a case of feudal cruelty than was ever devised in the Middle Ages. After the defeat of Bonnie Prince Charlie in the mid-eighteenth century, England had sought to undercut Scots nationalism deviously by transferring ownership of land from individual crofters to clan chieftains. So the crofter's bare subsistence from his tiny, infertile holding was reduced further by the rent he paid. Then, many chieftains, seeking to live like great lairds, found the income from rents insufficient for their newly expanded needs. In one or two generations, several Highland estates were facing ruin. The landowners, often with the advice of southern land sharks, could see only one practical, economic solution. Like most practical, economic solutions, it was harsh and inhumane: it meant forcing the crofters off the land and opening the estates to sheep farming.

The worst of the clearances took place on the Sutherland estates, where crofters were wrenched off land that their families had tilled for centuries and sent – uncompensated, often penniless, with no food or shelter waiting for them – to bleak fishing areas on the coast. Naturally, those who could, emigrated; those who could not, starved.

Selkirk had been among them (as he had been among the Irish) to see their plight for himself. He also saw that the bulk of the emigrants went to the U.S.A., and he regretted the loss to the Empire of these hardy, thrifty, reliable people. Soon his blandishments took effect on the government. In 1803 Selkirk managed to deflect some 800 Scots from the U.S.A. and settle them on land granted to him by the Crown in Prince Edward Island. There, once they adapted, they thrived. Selkirk's next century, bringing colonists to Baldoon (Ontario), proved less successful and was abandoned after the Americans overran it in 1812.

But during these years the Earl wandered through Canada, gathering knowledge and experience to reinforce his dreams. He noted that the fur traders controlled the west, and that the support of one of the great companies would be needed before a colony could begin to be established in the interior. He also became acquainted in 1804 with the Northwesters, and was fêted at their uproarious Beaver Club in Montreal. But it was H.B.C. with its Charter and imperial ties that interested him most.

The association between Selkirk and the Northwesters was renewed in 1808 when Sir Alexander Mackenzie used Selkirk as his agent, or buyer, in his bid to obtain a controlling portion of H.B.C. stock. But apparently Selkirk, during this assignment, also bought for himself. During the previous year, he had married, and his wealthy and successful brother-in-law was as interested in H.B.C. trade as Selkirk was in H.B.C. land. Together they acquired a sizeable portion of H.B.C. stock; slowly the arrangement with Sir Alexander was dropped. The Northwesters seem to have had no inkling of Selkirk's colonizing impulses, until they saw Sir Alexander's bid fail and Selkirk's succeed. He and Andrew Wedderburn (later Colvile), his brother-in-law, held a commanding position on the Company Committee.

Next Selkirk asked H.B.C. for a grant of land, in order to place a settlement on Red River. The Northwesters howled objections. His Lordship was merely trying to carve a personal estate out of the northwest. A colony would wreck the fur trade; colonists would be massacred by Indians. Nevertheless, the powerful Selkirk faction carried the proposal, and the grant was made.

It gave Selkirk 116,000 square miles of Rupert's Land – an area five times as big as Scotland, lying mostly in the present province of Manitoba, but dipping into Saskatchewan and down into the present states of Minnesota and North Dakota. The area was named 'Assiniboia'. The terms of the grant required the Earl to set aside one-tenth of the land for H.B.C. men who might retire there; and it required him to settle 1,000 families in Assiniboia within ten years. He and the settlers were forbidden to engage privately in the fur trade, but could use H.B.C. facilities at the Bay to bring in supplies.

For all this, Selkirk paid a token fee of ten shillings; but he was to finance the entire operation. The Company, in theory at least, would profit: not only would the colony be a haven for retired employees who wanted to stay in the west, but its agriculture could be a source of food for H.B.C. posts, diminishing the need for English supplies. And the colony's presence, solid and permanent, would reinforce H.B.C.'s title to the land.

The North-West Company was well aware of these advantages, especially the last. It also saw that the colony would straddle the Northwester's main routes from the east, and might interfere with their lines of communication. More important, the colonists might threaten a vital source of fur-trade food, the vast buffalo herds of the Red River plains. So the Northwesters prepared themselves to ensure the colony's failure by means of every technique, underhand or otherwise, in their well-stocked repertoire.

Meanwhile, the enthusiastic Earl planned and organized for his first group of settlers. It is unlikely that he realized how determined the Northwesters were to oppose him, or to what lengths they would go. It is also doubtful whether the Northwesters realized the depths of the Earl's own determination and fighting spirit. By the time the opponents had taken each other's measure, each was too deeply committed to give up. And the hapless colonists were caught in the middle.

The story of the first colonists in the west would be a nearly unbelievable account of hardships, dangers, misfortunes and mismanagement, even without the Northwesters' harassment. In many ways it is a heartbreaking story – mostly in terms of the colonists, torn out of their homeland, nervously going to a savage country where all their worst nightmares were to come true within months of their arrival, but also in terms of Selkirk, who had to watch his shining dreams of settlement grow tarnished and cracked, no matter how hard he worked or what compromises he made. Eventually his struggles and disappointments were to be the death of him. By then the process would have killed a number of settlers as well.

The first stages of Selkirk's plan began ambitiously. He sent out a prospectus to attract investment, hoping thus to help pay for the actual emigration. The prospectus praised the lands:

> . . . there are immense open plains without wood, fine dry grassland, much of it capable of immediate cultivation . . . This is an advantage that no other part of British America possesses by nature. . . .

But, countering these superlatives, he did not deny that settlers might be 'afraid of venturing to a new and [to them] unknown country'. He was not offering shares in the project as a quickly profitable speculation, but as a solid and long-term investment in empire. His opponents soon capitalized on his candour. Bishop John Strachan, who had some experience of the New World and who led the array of critics, termed Selkirk's plan

> one of the most gross impositions that ever was attempted on the British public, and must be attended with the most baneful consequences to all those unfortunate men who, deluded by the false promises held out to them, shall leave their homes for such a dreary wilderness.

The Northwesters added a few forthright assertions, stating among other things that 'the difficulty of communication will prevent the colonists from receiving any supplies, unless at an enormous expense', that 'there is the strongest possibility that the first colonists will be massacred by the Indians', and that 'all the promises urged in the Prospectus to leave Great Britain are false and delusive'. Clearly, few holds were to be barred. And, in the event, the propaganda (along with political storm warnings in Europe) frightened off investors. Selkirk and his family, and a few friends, carried the expense themselves.

Selkirk now chose Miles Macdonell[1] to lead the first expedition, which would prepare the way for colonists. He had met Macdonell in Canada, and respected him as a strong man with military experience and first-hand knowledge of backwoods pioneering. Macdonell thus became the first governor of the colony, and, as a start, went to Ireland to seek recruits. A tough Scots fur trader named Colin Robertson went to the Highlands and the northern islands for the same purpose. (Robertson, of whom more will be heard later, was an ex-Northwester who had defected to H.B.C. after a disagreement over policy.) A third Selkirk recruiting agent visited Glasgow. All the recruits were to gather at Stornoway, the main Hebridean port, to embark on H.B.C. ships for the Bay.

But the opposition followed the agents and undermined their every effort. Anonymous articles in the widely-read Inverness *Journal* (actually written by a leading Northwester, Simon M'Gillivray) described in lurid detail the terrors that were in store for anyone foolish enough to join the venture. So the turnout was another disappointment: Selkirk had hoped for

[1] His name, like most Scots names at the time, receives almost as many different spellings as there are mentions of it. The variant used here seems the most probable.

about 200 men, but only 125 arrived. And this recruitment, remember, was only of men *hired* to go out and pave the way and then return, if they wished. Selkirk was offering a three-year contract, good wages, and 100 acres of land if a man wished to stay. Northwester propaganda offset even these attractions.

So already the Earl's plans were awry. Too few men had arrived, and many of those were nervous and doubtful. Then the ships were delayed in reaching Stornoway. Some men deserted; others threatened to follow unless their wages were raised. Expenses mounted. And the eager Northwesters were on hand, whispering, agitating, bribing. Finally in July 1811 the ships were loaded and set off, dangerously late, bearing an exhausted Macdonell and his disgruntled emigrants, now numbering only 105. (And some of those had been engaged as H.B.C. employees, and would go no farther than the Bay.)

Macdonell had intended to precede the real settlers by a year, so as to have homes built and crops planted by the time the families arrived, but the delayed departure and a rough crossing brought the ships into the Bay far too late, forcing the newcomers to winter at York Factory. There, Macdonell was astonished to meet hostility from the H.B.C. employees, whom he had naturally expected to be on Selkirk's side. Perhaps the Company men simply disliked this new 'governor' and his complaining crew of greenhorns; on the other hand the H.B.C. men were professional fur traders who could foresee, as well as the Northwesters, the danger to their way of life if settlement proved successful. Thus their attitude aggravated the distress among the new colonizers. And matters grew worse as Macdonell's men set out to build a camp for the winter – knowing little about axes and logs, jeered at by the H.B.C. men, and driven hard by Macdonell, who apparently favoured a brusque and overbearing approach.

As winter took hold of the Bay, discontent spread. Food soon became a problem, and scurvy broke out. Macdonell's men separated into regional groups and drew battle lines. Orkneymen fought with the Irish, the Glaswegians fought with everyone. On New Year's Day seven Irishmen and five Orcadians were in a critical condition after a general mêlée. Shortly afterwards, a prominent troublemaker among Macdonell's men led a group into armed mutiny. York Factory reluctantly came to the rescue, subdued the mutineers, and took them on as H.B.C. men to prevent further trouble in Macdonell's camp. Finally, after a series of lesser troubles, spring came, and Macdonell led his remaining colonizers south to prepare for the settlers who would be coming – all too soon – that summer. The journey was slow and difficult, more so because the emigrants had to learn about the special tribulations of western rivers and portages, forests and mosquitoes. But in August 1812, the first men of the Red River Settlement arrived at their destination: the Forks of the Red and Assiniboine rivers. Aside from Macdonell, only nineteen of the original recruits had completed the journey from Stornoway.

At the Forks H.B.C. had ignored requests to prepare for their arrival: no provisions were waiting. Also, the buffalo usually went south, away from the Forks, in autumn. Macdonell was forced to buy food from the nearest trading post – the Northwester's Fort Gibraltar. The enemy were friendly and polite, but villainy hid behind their smiles.

Now Macdonell began to hurry his men – to build a permanent settlement, to lay up stores of food. He chose a spot two miles from Fort Gibraltar and called it Point Douglas: there some of the men began building a storehouse and turning over the sod for a quick crop of winter wheat. Others went south along the Red River to Pembina (now in Minnesota), a fur-trade centre where both companies had posts, and where the buffalo grazed at this time of the year. There too the colonizers gathered provisions and set up winter quarters. Progress was slow due to their ineptness with axes, but eventually living quarters were more or less ready, stores of food put away at both bases, and an Indian hunter engaged at the Forks. Then the first settlers arrived at the Forks to help finish the work.

The new contingent of colonists had been recruited in the teeth of more and varied Northwester opposition. In Parliament, an M.P. who held shares in the North-West Company impugned Selkirk's motives. In print, M'Gillivray continued his anti-Selkirk persuasion in the Inverness *Journal*. At many important gatherings the deeply respected explorer, Sir Alexander Mackenzie, got a hearing for his attacks on H.B.C. and Selkirk. And a London Northwester, writing to the Montreal base, made it clear that they had not yet begun to fight:

. . . the opposition ought to be general and followed up at almost any expense. . . . The object in view is well worth making sacrifices for. . . . In short, no means should be left untried to thwart Selkirk's schemes.

In the west, the wintering partners were to take the directive literally.

Selkirk, however, blithely continued to gather emigrants from western Scotland and western Ireland, not trail-blazing men but families, women and young children. In June 1812 they sailed from Sligo, Ireland, about seventy in number, including eleven children under eight years old. Again it was a rough crossing, made worse by the tyrannical leader of the expedition, an Irishman named Keveny. (Selkirk was a notoriously poor judge of men.) The crew nearly rose in mutiny, but a seaman informed the captain, who forestalled trouble at gunpoint. The Atlantic was as turbulent as ever, and during one frightful storm, when all hands were sure the ship would go down, an emigrant woman – Mrs McLean – gave birth to a daughter.

But the ship stayed afloat, and reached York Factory, where the travellers met inadequate preparations and frequent delays; and the trip south was strenuous as always, or worse because the McLeans insisted on bringing along their sheep as well as babies. Reaching the Forks in October, the emigrants learned that Macdonell had decided to winter in Pembina (leaving five men to occupy Point Douglas). A band of Indians waited to guide the newcomers southwards.

The Indians were friendly (as they usually were with H.B.C. people) but not particularly gentle. They bargained harshly with the emigrants over their pay as guides; they took the children on horses but made the adults walk. Then, as the cavalcade plodded along, the Indians suddenly galloped away over the prairie, disappearing with the children and babies over a rise. The terrified emigrants – expecting anything from the armed and painted Indians – screamed and wept, sure they would never see their bairnies alive again. But, because there was nothing else to do, they began trudging along the trail the Indians had taken. And of course they soon came upon the band of practical jokers with the excited and happy children, perfectly safe, all laughing at the adults' terror.

Their first winter at the Pembina establishment, now named Fort Daer,[1] gave an extended foretaste of the special hardships to be met in the northwest. The buffalo chose to forage elsewhere that winter, so hunters (half-breeds and Indians) had to be hired: the emigrants knew little of guns or hunting. But the settlers themselves had to bring the meat in, for the proud hunters would not fetch and carry; and many were trapped by blizzards and forced to eat the food they had gone to get. Food became more scarce, and Macdonell had to send the more mobile people 100 miles to another fort. At other times he had to beg or buy food from the H.B.C. post or, as its supplies ran short, from the Northwesters.

By this time ill feeling had grown up between Macdonell and the local H.B.C. men. The latter resented the governor's militaristic ways and his insistence on his independent authority. They sought to poison Selkirk against him (in vain); they intrigued with his men. Remaining friendly on the surface, the Northwesters, too, worked to subvert the settlers. One of the leaders in these subtle attacks was Macdonell's cousin and brother-in-law, Alex Macdonell: the fierce Northwester opposition could even cut across Scots blood ties.

Spring came but hardship continued. Macdonell initiated organized farming – at a spot which he named Colony Gardens – but the colonists were poor farmers. They planted badly and too late, a spell of drought damaged the crops, and in the end only potatoes and turnips were salvaged. Also, the organizers of the expedition had failed to send proper farm implements: only hoes were available to break the tough prairie sod, and the harrows lay broken and toothless. Those of McLean's sheep that survived the winter were killed in the spring by dogs and wolves. In summer, the fish and wild berries were scarce as well, as if nature herself were siding with the Northwesters.

But one small morale-booster had appeared. Northwester-inspired fears of Indian massacre proved baseless. The local Indians, mostly Saulteaux,[2] were friendly and tolerant. At one point, Macdonell approached them to 'buy' the Selkirk land from them – in a diplomatic attempt to stave off resentment – and was surprised to learn that they modestly claimed no title

[1] Daer was the title held by the heir to the Selkirk earldom.
[2] A branch of the Ojibwa tribe of Ontario, so called because their gathering place was at Sault Ste Marie.

to it. It had been free territory, they said, and had then belonged to the Assiniboines. Now it was anyone's. So the Saulteaux were satisfied with a token gift and an assurance of friendship. But Macdonell was aware that the attitude of the métis[1] would not be so reasonable.

The métis – as the offspring of white and Indian unions are properly known – were, from this point on, to play a central role in the great events of the west. Marcel Giraud, the French ethnologist, states – like a practical man – that there had been métis in the west as long as there had been white men, with an initial lag of a few months, but adds that they did not come into their own as a separate community until the early nineteenth century, about the time that the Red River Settlement was beginning. By then a considerable number of métis were scattered through the west, usually in small bands around the trading posts. The French métis outnumbered the English and Scots; but then the French – as fur traders before 1763, then as *voyageur* employees of the later fur companies – had undoubtedly outnumbered the British in the west.

Métis communities were closely knit, bound by pride of race – or both races. The métis themselves were independent and self-reliant; many were well-educated, for their fathers would send promising sons to school in Montreal or even Europe. Even at this time a few métis were turning to the soil, cultivating gardens or small farms around posts in fertile areas (mostly in Red River, but also in Saskatchewan's Qu'Appelle valley). The majority, however, preferred to live off the land: a little trapping or serving as guides, but mostly fur trading and hunting.

As fur traders – literally born to the trade – the métis were indispensable to the British and Canadian companies, who relied on them as go-betweens with the Indians and also as skilled woodsmen who had learned the ways of the wilderness from infancy. On the plains, the métis were buffalo hunters supreme, masters of the art of 'running' the buffalo – in which a herd would be stampeded while the métis, on their wiry little plains

[1] The word is French for 'mixed blood'. Métis also received the more or less disparaging name of '*bois-brulés*', referring to their complexion. A more common term today, 'half-breed', also carries a sneer. In this book, then, the French term '*métis*' will be used for all these people, with distinctions – French métis, English-speaking métis – made when necessary.

ponies, galloped alongside or even among the buffalo, loading their muskets without slowing, and firing along their horses' necks. It was a wild, exhilarating, deadly dangerous activity, for the herd might easily turn, or a horse stumble. (Indians hunted this way too, but preferred the safer method of driving the buffalo into a compound and killing them at leisure, or stampeding them over a steep embankment to their death.) To the métis, running the buffalo was a sport and a way of life, symbolizing their freedom and their mastery of the plains. The hunt also gave solidarity and organization to the métis communities. To this social structure came laws to govern both the hunt and the community life – and from it came their justifiable sense of being the true children of the west, a separate nation.

The Northwesters must be solely and explicitly to blame for the fact that the emergence of the métis as a nation was marked by violence, cruelty and wholesale murder. Though they were always wild, proud people, they showed no particular communal bloodthirstiness until they were stirred up by the Northwesters' subtle anti-colonist campaign.

In 1813 a new group of settlers from Britain walked into the middle of a crisis. The new contingent was composed almost entirely of Sutherlanders from the parish of Kildonan, where riots against the Clearances had almost developed into organized revolt. Selkirk's recruiting had drained off some potential rebels, and had given the others some hope to set against desperation. One hundred Kildonans arrived in 1813; seven times that number waited in Scotland to emigrate when they could.

The Kildonans were not spared the misfortunes that seemed to haunt every step of the Selkirk enterprise. Typhus had swept through their ship, and several had died. More lay ill as the ship (after a mercifully quick passage) entered the Bay. Then, out of what was apparently sheer stupidity, the captain put in at the northern port of Churchill – not at York, where food and medical supplies were waiting. The captain's ineptitude declined into stubbornness, and by the time he had been persuaded to sail down to York, winter had set in and trapped the vessel. With typhus still raging among them, with little food, no shelter and no medical help, the Kildonans wintered on the bleak northern coast.

It speaks well for their immense hardihood that, though

unfamiliar with axes or guns, they managed to throw up log shanties and shoot enough game to eke out a living through the stormy winter. (Again H.B.C. showed its unwillingness to co-operate: the local traders complained that the Kildonans were taking all the game, and tried, unsuccessfully, to impound their guns.) Before spring broke, however, the Sutherlanders could no longer wait. Several had died during the winter. The able-bodied survivors knew that somehow they had to break out of their isolation, or more would die. From Indians they obtained snowshoes, of which they knew nothing, and they built rough sleds to carry what food they could gather. Then, in April, before the ice had left the rivers, they set out to *walk* to York Factory.

For four hundred miles, on short rations, through a frozen wasteland that must have seemed like the backyard of hell, with feet aching and cramped in the unfamiliar snowshoes, they trudged southwards – obstinate, indomitable, the bag-pipers skirling around them as they went.

And they arrived safely – thirty-one men and twenty women – having left about thirty old people, women and children at Churchill. When the ice cleared, they set off for the Forks (the others came later). They arrived in the best of spirits, and plunged lustily into the work of making their new homes habitable.

Their arrival boosted morale at the Forks immensely, and might have proved the turning point in the colony's fortunes. But Miles Macdonell had been planning to take the initiative in the cold war then brewing with the Northwesters. It was a foolish, rash plan, typical of the man, and it precipitated what was called the Pemmican War.

Pemmican had long been a staple food of the nomadic Plains Indians, and the far-ranging fur traders acquired it from them. It was made of buffalo meat, usually from the hump, pounded and dried and moulded with buffalo fat into lumps. (Wild berries and other plants were sometimes mixed in for a balanced diet, and often dirt, insects and similar substances found their way in as well.) Pemmican keeps almost indefinitely, and is eaten by travellers when game is scarce or when they are moving too fast to live off the land. The stuff is hardly palatable, though reasonably nutritious, and travel in the west would have been impossible without it.

It was especially vital to the Northwesters, with their long supply lines and their extensive work in Athabasca where winters are long and wild life wary. For them Red River was a major pemmican depot, at which the canoes coming west picked up their supplies. And now pemmican, even more than furs, was theatened by the Red River settlers, who (the Northwesters feared) would drive away the buffalo or reduce their numbers. Macdonell's initiative kindled their fears.

H.B.C. policy had always insisted on passivity, giving the enemy no provocation. Selkirk had advised the same. But Macdonell, high-handed as ever, was the governor, and he asserted himself. He claimed to be afraid of a continuing food shortage in the colony, and of the likelihood that the Northwesters might try to starve the settlers out. Probably he was right on both counts, but he could not have chosen a worse way of achieving security. In early 1814 he issued a proclamation – itself an insult, in that land of free men – which forbade the 'export' of pemmican from the colony of Assiniboia except under his special licence. The bulk of the pemmican made in the colony was to be consumed there, so that enough would remain to meet the colonists' needs. Then he added a more dangerous corollary: to keep the meat supply near at hand, he forbade the métis to run the buffalo, for they drove the herds too far afield.

If it had been obeyed the embargo would have ruined the Northwesters' organization; but, of course, Macdonell could not enforce the order, and they went right on moving pemmican out. Similarly, the fiery métis' blood was up and they ran the buffalo more often than they needed. (They were twice harmed by the double ban, for as the principal hunters they made much of their livelihood by supplying the fur traders' pemmican.) Macdonell, who had appointed one John Spencer as colony sheriff, then began the first manœuvres of the Pemmican War.

They were mild, almost funny, for a while. Spencer pursued caches of pemmican through the colony, rushing to a riverbank hideout one day, ransacking a canoe another day, always one jump behind the well-informed Northwesters and rarely finding anything. Then, losing patience, he marched into a Northwester fort and impounded a big supply. The Northwesters retaliated, capturing an H.B.C. man and sending him to

Montreal to be tried for larceny. (Canadian courts had theoretical jurisdiction over the northwest, though in the absence of law-enforcement officers their effect was minimal.) Next Macdonell set up guns overlooking the Red River and, under them, captured two canoes full of Northwesters.

By now, Northwesters were starting to gather from all over the country, but from among them issued some calm voices suggesting negotiation. Macdonell was amenable, and eventually some of the pemmican was given back and the captured Northwesters went free. An agreement was reached: the Northwesters could take out food if they guaranteed to bring other food in for the colonists. A nervous peace settled temporarily over the colony. Under the circumstances, no more emigrants arrived that summer.

It was just as well, in the light of a letter intercepted by Macdonell and written by his cousin Alex, which read in part: 'Nothing but the complete downfall of the colony will satisfy some by fair or foul means.' Incidents continued: Sheriff Spencer himself was 'arrested' and shipped to Fort William, the main Northwester base on Lake Superior. And the métis went on defiantly hunting. When a Macdonell man arrived to protest, the métis took him prisoner. Macdonell countered by arresting a métis leader. The métis retaliated by capturing four Macdonell men. Impasse: Macdonell backed down, and each side released its prisoners.

Where Northwester subversion had failed, fear was beginning to succeed. Prompted by the Northwesters, the métis were beginning to assert that *they* were the rightful owners of Red River, and that the colonists were usurping the land of the métis nation. And they reinforced their claim by harassing the colonists. Often at night a horde of mounted métis would circle a farmhouse, whooping and firing their rifles, while the terrified settlers huddled away from the windows. Fences were broken down regularly, crops trampled and burned. Then one night in June 1815, the métis declared outright war. A group of them attacked the colony, breaking into several houses, threatening the inhabitants, plundering property, driving off the few sheep and cattle. No settlers were killed, but several were injured in the general mêlée.

At this point Macdonell disappeared. It is thought that he wanted to allow the colonists to desert if they wished, without embarrassment. But most stood fast. The skirmishes were continued, the Northwesters now openly joining in assaults on farms, in which some colonists were taken prisoner. Macdonell reappeared and, realizing that the colonists had little chance, ended the fighting by giving himself up. He was sent as a prisoner to Fort William.

The remaining settlers were driven off the colony at gunpoint and travelled eastwards, making a temporary camp while they waited for help. Meanwhile the métis completed the destruction, setting fire to the colony's buildings, trampling and burning the remaining crops. Little of value was left intact.

In London, Selkirk, knowing nothing of the outbreak, had been trying to get some protection for his colony, but the government officials were either indifferent or under Northwester influence. In the end, Selkirk took matters into his own hands. By this time he and his wife's family had acquired a controlling voice in H.B.C. affairs; thus his plan of action aimed at protecting the Company, in the long term, as well as the colony. And for once he chose the ideal man for the job: the tough and fearless ex-Northwester, Colin Robertson, who had long been advocating that H.B.C. fight its rivals with their own weapons. Robertson was sent to establish more settlers at the Forks, and then to gather a band of men to undercut Northwester rule of the greatest fur land, Athabasca.

Robertson moved out from Montreal with an advance party of twenty men. As they approached the plains, they met the remnants of the colonists, and heard for the first time of the colony's fate. The unhappy ex-settlers, even worse off at their camp, readily succumbed to Robertson's optimism and agreed to go back and try again. In August 1815 the group reached the Forks.

There, to their astonishment, they were confronted with the sight of ripening grain, neat stacks of hay, mended fences, and smoke issuing peacefully from a cabin. Inside was one John McLeod, a stolid Scot who had simply stayed on, in spite of the métis (who were hunting buffalo and so left him alone) and the hardships of running a colony alone. With help from one or two H.B.C. men McLeod had tended the few fields which the hasty raiders had insufficiently damaged, and had even begun to build a new Fort Douglas. It is too bad that dour stubbornness is not a favoured quality for popular heroes. Certainly there should be a ballad of John McLeod.

While Robertson's men began labouring to reproduce Colony Gardens, a new contingent of settlers – more Kildonans – arrived from the Bay. (Remarkably, they had had a smooth and trouble-free passage.) With them came the colony's new governor, named Semple. He was a well-educated and well-travelled gentleman, who believed with a near-arrogant confidence that civilized Britishness would invariably win any conflict with savages and rabble. And while the colonists brought in the reasonably healthy crops that McLeod had tended, while they worked as only Kildonans could to build a fort and their own houses, Semple began to wonder what all the fuss had been about. Clearly the leadership had been at fault; the Northwesters would have no effect against a display of firmness and resolution. He wrote to Selkirk: 'Nothing but the grossest mismanagement on the part of those of the Colony could have enabled such miserable opponents to triumph over them.'

Robertson knew better. He had gone to meet the métis and had assured them that H.B.C. would win out; impressed with him, many of the métis changed sides and worked as hunters for the colony, or at least remained neutral. He had also broken a new Northwester attack on the Company, when Alex Macdonell had led a small force to threaten an H.B.C. post at Qu'Appelle. Robertson promptly arrested a leading Northwester at Red River, Duncan Cameron, and used him as a hostage to obtain a guarantee of peace both at Qu'Appelle and at the Forks.

In the meantime, Selkirk had decided to visit the country personally, to seek peace negotiations with the Northwesters. When he arrived at New York he heard for the first time the story of the colony's destruction. Shaken by this, he was doubly distressed in Montreal, when the Northwesters brusquely rejected his advances, stating flatly that they would get out of Rupert's Land when forced to by law and not before. (But, as always in previous years, H.B.C. was unwilling to risk a test in court of the old Charter's legality.) Worse, eastern officialdom was even more under the Northwesters' thumb than London, and Selkirk found no way of assuring protection for his colony.

Then came the hardest blow. In the winter of 1815 the

entrenched Northwesters wrecked the H.B.C. spearhead in Athabasca. Robertson, unfortunately, had been needed in Red River, and the H.B.C. attempt suffered from his absence. As in the earlier attempt,[1] the enemy had diverted provisions, and frightened game and Indians away from the H.B.C. men. Soon, having done no trade, established no posts, starving and freezing, the H.B.C. men were forced, for survival, to turn to the Northwesters for help. They were fed and provisioned and ushered unceremoniously out of the Athabasca country.

The news of the Athabasca débâcle undermined much of Robertson's pacifying work with the métis. In spring, he himself left Red River, having intercepted some Northwester correspondence and read of new plans to wreck the colony. With Semple's reluctant permission, he again arrested Duncan Cameron as a hostage – but this time took him off to the Bay. At the same time, acting on Robertson's advice, Semple and some colonists attacked Fort Gibraltar, the nearby Northwester post, and tore it down.

These were good tactics, but they came too late. The métis had once again come under Northwester influence. Cuthbert Grant, the métis leader, intelligent and well educated but one of the wildest of them all, was the son of a Northwester: his sympathies were not with colonists. He and his armed followers left the buffalo herds and set up an ominous camp north of the colony. Semple, aware of their presence, prepared for battle. The métis did not keep him waiting.

In May 1816 Grant and fifty métis ambushed and captured an H.B.C. convoy, or brigade, of boats carrying supplies. A few days later they raided and plundered an H.B.C. post on the Assiniboine, Brandon House. But these were merely opening skirmishes. Alex Macdonell was moving on the colony with a party of métis and traders. From the Northwester base at Fort William another war party was marching towards the Forks. These forces were intended for emergencies or for mopping up, however; the real work was to be done by Grant.

Macdonell had several times tried to recruit the Indians to help clear out the colonists. In June he tried again, haranguing a party of Saulteaux under their strong old chief, Peguis, warning them of the danger to their livelihood from the settlers. He urged them to help him kill the interlopers: 'If the settlers

[1] See page 20.

39

resist,' he is reported to have said, 'the ground will be drenched with their blood.' But the Indians had no quarrel with H.B.C., or with the colony, preferring them to the lawless Northwesters. Peguis had in fact helped the colonists when the métis had first destroyed the colony. Again, he refused any part in the fight. At the same time, unwilling to provoke trouble with the North-westers and métis, he did not join the colonists. He remained neutral, and watchful.

On June 19 the eruption came.

Cuthbert Grant and a band of métis, armed and painted for war, rode towards Fort Douglas. Warned by scouts, the settlers scrambled for safety inside the fort. Presumably Semple feared a siege, which would endanger women and children, so he gathered and armed twenty-six men and led them out – bravely, if rashly – to meet the métis. He was still convinced that a show of British firmness would overawe his 'miserable opponents'. It did not.

The two parties met near a clump of trees called Seven Oaks. Harsh words were exchanged. Then a métis, screeching insults, rode up to Semple – and the governor, enraged that a savage should so address him, seized the man's bridle. Another métis fired, and one of the settlers fell. As if the shot had been a signal, a second party of métis, sent by Grant on a flanking movement, rode out of the brush behind Semple's group, cutting it off from the fort.

The conflict that followed did not last long. Semple's men stood and fought, but they were surrounded, outnumbered, and on foot. The métis were mounted and famous for their marks-manship at full gallop. In a few moments most of the settlers, and the governor himself, lay dead or wounded. Three escaped to the woods in the turmoil. One métis was killed, their only casualty.

As the last settler fell, the frenzied métis leaped from their horses, wielding knives and hatchets to finish off the wounded. They stripped the bodies and viciously mutilated them, leaving them where they lay. The scene was later to be rightly known not as the battle but as the *massacre* of Seven Oaks.

The remaining settlers in the fort, ordered by Grant to surrender, had no choice. They were herded into boats and sent off to Fort William. By that time the two other Northwester parties, which had stayed in the background, had moved up to gloat over the dead, on whom wolves and birds had already begun to feed, and to join the métis in a wild celebration of the final ruin of the Selkirk settlement.

Lord Selkirk, however, was still in Canada. Ignorant as yet of the massacre, he had finally received permission to gather an armed force – and had found some Swiss mercenaries from the regiment of a Colonel De Meuron. These were at a loose end after the close of the war of 1812, and eighty of them, along with some Scots and Canadian ex-soldiers, signed on as potential Red River guards *cum* settlers. Selkirk sent some ahead, following in June with the rest. Then in July, while at Sault Ste Marie, he heard the news of the massacre. In a fury, he recalled the advance party and marched on the Northwester post of Fort William.

He met no resistance from the surprised fort. He arrested the inhabitants, took over the supplies and furs, and searched for documentary evidence of the Northwester crimes against the colony. He paid for the provisions, however, and also obtained a promise from a Northwester official at the fort that the dispute would be arbitrated. But the man had no real power to give such a promise, nor to sell the goods. Legally, Selkirk had seriously compromised himself. The Northwesters immediately began one of their expert propaganda campaigns, in Canada and Britain, representing the Earl as a high-handed robber baron taking the law into his own hands.

As prejudice built up against him in civilized parts, Selkirk consolidated his position in the west. His soldiers marched (in deep winter) to Red River, overran Fort Daer at Pembina, and staged a surprise attack on Fort Douglas that gave them a victory over the few Northwester residents without firing a shot. Then he sent word to the temporary camp of surviving settlers, who were spending a wretched winter on H.B.C. provisions. And in spite of all the horrors they had been through, most of them – especially the Kildonans – jubilantly returned to the colony when spring came. It seems as if they had come to feel it was home.

That spring they rebuilt and repaired and replanned. And when the buffalo again went far afield, Chief Peguis and his Saulteaux arrived to help, not only hunting for the settlers but bringing in the meat – which, ordinarily, Indian hunters believed was women's work and beneath their dignity. Cuthbert Grant led a few tentative forays against the new settlement, but the settlers were vigilant and each time reached the protection of the fort. Each time, also, the métis withdrew, proving what Semple might have known: that the restless métis were unlikely to lay a prolonged siege.

Then Selkirk arrived at Assiniboia with his soldiers, to put the colony finally on its feet. He apportioned the land at the Forks, giving free land to those who had lost everything from the métis' raids, settling the De Meuron soldiers on good farm sites; giving the colony sites for a church and a school, planning roads and bridges. Finally, with the help of Peguis, he approached the Saulteaux and Cree Indians within the borders of Assiniboia to draw up a treaty. It gave him full title to the land for an annual 'rent' to the chiefs of 100 pounds of tobacco. It was the first formal treaty to be signed between Indians of Rupert's Land and a British subject.

For the settlers, the turning point had been reached. But not for Selkirk. The Northwesters had now begun to fight on another ground: legal action. By sending his Northwester captives to Montreal for trial, Selkirk had precipitated what both H.B.C. and the Northwesters had always avoided – a court conflict.

He had already been, prejudged however, by many influential men. The British Colonial Secretary, for one, believed him to be the villain of the piece, and – under subtle Northwester pressure – ordered his indictment. Selkirk went east to Canada to begin the long and dispiriting battle in the courts. It may be enough to say that the Earl was facing not only the Northwesters' immense vested interest, but oligarchic government in Canada, a pliable judiciary which did what it was told by the government, an indifferent or hostile British public, and a backlog of prejudice built up from the beginning of his Red River enterprise. After the trials, which dragged on and on, melting down the Selkirk fortune, a British lawyer thus summed up the Northwesters' successes in court:

> Private vengeance arrogating the functions of public law; – Murder justified in a British Court of Judicature, on the plea of exasperation commencing years before the sanguinary act; – the spirit of monopoly raging in all the terrors of power, in all the force of organization, in all the insolence of impunity.

42

After a series of defeats in the courts, Selkirk turned his back on the wrangle and left for Britain in 1818 – a sick man, having in the course of things contracted tuberculosis. By this time, a number of his powerful friends had instigated counter-propaganda, forcing the British Government to exercise some form of objectivity. But the new hope came too late. His illness worsened, and in 1820 he was dead.

Selkirk did not live to know that the Northwesters, too, had been hard hit by the process: the expenses of litigation had eaten into their profits, and their famous company spirit had been damaged. Once again they relearned their lesson: trade wars do no one any good. And once again – as during the rivalry with the Pangman–Mackenzie group, or with the XY Company – they began thinking about amalgamation. Selkirk had always opposed the idea; but after his death H.B.C. began to see its value. Apparently Colin Robertson acted as one of the intermediaries when the Northwesters started to put out feelers. Negotiations were brisk and to the point: both sides were willing, and concord was swiftly reached. In 1821 the two companies became one. The great rivalries over the fur wealth of the northwest had finally ended.

As usual, the English had lost most of the battles but not the war. The new union of fur traders was to be called the Hudson's Bay Company (due to the remaining strength of the Charter); there would be no more Northwesters. H.B.C. was now dominant not only in Rupert's Land but in the areas opened up by their erstwhile rivals, where the Company had never been: Athabasca, and the Pacific west. It seemed at first, however, that the Northwesters had profited more by the union, for they received 55 per cent of the new company's shares. In fact this percentage was divided into 30 for the Montreal agents and 25 for the wintering partners; and the Montreal percentage soon became virtually worthless, since the winterers could now use the shorter route to the outlets on Hudson Bay. In a very few years the great Montreal firms of the North-West Company were bankrupt and disbanded. Thus Selkirk was partially avenged.

At Red River, furthermore, Selkirk was justified. The twice-shattered colony slowly began now to put down roots to make itself permanent. Groups of newcomers arrived to swell the population; ex-H.B.C. employees, pioneers from Canada, more immigrants from abroad. (Selkirk had sent an agent to Europe, who had gathered about 100 Swiss – including a number of unattached women, who the Earl hoped would help the rowdier De Meuron soldiers settle down to agriculture.)

From then on all the colony's hardships were natural, but they were no less frequent. A promising crop in 1818 was destroyed by an infestation of grasshoppers – which would be a recurring plague on Red River. The insatiable insects flew in masses that obscured the sky like thunder-clouds or dust storms. Where they landed green changed to brown, as tree tops and grass blades, crops and gardens, were stripped to the bare earth. The colony recovered, turning again to the buffalo for survival, and now being more skilful with snowshoes and guns. Then in spring came the grasshoppers' legacy; the larvae hatched out, and ate the new crops to the last leaf.

This blow sent some of the less capable settlers, mostly De Meurons, out of the colony towards more civilized territory – namely, the nearest U.S. settlement at Prairie du Chien on the Mississippi. Other settlers went that way too, but only to buy new seed-grain. In spite of the hostile bands of Sioux that wandered south of the border, the path southward from Red River to the U.S. frontier settlement became well trodden – and was to become more so in later years.

By this time the International Boundary, established in 1783 at the 49th parallel as far west as the Mississippi,[1] had been extended along that parallel to the Rocky Mountains. (The 1818 boundary agreement discreetly shelved the issue of the Oregon territory, for which see Chapter 3.) But with the agreement, a sizeable piece of Selkirk's grant of land had become American. With it went the settlements at Pembina – Fort Daer, trading posts, métis and all. The fort was dismantled and floated down the Red to the Forks, and the métis soon moved north as well. But many of the Pembina residents of the Selkirk colony preferred to stay and become Americans. Soon a natural disaster drove even more Red Riverites into the U.S.A.

The winter of 1826 produced unusually heavy snowfalls; then in spring the snow melted with excessive speed. The result was a catastrophic flood – both the Red and the Assiniboine

[1] See page 19.

44

bursting their banks and covering land for miles around. The colonists scattered to higher ground, helped by prompt action on the part of the H.B.C. Only one life was lost, but the colony and the settlers' possessions went under the water.

When the flood subsided the more stolid among the colonists started the work of reclamation. Two positive side-effects of the disaster then emerged: the soil was even more enriched by its inundation, and the more restless and unproductive of the settlers decided they had had enough and left for America. (Again these were mostly De Meurons and others from among the Swiss who had not taken to farming.) Some Irish and a few Scots moved east, to the more placid backwoods of Canada. The most valuable pioneering stock remained: the sturdy Kildonans, the former H.B.C. men (mostly Orcadians) and, of course, the métis.

The métis population multiplied rapidly, and was becoming socially as well as numerically dominant in Red River. The colony's leading citizens were now the experienced and prestigious ex-H.B.C. men – comparatively well off, and well adjusted to the west – many of whom were métis, while others, though white, had métis or Indian wives. They settled near Grand Rapids, or around Fort Douglas; they built the largest houses, often of stone; they were looked up to by colonists of all nationalities.

The bulk of the métis community, however, lived some miles away on the White Horse Plain. There Cuthbert Grant had set the pattern, settling down to some farming, and taking up the title of 'Warden of the Plains'. It made him an unofficial magistrate, and it tamed him considerably. But the other métis had not exchanged guns for ploughshares. The cohesive force keeping the community together was still the buffalo hunt, especially the great spring hunt, when many métis bands came together on the open plains to wreak immense slaughter among the herds. Sometimes the hunt was enlivened by a different kind of action; a clash (usually on the southern plains below the border) with a war party of Sioux. The métis, always ready for trouble, fought by forming their carts into a circular barricade, as in old western films, and withering the Indians' charge with their deadly marksmanship. Thus the métis under-lined their predominance in the west. They were the hunters who fed the traders and settlers; they were also the fighters

45

who could withstand the northwest's fiercest Indians. (In 1857 came the métis' finest hour in their running war with the Sioux: about eighty métis drove off a vastly greater force of Indians after a pitched battle lasting two full days.)

Within Red River, then, a balance was being struck (though not so rock-firm that later events could not destroy it) between the old wild ways of fur trade and buffalo hunt, and the new embryonic growth of agricultural civilization. The Red River settlers were hard-working and quiet-living. Breaches of the peace were surprisingly few (once the De Meurons had left), considering the rawness of the land and the absence of any peace-keeping force. Authority in the settlement remained in the hands of Selkirk's heirs, who continued to appoint governors of Assiniboia as the sole nominal government. (Semple's successor was H.B.C.'s former arch-enemy, Alex Macdonell.) But H.B.C., through the local officers and also in the person of the supreme company power, the Governor of Rupert's Land (George Simpson after 1821), exercised considerable *ex officio* authority at Red River.

Then in 1834 the new Lord Selkirk reconveyed Assiniboia to the Company. To the settlers, the action appeared mostly a formality: H.B.C. continued to appoint governors, through whom it imposed 'the cool and languid care of a step-mother',[1] as well as appointing justices of the peace and establishing a court. (The 1834 reconveyance, incidentally, restored the unsettled parts of Assiniboia to Rupert's Land – so 'Red River Settlement' thereafter meant only the settled areas on the rivers.) By this time the governors had acquired councillors, in the form of influential Red River citizens appointed to a 'Council of Assiniboia' – but as advisers, not legislators or executive. And Red River authority remained in this overall form for years.

As farmers the Red Riverites remained more or less primitive for some years. They turned the sod with ploughs of iron and sometimes wood; they sowed their crops (mostly wheat, oats, barley and potatoes) by hand. Their farms were formed as 'river lots', having a narrow frontage on the river, for wood and water, then extending back on to the prairie in a long strip of land. All settlers firmly believed it would be impossible to

[1] An apt description provided by Alexander Ross, a mid-century inhabitant and chronicler of the settlement.

cultivate the grasslands of the open prairie, which lacked either tree or stream, so they used the prairie only as grazing for the stock brought up from the U.S.A. and for the horses that were so vital to the métis' livelihood.

Crops were harvested in the early days by hand, with sickles and scythes. Women and children raked the wheat and 'stooked' it; the sheaves were threshed with flails and winnowed in the open air, in all weathers. Much of it was then stored in casks – whether wet, dry or frozen – for sale or for later milling. And it all went to the mills, rotten wheat and sound, along with the flotsam it had picked up in the process. The flour (from the hand-mills or erratic water- or wind-mills) made a cruelly coarse, dark bread, notorious throughout the west, that required true pioneer hardihood to eat. Yet it was eaten. That, and the unmilled wheat, supplied many H.B.C. posts as well as the colony itself.

Fortunately the Red River soil grew excellent oats, which (especially for the Scots) compensated for the dreadful wheat. Also the gardens produced magnificent vegetables, and in a good year abundant game added extra nourishment to Red River fare. At any rate no one died of it. And some of the wheat and barley was diverted to private stills, which must have made the food more edible and brought joy to long winter nights.

To improve agricultural conditions the settlement, following a dream of Selkirk's, set up a series of experimental farms. Each failed disastrously, due to various tricks of nature: frost, drought, hail, grasshoppers, and so on. The Company underwrote the losses of these experiments, and also paid for other ill-fated business ventures designed to make the settlers financially self-sufficient. One such was the hopefully named Assiniboia Wool Company, which disproved Selkirk's idea that sheep would thrive on the prairie grass. Only a few bales of poor quality wool were produced, which made some poor quality clothing for the settlers. The enterprise collapsed when wolves and local dogs made meals of the sheep. A similarly abortive attempt was made to export buffalo 'wool' but the entrepreneurs found that coarser hairs had to be removed by hand, which multiplied the costs, and that the thick curly hair resisted all dyes except black. So the Buffalo Wool Company was liquidated as well.

With ventures of this sort breaking the monotony of hard work and more work, the colony advanced through the 1820s and 1830s firmly set in its comfortable frontier pattern. Now fully experienced in the ways of their country, the Red River settlers looked forward to a future of peace and quiet growth, in spite of their isolated position as the first and only outpost of settlement west of the Great Lakes. But shortly that isolation would be shattered, and from the south and east new forces would disturb their peace and considerably speed their growth.

3

To Make a Nation

While the Red River Settlement, on the eastern side of the west, plodded towards civilization, a similar embryo of civilization began to take shape on the extreme western edge – the Pacific coast.

The Hudson's Bay Company, monopolistically supreme in Rupert's Land after the amalgamation in 1821, had extended its power over the areas opened by the Northwesters. Britain had made the extension official by an 'Act for regulating the Fur Trade . . .' which gave the H.B.C. an exclusive licence to trade with the Indians[1] in all unsettled parts of North America. The licence would need renewing in twenty-one years, but meanwhile the Company acquired a clear monopoly over the Athabasca and Mackenzie regions.

On the Pacific, however, the Americans claimed equal rights in the fur-rich territory called Old Oregon (made up of the present states of Washington and Oregon, pieces of Idaho and Montana, and much of the present province of British Columbia). In the agreement of 1818 title to land *beyond* the Rockies had been left open – it was not a 'no-man's-land' but an 'every-man's-land' – and the Americans paid little attention to grants of exclusive trade issued by a British Parliament. As American traders infiltrated Old Oregon, H.B.C. prepared itself for competition. Then, at the beginning of the 1840s, settlement became a factor in the clash of opposing claims as a tidal wave of American frontiersmen washed into Oregon. These squatters

[1] The Act also sought to prevent further use of liquor in the fur trade. But, while the quantities were certainly reduced after 1821, the traders found that more independent tribes like the Plains Indians (obtaining most of their needs from the buffalo), or the transmontane Indians (living on salmon), would not trade furs unless they were given guns, ammunition and drink.

49

had hardly struck their ploughs into the rich soil before they were demanding that Washington (D.C.) take action to make Oregon an American territory. And Washington was listening.

The Company became nervous. It, too, had tried something resembling colonization when, in 1839, it had set up a subsidiary company devoted to agriculture, called the Puget Sound Agricultural Company. The subsidiary's farms were placed on Puget Sound, an inlet on the coast south and east from the tip of Vancouver Island. These farms, and others established on the Cowlitz river, were intended to supply produce for H.B.C. posts along the coast, though many of the posts had extensive, thriving gardens of their own. Then H.B.C. went to look for colonists to operate the farms. They looked in vain. Events in Red River, tales of which had filtered back to Britain, losing no colour en route, had sent other would-be colonists off to safer climes: eastern Canada, or Australia and New Zealand, or even America. In the end, H.B.C. had to turn to Red River itself to find farmers to man its agricultural ventures. In 1841 some twenty-one families, altogether over 100 people, struggled across the prairies and through the Rockies to cultivate the soil of what is now the state of Washington.

This handful of newcomers made little impression in comparison with the inpouring of Americans. That wave had begun slowly; in the first years only about 100 arrived each year. But in 1843 1,000 Americans moved in and called themselves the 'Great Immigration'. In 1845 the arrivals numbered 3,000. The Company began to feel thoroughly crowded. It had always realized that a boundary settlement would have to come, but had believed that the logical (natural) boundary would be the Columbia river. Thus the Puget Sound and Cowlitz enterprises had been placed on land that H.B.C. was sure would be British. Now the Company became pessimistic; there was every chance that the line along the 49th parallel would be extended to the sea. That would mean the loss of some further posts – including Fort Vancouver (no connection with the present city), H.B.C.'s Pacific headquarters. A new site for the HQ had to be found. In 1843 the southern tip of Vancouver Island was chosen, and there Fort Victoria was built.

The move had been made just in time. In 1844 American expansionist energies threw up a politician named Polk, who campaigned for the presidency on a policy that asserted the U.S.A.'s right not only to Oregon but to the entire Pacific west, up to Russian-owned Alaska. His platform was soon condensed into the catchy slogan: 'Fifty-four Forty or Fight' (referring to the latitude on which the southern tip of the Alaskan panhandle rests). He was elected, and the whole of British America was alarmed.

But Polk the President proved less anxious to fight than Polk the campaigner. Britain responded with diplomacy and talk of war was stifled: the Oregon question went amicably to negotiation. In 1846 the Americans pressed some uncompromising demands, and came out largely the winners: the International Boundary was extended to the Pacific along the 49th parallel, though it jogged down to make Vancouver Island all British. The H.B.C. had lost the Columbia valley, and had to reorganize its Pacific west department.

(Incidentally, the wording of the Treaty of Washington of 1846 left a loophole that was to provide fuel for further Anglo-American disputes. It said:

... the line of boundary ... shall be continued westward along the said forty-ninth parallel ... to the middle of the channel which separates the continent from Vancouver's Island, and thence southerly through the middle of the said channel, and of Fuca's straits, to the Pacific Ocean. ...

As the San Juan dispute blew up in later years, it became clear that more than one stretch of water could be taken as 'the said channel'.)

About thirty miles from the mouth of the Fraser, Fort Langley was the first fur post to feel the effects of the new boundary. Because of its position on a great salmon river it had always been an important source of provisions (it had even exported salmon to the Sandwich Islands, now Hawaii). Langley rested on ground good enough for cultivation; but in 1840 a fire destroyed the fort, and a new Langley arose a few miles away on an even better site, with rich alluvial soil. H.B.C. employees turned to farming, and got about 200 acres under cultivation in spite of recurrent floods and frosts. Dairy cattle did well there, too, adding to the value of the area. And, with the flourishing fishery and agriculture, Langley was ripe for civilization.

51

Langley gained further prominence when Indian wars south of the border in 1848 forced H.B.C. to finally abandon the Columbia trade route (which they had kept up with U.S. permission). The Fraser, for most of its length, was unnavigable, so a largely overland route developed. But boats could use the great river as far as Langley, which became a major clearing house for the new route. Goods passed through the post on their way to the interior, furs were gathered there on the way out. And the new route led to the building of other posts in the interior.

The overland route was travelled by vast 'brigades' of horses. They began in the north, at Fort Alexandria, the centre to which came the furs of New Caledonia (as the northern interior was called) by means of difficult but manageable waterways. From Alexandria the brigades made their way to Fort Kamloops, a thriving post on the Thompson river, the Fraser's great tributary. And from there – having picked up the output of the Thompson valley – they trooped across country to Fort Hope on the Fraser, farther inland from Langley, at the point where the river makes a huge turn westwards on its way to the Pacific.

These posts, being central clearing houses and crossroads, gradually became provisioning points. Farms sprang up along the route at the bigger posts, and at least gardens at the smaller. Wheat was grown as far north as Alexandria; stock was raised at every post where it was practicable. Kamloops, especially, began raising horses for the brigades, and revealed the vast potential of the Thompson valley for this purpose. The interior west of the mountains began to reveal itself, in many regions, as a settler's paradise. But when the H.B.C. entertained thoughts of colonization, the area they chose for the first steps was Vancouver Island.

Since its foundation as the headquarters of H.B.C. on the Pacific, Fort Victoria had been proving a well-chosen site. Its port was good enough to take the incoming British ships (from which goods were transferred to a small steamer and sent to Langley), and only a few miles away lay a perfect natural harbour, Esquimalt. Victoria was also showing itself capable of supporting a sizeable population. The farms round about – revised versions of the Agricultural Companies swallowed up by the U.S.A. – were enormously successful; other natural resources seemed substantial, and the climate was idyllic. The H.B.C. employees (or retired employees) who manned the farms found themselves in a potentially ideal settlement, and the Company developed plans for translating potential into reality.

The impetus that made H.B.C. think in terms of settlement against the grain of the fur trade came from simple fear of the U.S.A. The threat of American land hunger had become very real by the mid-1840s. A line drawn across a map offered a poor barrier to the U.S.A.'s 'manifest destiny' – a rhetorical phrase coined in the 1840s by an American journalist as a euphemism for the country's expansionist appetite and continental power urge. Oregon gained territorial status by 1848; by that time California, too, was American. Their people began looking hungrily north at the thriving farmlands and unclaimed territories of the Hudson's Bay Company. Not that the Oregonians desperately needed land; it seems almost to have been an automatic reflex.

Gradually the hunger must have become irresistible, for squatters filtered across the border to take up land, defying H.B.C. attempts to uproot them. The Company foresaw the trickle of squatters becoming a rush, after which the U.S.A. might simply claim the area, settled by Americans and no others, as hers by default. Those were the usual tactics of manifest destiny. Since the H.B.C. could not lean too heavily on the squatters – it had only a trading licence, not chartered rights of sovereignty – *British* occupation of the land seemed to be the only way to counteract the menace.

So the Company devised a proposal whereby it, H.B.C., would organize and finance the colonization of strategic areas of the Pacific west. In return it sought possession and control of the lands west of the mountains. The British Government hedged a little, agreed in principle, but in the ensuing negotiations restricted H.B.C.'s title to Vancouver Island alone. (By this time Britain had grown more interested in colonization, with hunger, unemployment and famine in Ireland. Also, she was growing mildly concerned about creeping americanization – though not so concerned that she would give a trading company outright ownership of such a vast and wealthy territory.)

By a Royal Charter of 1849 Vancouver Island became H.B.C. property, and Fort Victoria became the second western settlement. The Company was required by the charter to encourage settlers by selling lands 'at a reasonable price'; it was also required to prove to Britain, on demand, that a suitable colony had been established. The charter also specified that when H.B.C.'s trading licence came up for renewal again (it had been renewed in 1838), Britain could buy the colony back if it had not been sufficiently developed – paying whatever sum H.B.C. had spent to that date.

Thus the threat of American expansionism had provoked H.B.C. to take a major decision, and had created some concern in Britain as well. And more: the earlier threat over the Oregon Territory, with President Polk's sabre-rattling, had aroused interest even among the insular and parochial colonies of eastern British America. More concern and fears – in H.B.C., Britain and British America – were to be felt as the U.S.A. flexed the muscles of her manifest destiny in the direction of Red River.

The encroachment against Red River wore a face more friendly than that of territorial dispute. Economic links had developed in the 1840s between Red River and its southern neighbour, growing out of the fur trade. This development had started when a Canadian named Norman W. Kittson, working then for Astor's American Fur Company, set up shop at Pembina just below the border. Previously, many Red River métis had filled out the empty winter days with hunting and trapping, putting their share of furs into the H.B.C. posts; but with Kittson's presence, competition grew. Scores of Red River métis slipped across the border with furs, and slipped back again with American goods and liquor. The Company passed various laws to block the free traders, which the métis characteristically ignored at first, and then resisted.

A petition was presented to the Crown in 1846 (among the signatories was a J. Louis Riel, father of a soon-to-be famous son) asserting that the H.B.C. monopoly was bringing ruin on the colony, and insisting on the métis' right to trade privately. But Britain decided that the petitioners were a handful of mere agitators. Besides, the British feared (with good reason, given the precedents) that wide-open trade would result in ruinous competition, near extinction for the beaver, and widespread alcoholic degradation of the Indian.

In the same year, 1846, when the Oregon crisis was at its height and all British America was nervous of U.S. intentions, a regiment of British soldiers arrived at Red River. Their presence calmed some of the more restless spirits, and the private trade in furs dwindled accordingly. But the soldiers were withdrawn in 1848, the privateers took up where they left off, and the last fur crisis reached its climax.

The Company, deciding on a show of force, arrested some métis for illegal fur trading, and held a trial at Fort Garry,[1] clearly intending to make an example of them. But the plan backfired. A muttering crowd of armed métis, dominated by the elder Riel, gathered around the courthouse; rioting and worse would break out if the verdict was too harsh. Presumably the jury took note of their danger, and then again H.B.C. had chosen a very poor test case, for the accused took furs to H.B.C. posts at least as often as they visited America. Seizing on to this escape route, the jury halfheartedly convicted the prisoners of illegal trading, but recommended mercy because it seemed to them that the métis 'were under the impression that there was a free trade'. H.B.C. accepted the recommendation and dropped the case, with the result that most of the waiting crowd believed, from then on, that the court had in fact thrown the fur trade open.

So, for all intents and purposes, trade *was* free. H.B.C. resigned itself to the fact that numerous small traders operated on the Assiniboine and Saskatchewan rivers. The Company might not have been so willing to live and let live had the métis, or any other group of private traders, set up an organization to threaten the fur lands of the north, where the real profits lay. But instead, the métis traded in a scattered, individualistic way; like mice in an old house, they were not worth the bother of exterminating so long as they were not too much of a nuisance.

At the same time as this breakthrough was accomplished in the fur trade, the American region below the border gained the new status of the Territory of Minnesota. Almost at once the importance of the fur trade, for Red Riverites, was equalled by the importance of a general mercantile trade, and Red River's long isolation was ended as Minnesota reached out commercial arms to embrace it.

[1] The H.B.C. fort built at the Forks after the amalgamation, to replace the Northwesters' Fort Gibraltar, and named after the H.B.C. Deputy Governor Nicholas Garry.

Norman W. Kittson, always in the van, shifted his operations to the town of St Paul, which was then burgeoning forth as Minnesota's metropolis-to-be. As the 1850s progressed, the passage of goods between Red River and St Paul exceeded the amount passing between the settlement and the H.B.C. centre, York Factory. Not even the economic depression of 1857, the 'Panic', could do more than temporarily slow the American progress. In the following year, 1858, Minnesota became a state with a population of about 100,000, and Red River's role had been defined: that of the dependent parasite, at best symbiont, fattening on the southern settlement's prosperity. And Minnesota fell victim to the dream of manifest destiny, of encompassing the rich and comparatively empty lands to the north – not only Red River, but beyond. A Minnesotan, J. W. Taylor (nicknamed 'Saskatchewan' because of his propaganda for expansion in that direction), wrote glowingly of his state's aspirations as 'continental in their grandeur'.

The Minnesotans were well aware that through their state ran the easiest and quickest overland route to the east, whether to Montreal or to New York. (The route's importance increased when in 1859 an indomitable entrepreneur named Anson Northup placed a steamboat on the Red River, in spite of its tendency to flood in spring and virtually dry up in autumn.) Even H.B.C. shipped goods through the Minnesota route – because it was open all year round, which York Factory was not – thus swelling the profits of its commercial rivals. And the métis found a new form of livelihood: working as freighters on the great brigades of carts and wagons that had begun regularly to ply between Red River and St Paul.[1]

As Red River's dependence on American goods and goodwill deepened, some latent nationalism was being awakened in British America. It was stirred further by pronouncements such as that of Saskatchewan Taylor, or such as the crow of a St Paul newspaper, in 1859: '. . . we will make British Canada as much tributary to Minnesota as if the Star Spangled banner floated from the flagstaff of Fort Garry. . . .' To a Red

---

[1] The Red River cart, a description of which appears later in a discussion of pioneer transport, had by then fully come into its own as essential western equipment. In 1844 only six carts had rolled over the trail between Red River and the U.S. centres. By 1858 the number had reached 600; by 1869 annual brigades numbered 2,500 carts.

Riverite, the only flaw in that statement was its use of the future tense.

But while the new Red River newspaper, the *Nor'wester*, intoned dire warnings of American takeover, the settlers generally seemed to have agreed that the Minnesotan attachment was better than none. They went on buying American, spending more than $100,000 in St Paul every season. The *Nor'wester* itself was printed with type and machinery freighted up from Minnesota, and every issue carried (along with patriotic warnings) columns of advertisements for St Paul merchants. By this time many of those merchants, including Kittson, had opened up branches in Red River. From Minnesota streams of farm machinery – rare in the settlement before this time – furniture, clothing, hardware, even groceries, poured into Red River hands.

And when, by the early 1860s, the Minnesota settlements spread farther over the Red River valley and approached the border, it seemed as if the new state was very close to fulfilling its manifest destiny. (By this time, furthermore, Dakota, Idaho and Montana had become fully fledged territories.) As Saskatchewan Taylor put it, if Britain wouldn't colonize her northwest, Minnesota would.

But then Minnesota's advance was slowed by two tragic developments. First, the Civil War broke out, and drew men and money away from the joys of manifest destiny to waste them in war; and second, the Sioux rose in Dakota and Minnesota against the invaders of their ancestral lands, in a series of terrible massacres which drove out many of the surviving settlers.[1]

The breathing space which these horrors unhappily provided gave Red River a chance to gather itself and ponder its own future, that is, whether it preferred to remain British or become American. By that time, in the east, others had also begun to ponder the fate of the western settlements.

· · · · ·

[1] During these risings, the Sioux first learned the value of the 'medicine line', the boundary across which the Cavalry could not pursue them. Britain's refusal to let the U.S. Army into Red River, which the Sioux used as a hideout and base for raids into Minnesota, and her ineffectual attempts to restrain the foreign Indians, worsened the strained Anglo-American relations of that time.

Concern for the west among the residents of eastern Canada had always been, at best, limited, but in the mid-nineteenth century a few men perceived some of its possibilities – especially the Liberal politician George Brown, turbulent editor of the Toronto Liberal newspaper the *Globe*, and indefatigable booster of Canada West.[1] Brown acquired his interest in the west in the 1840s, when the Oregon dispute was in the news. But, unlike most, he retained his interest afterwards, and the *Globe* reflected it. He campaigned against the H.B.C. monopoly, and insisted at every opportunity that Canada West's future lay in its connection with a colonized west. (By that time steamers were plying the Great Lakes from Toronto to Lake Superior, and Brown knew that if the west's resources could be exploited, they would be funnelled down this route to enrich his province.) In the 1850s, an associate of Brown's, William McDougall, editor of the Toronto *North American*, took up the same hobby-horse, and the idea of annexing the west also became an important plank in the Liberal platform. A speech of Brown's in 1858, often and justly quoted, declares the Liberal view:

> . . . it is my fervent aspiration and belief that some here tonight may live to see the day when the British American flag shall proudly wave from Labrador to Vancouver Island and from our own Niagara to the shores of Hudson Bay.

Brown's vision was infectious, as was the implicit (but less publicized) vision of immense tracts of land, untapped resources, and fortunes to be made. A third enticement grew from the familiar dog-in-the-manger anti-Americanism, the British American's nationalism that remained (and remains) dormant until activated by a fear of American manifest destiny. Brown's political enemy, the affable, shrewd manipulator of men, John A. Macdonald, expressed the feeling perfectly:

> I would be quite willing, personally, to leave that whole country a wilderness for the next half-century, but I fear that if Englishmen do not go there, Yankees will.

He made the remark in 1865; the west, at least, had known the truth of it for years.

[1] The old provinces of Upper Canada and Lower Canada had been merged in 1840, a shaky marriage that cut across national and religious differences. Thus most Canadians still thought of Canada as twofold, and called its parts Canada East and Canada West.

But if the west was ever to be made Canadian, first it would have to be removed from the rule of the Hudson's Bay Company. Some cracks had appeared earlier in H.B.C.'s monolithic sovereignty, in the late 1830s, when it sought for the first time to renew its exclusive trading licence for the territories beyond Rupert's Land.[1] The British Colonial Office seemed to have become newly aware of the extent of the H.B.C. hegemony, and suggested an amendment to the licence that would reserve Britain's right to establish colonies within H.B.C. territories. The Company, of course, accepted. In the 1850s, when H.B.C. began seeking a second renewal, an even harsher spotlight was turned on the application. New pressures forced a reappraisal: the U.S. encroachments on the west, Canada's growing interest in the west fostered by George Brown, and a general British feeling that monopolistic trading companies should be brought to heel. In 1857 Britain set up a Select Committee to examine H.B.C. and its western lands. In the same year the Committee reported.

It found an immense variety of opinion on the question of the fertility of the western prairie. H.B.C. interests tried to understate the case: Sir George Simpson, the Governor of Rupert's Land, said flatly: 'I do not think that any part of the Hudson's Bay Company's territory is well adapted to settlement.' He expanded his opinion with references to 'poverty of the soil', 'rigorous climate', and so on. But the Committee pinned him with a contradiction, quoting from a book that Simpson had written ten years earlier – an exercise in the picturesque – in which he referred to an area of southeastern Manitoba as 'the fertile shores of the spacious lakes' and foresaw the Rainy River as having, in future, 'crowded steamboats on its bosom and populous towns on its borders'. Thus confronted, Sir George muttered that perhaps a 'slip of land' in the area was fertile, but the rest was 'deep morasses which never thaw'. The Committee was not convinced.

Then A. K. Isbister, a prominent member of a British métis family which had served H.B.C. for generations, told the Committee that the Company had long been 'an obstruction to the colonizing spirit', and asserted that he himself had 'raised corn as far north as Fort Norman, which is near the Arctic Circle, on Mackenzie's River'. Isbister also pointed out

[1] See page 49.

59

(anticipating John A. Macdonald) that H.B.C. was bound to lose its territorial rights one way or another:

> I believe it is our interest to people that country, because the United States are fast peopling the territory along the frontier, and they will have that territory from us unless we do people it.

The Committee's report came down strongly on the side of settlement, and of Canada's western ambitions:

> . . . Your Committee consider that it is essential to meet the just and reasonable wishes of Canada to be enabled to annex to her territory such portion of the land in her neighbourhood as may be available to her for the purpose of settlement, with which lands she is willing to open and maintain communications, and for which she will provide the means of local administration. Your Committee apprehend that the districts on the Red River and the Saskatchewan are among those likely to be desired for early occupation.
> . . . Your Committee trust that there will be no difficulty in effecting arrangements as between Her Majesty's Government and the Hudson's Bay Company by which these districts may be ceded to Canada on equitable principles. . . .

But of course there was difficulty in plenty.

First among the obstacles was sheer ignorance, in Canada and Britain, of the nature of the west. Brown's and McDougall's newspapers tried to inform the east, but other journals printed quantities of misinformation about the west's climate and fertility – some of it, clearly, sponsored by H.B.C. First-hand knowledge was seen to be necessary. In 1857–8 Britain sent a team to examine the west: a geologist and a botanist, led by a young army officer named Captain John Palliser, who had hunted on the western prairies.

Their topological reports have become classic. It was Palliser who first noted that the prairies take the shape of a rough triangle, bounded by the Rocky Mountains, the U.S.A. border, and the Pre-Cambrian Shield.[1] He also found that the prairies

[1] A geological and topographical term for a vast, shield-shaped sweep of unbelievably rugged country. The western side of the Shield curves down from the north through northern Saskatchewan, diagonally through central Manitoba, into Ontario – to embrace the Great Lakes. Then its boundary swings east again, curving through Quebec.

rise in three 'steppes', from the low flat land at Red River to the heavily rolling terrain approaching the Alberta foothills. And he distinguished between the two basic forms of prairie land in the west: the park belt, and the 'true' prairie.

The park belt stretches diagonally from southeast Saskatchewan to northern Alberta; its northern edge can be roughly placed at the North Saskatchewan river. Within it, the land undulates slightly, and contains long, lush grass interrupted by groves of trees, ranging from a clump of half a dozen poplars to a wood of several acres. The true prairie is an extension of the U.S.A.'s Great Plains, jutting into southwest Saskatchewan and southeast Alberta. It is flat and dry, with coarse short grass and absolutely no trees[1] except on sheltered riverbanks.

Palliser pronounced the park belt immensely fertile, and the true prairie equally arid. (Later expeditions were to find that he overestimated both the extent and the aridity of the latter.) His report, in the end, was positive: the fertile region contained millions of acres of land that was ideal for agricultural settlement. And he offered a possibility for the future: a railway, he said, might easily be built from Red River west across the prairie, through available mountain passes to the Pacific. But, he added, the only practicable route from the east to Red River dipped down beneath the Great Lakes through the U.S.A.

Here Palliser had stressed the single greatest obstacle that confronted the settlement of the west. Canadians had no clear road to the west through their own territory. In the U.S.A., a settler could load an axe, a plough and a rifle on to his wagon and roll westwards without natural impediment other than a few great rivers. As far as topography alone was concerned, the frontier could be pushed back fairly readily. But in Canada the main resistance to the westward flow of settlers *was* topographical. From the east up to about Sault Ste Marie the terrain was rough but manageable, but beyond there – above the greatest of the Lakes – it was simply impenetrable. Jagged outcroppings of rock; quaking, sucking 'muskeg' (an Indian word for bog) in the hollows; forest and bush as tangled as any jungle; lakes scattered like pockmarks every few miles. So, until adequate transportation could be contrived, the badlands

[1] Until, of course, the settlers planted windbreaks on their farms.

above Lake Superior imposed a barrier that effectively cut off western Canada from the east. (To some extent they still do: the wilds of northern Ontario have by now been bridged, by railways and highways, but not altogether tamed.)

While Palliser was in the west for Britain, Canada sent out her representatives. A surveyor, S. J. Dawson, considered the area between Lake Superior and Red River and reported – optimistically – that a road could be built through that area, linking navigable waterways to create a land-and-water route between the prairies and the east (utilizing steamers on the Lakes). Later, indeed, work began on the Dawson Road, and eventually travellers could move along an all-Canadian land-and-water route. But few did. The road was constantly in an appalling condition for most of its length; and the many shifts of passengers and freight from wagons to boats and back again made the journey long, exhausting and expensive. Nevertheless, when Dawson reported, the outlook seemed bright – and even brighter when Professor H. Y. Hind studied the prairie soils and proclaimed that the fertile region was even more extensive than Palliser had estimated.

So knowledge and interest grew in place of ignorance and indifference. Vision grew as well: the sweeping dream of a transcontinental railway through Canadian territory had been born earlier, but was reinforced by Palliser. Thus, stimulated by the vista of rich land aching for exploitation, the practical men in Canada occupied themselves with the task of prying loose H.B.C.'s grip on the west.

They chose the simple method of a direct challenge to the Charter, based on the arguments used by the French during the eighteenth-century fur wars. Canada stated that the French (La Vérendrye and the rest) had discovered the western interior, and so by right of discovery the land belonged to New France – in its nineteenth-century guise as Canada East. All that H.B.C. owned, in this view, was a narrow coastal strip along the Bay. When H.B.C. hotly disagreed, a succession of Colonial Secretaries (Britain was then changing governments like petticoats) struggled to mediate between the two claims.

A shake-up in the H.B.C. hierarchy in the 1860s made little difference to the negotiations. An enterprise called the 'Northwest Transit Company' had been preparing to construct a road and telegraph line across the few hundred miles separating Lake Superior from Red River. H.B.C. was unwilling to co-operate. The Transit Company got round the difficulty in true tycoon style – by forming a company which in 1863 bought out the proprietors of H.B.C. But while the new owners seemed, in principle, more interested in settlement, they were just as determined as their predecessors to guard their rights in the wrangle with Canada. And Canada remained as determined to annex the west at the minimum cost.

Deadlock resulted. And deadlock remained, through the 1860s, as Canadian energies came to be diverted into a new preoccupation – with the political currents that were leading it towards Confederation.

The progress of the eastern colonies towards federal union followed the traditional pattern of a heroic poem, or a soap opera; a brave and banner-waving start, soon bogging down in misfortune, muddle, and unexpected opposition; then risky eleventh-hour manœuvres, and perhaps an intervening *deus ex machina*, bringing the plan to accomplishment.

The Confederation idea grew out of a simple realization among British North American leaders that the colonies had a limited future, or none at all, in their separate and isolated state. On a map the provinces seem jammed together. But in the mid-nineteenth century the distances were considerable, and were enlarged by regionalism and mutual mistrust. New Brunswick and Nova Scotia maintained some communication; but Prince Edward Island remained stubbornly regionalist. And Newfoundland was too far offshore to be much concerned, or considered, in mainland affairs. Again, the two Canadas had close links – though, for many fiery Catholics and truculent Orangemen, far too close. Their union had been a Colonial Office attempt to resolve the religious and racial difficulties, but it had failed; and Canada's political parties slowly strangled in a series of party splits and toppling minority governments. So that colony, too, turned in upon itself, away from the Maritimes.

This isolationism might have been awkward enough as regards expansion, trade and communication. It became downright dangerous in the light of the U.S.A.'s continental ambitions, and of the U.S. military might that was displayed in the Civil War. Fear of America, in fact, was the *deus ex machina*; for every time the spirit of Confederation flagged and threatened to vanish, some stirrings in the U.S.A. would send the British American provinces huddling together, remembering the adage about unity and strength. Of course, hopes of greater political power and financial achievements also served to nourish the Confederation spirit. And – because it would be too cynical to believe that *only* fear and greed activated the Fathers of Confederation – among the colonial leaders were men of vision, able to construct a dream of a transcontinental nation of federated provinces under the British flag.

But the dream failed to impress many people in either Britain or the U.S.A. The mother country was feeling far from motherly: the great imperial surge that had placed the Union Jack permanently in the sunshine had faded, and ownership of colonies for their own sake had come to be rejected. Though the naval uses of the Maritimes remained, British America as a whole had become more trouble to Britain than it was worth. Free trade undercut the value of colonies as markets; and British America had only a limited value as a source of raw materials. 'Our colonies are rather too fond of us, and embrace us, if anything, too closely,' editorialized *The Times* in 1849, presumably echoing Colonial Office sentiments. The mother country would have been relieved if her children had issued a Declaration of Independence.

But then by that time the provinces possessed some measure of independence, or self-government. (The colonial structure of government remained more or less the model for later provincial governments, east and west, so it should be sketched briefly here.) Westminster, of course, had been the sole colonial authority (through various ministries until the Colonial Office was established in the early 1800s – though the position of Colonial Secretary did not appear until 1854). And Westminster ruled through governors. Each Maritime province had its Lieutenant-Governor; the whole of British America was overseen by a Governor-General, who also administered the Canadas.

Governors had oligarchic 'councils' of appointed advisers, and for a long time had little else to check them. Eventually legislative assemblies appeared (Canada acquired one in 1791), elected by a franchise based on property. But they were mostly debating societies. And this backdoor gesture towards representative government was balanced by the development (from the advisory councils) of *legislative* councils – appointed, and for life – and by the governors' power of veto.

The brief and bloody revolution in the Canadas in 1837 proved the need for reform; and Lord Durham's Report on British America emphasized the need. Governors began to allow the assemblies and councils more freedom, and – in a very British process – a change to partial self-government *evolved* slowly and naturally, though never officially declared as such. The councils became ministerial cabinets in everything but name; the assemblies gained wide control over the composition of councils. Governors rarely overrode ministerial or assembly decisions; nor, it seems, did Westminster, unless the decisions were clearly at variance with British law.

Britain retained full control over foreign affairs, defence, and (in part) trade; the colonies dealt with domestic matters. But because there was no explicit statement of the division of responsibilities, the colonies always encroached on imperial areas. Thus, in mid-century, in the face of Britain's passionate commitment to free trade, British America not only retained but increased its protective tariffs.

But it seemed as if this much autonomy had satisfied the colonies. They were reluctant to sever the apron strings completely – because of honest British loyalty, but also because of a not unreasonable knowledge that the U.S.A. was belligerent and land-hungry. The colonies might have spent every available cent on defence and still have caused the U.S. Army little inconvenience. So the colonies preferred Britain to provide, and pay for, their defence. And Britain disliked both the cost and the danger of being dragged into a confrontation with the U.S.A. over these unwanted colonies.

The U.S. had good reasons, other than mere territorial appetite, for menacing the British provinces. Its anti-British stance had carried over from revolutionary days, when Nova Scotia had refused to join the thirteen New England colonies, and from the abortive War of 1812, which damaged American pride. At the beginning of the Civil War, the British American provinces angered America again. The colonists inveighed against slavery and gave sanctuary to fleeing slaves, which enraged the South. And some clever political minds, mainly

Conservative – who, seeing in the secession the possibility of a new balance of power on the continent that would take some pressure off British America, publicly hoped for a Southern victory – enraged the North. (George Brown and the *Globe*, incidentally, provided a focus for those who were wholly pro-North throughout the war.)

With the growing tension between British America and the U.S.A., it was high time to think in terms of colonial unity. Then the need was underlined: Britain decided to reinforce her Maritime garrisons, and the paucity of intercolonial communications was revealed. For the best route, the only real route, between the Canadas and New Brunswick went *through the U.S.A.* British soldiers were forced to travel the long way round, slowly and with difficulty, being transported part of the time on farmers' sleighs.

The first step towards Confederation was taken when the Maritimes began discussing union among themselves. (Interest in the west took a back seat in the mid-1860s as the east concerned itself with problems of provincial union. So the progress of Confederation, being outside our subject, will be only sketchily traced to its conclusion – which is *not* outside the subject.) They had talked of it before, but now the first of many 'international incidents' arising from the Civil War lent urgency to the talks. In November 1861 a Northern ship had intercepted the British vessel *Trent*, and had removed from the ship two Southern gentlemen. Britain reluctantly issued a formal protest, and demanded the Southerners' release. The colonies held their breath. But President Lincoln, reportedly expressing a preference for 'one war at a time', authorized the release.

Yet 'one war at a time' held an ominous implication for the future. It became more ominous in 1863, with the *Chesapeake* incident: when U.S. warships invaded Nova Scotian waters to capture a Southern privateer. This crisis, too, was overcome through some desperate diplomacy, but it in turn gave on to the next and worst incident, the notorious St Alban's raid. In 1864 some Confederates leaped across the border from Canada into Vermont, attacked and robbed the town of St Alban's, and fled back to Canada. There they were captured – but a Canadian magistrate rashly claimed he had no jurisdiction, and released them. The U.S. was furious, and the two countries were never so close to war. But Lincoln and other cooler heads averted any irrevocable moves.[1]

So the colonies were spurred into action. Maritime talks led to a full-scale conference on federation. And at this point Canada joined in. Brown and Macdonald had buried their antipathies in a short-term coalition, to overcome their political stalemate. For more permanent peace, politically, Brown suggested a loosening of Canada's own union into a federation of Canada East and Canada West; while Macdonald favoured the idea of the province adding itself to the Maritimes in an overall federation. The question was still open when the Canadians unofficially joined the Maritime Conference at Charlottetown in 1864.

There the spellbinding Brown and the persuasive Macdonald won Nova Scotia to the broader cause of British-American Confederation. New Brunswick remained cautious; Prince Edward Island, insular to the end, was opposed. But another conference was held later that year, at Quebec, to discuss formally the concept of Confederation. And there seventy-two resolutions defining the possible nature of the new nation were hammered out. One read:

> The North-West Territory, British Columbia and Vancouver [Island] shall be admitted into the Union on such terms and conditions as the Parliament of the Federated Provinces shall deem equitable. . . .

But when the provinces sought to ratify the resolutions, the whole idea nearly vanished for ever in a welter of colonial politicking and what D. G. Creighton (in *The Road To Confederation*) calls 'suspicious and narrowly parochial local patriotism'. This quality, on which no one province had a corner, frustrated Confederation for nearly two years. Opposition parties opposed the idea on principle; New Brunswick's government fell; Canada ratified the resolutions, then nearly undid the job in a new outburst of quarrelling between Brown and Macdonald that threatened the coalition.

But eventually, in 1866, further movements of the U.S.A. provided another spur – and, as it proved, the last. The end of the Civil War had left an army 800,000 strong with no one to fight, and British America feared that this military machine

[1] But America's abandonment of a reciprocal trade agreement clearly grew out of anger left over from this incident.

might be directed northwards. Then, too, there were the Fenians. Though the U.S. Army was by far the most real threat, the Fenians somehow occupied at least as many British nightmares.

The Fenians were an organization of Irish–Americans who, apparently, believed that the cause of Ireland's freedom from British rule would be furthered by raids on border towns in Canada. Their avowed aim was invasion; as a line of their marching song put it, revealingly: 'We'll go and capture Canada, for we've nothing else to do.' They were a trifle ridiculous, but their violent anti-British noise (grown noisier when news of the proposed Confederation reached them) frightened Canadians. In 1866 the New York *Herald* wondered aloud whether British–American Confederation 'does not portend evil', but added that such evil could be forestalled by 'a word of encouragement to the thousands of Fenians who are eagerly awaiting invitation to invade Canada'. The newspaper numbered the Fenians correctly, but credited them with too much politeness. It was not an invitation, but St Patrick's Day, that they claimed to be waiting for.

And then St Patrick's Day came and went without incident. Where were the Fenians? In April they were in Portland (Maine) glowering across the border – 500 of them, all armed. Britain sent ships, Canada's militia bravely forgathered. But in the event the Irish mountain brought forth an exceedingly harmless mouse: the main event of the Fenian attack was the theft of a British flag from a New Brunswick island.

During the scare, however, Confederation had gained mightily in popularity. With regionalism and factionalism set aside for once, the politicians were seen to be amazingly rapid and efficient workers. Shortly a group of delegates from the committed provinces met in London, presented a plan to H.M. Government, and with British help worked out the British North America Act. Preoccupied with domestic affairs, the British Parliament debated it briefly and passed it readily.

On July 1, 1867 British America was reborn as the Dominion of Canada, a federation of four provinces: Nova Scotia, New Brunswick, Ontario and Quebec. Almost immediately, the new Dominion began the process of gathering into the fold remaining provinces and territories, according to the clause of the B.N.A. Act which specified:

It shall be lawful for the Queen . . . on addresses from the Houses of Parliament of Canada, and from the Houses of the respective legislatures of the Colonies or Provinces of Newfoundland, Prince Edward Island, and British Columbia,[1] to admit those Colonies or Provinces, or any of them, into the Union, and on address from the Houses of Parliament in Canada, to admit Rupert's Land and the North-Western Territory, or either of them into the Union. . . .

Perhaps, when Canada was born, no shots were heard around the world. But some of the noises – from that clutch of tiny outposts of Victorianism on the St Lawrence and the Atlantic – were being listened to very closely in the even tinier outposts of the west.

[1] By this time, as Chapter 5 will show, Vancouver Island and the mainland had been united as the Crown Colony of British Columbia. Red River and Rupert's Land remained mere settlements, lacking any measure of responsible government.

4

The First Western Province

Confederation, with all its attendant reorganizations and administrative tangles, rocked the east like an explosion. The blast wave took two years to reach the west: but when it came, it created a major turning point, the importance of which cannot be exaggerated. The year 1869 marked the first death-throes of the old wild free western life of fur trader and métis, beaver trapper and buffalo hunter. (The last throes, in 1885, would be considerably more violent, as the conclusion of a transition period begun in 1869.) Confederated Canada would ensure that agriculture – so far represented in the west by a few scratchings on the banks of the Red River and on Vancouver Island – would inherit the emptiness. Civilization began to make its first irresistible thrusts against the frontier.

A renewal of the American threat acted as a spur on Canada's westward ambitions. After the Civil War, and after the cavalry had crushed the Sioux uprising, Minnesotans had returned in force to lean heavily on the flimsy barrier of the boundary. On the Pacific, in 1867, the U.S.A. had bought Alaska from the Russians. Canada's dream of an ocean-to-ocean dominion was in jeopardy: the land beyond the mountains would be unlikely to remain British for long unless someone threw it a lifeline. An ex-Canadian in America, George Sheppard, had written at the end of the Civil War that a little tightening of the economic ties binding Red River and St Paul would cause the British settlement to 'drop like a ripe plum' into U.S. expansionist hands. And Britain's Pacific possessions were ripening as well.

To forestall an American takeover, Canada might have admitted the west into Confederation, conferring provincial status (and a measure of self-government) on Rupert's Land

and the Northwest. Or Britain might have made the west a Crown Colony, with all the appurtenances of governors and colonial administrations. But instead Canada wanted control. The Dominion favoured outright *annexation* of the west, whereby it would be governed directly from Ottawa. In other words, Canada – while herself still a colony – wanted to turn the west into a Canadian colony. But there remained the obstacle of the Hudson's Bay Company, with its powerful connections in Britain and its monolithic influence in the west.

H.B.C. was not opposed to the principle of western colonization: the new management, which had taken over in 1863, brought a keen interest in railways, telegraphs and settlement into its operation of the fur trade.[1] But even so the Company intended to protect its rights – against the Canadian hope of acquiring (annexing) the west at little cost. Canada had previously begun its assault, as Chapter 3 showed, by challenging the H.B.C. charter. But this ploy was countered, in 1867, by the pragmatic politicians of the Colonial Office, who pointed out that the charter had been treated as valid since 1670, and that it was therefore no time to be dredging up objections. Britain was determined to respect the claims of the Company.

So a long-drawn-out negotiation began, a series of offers and counter-offers, with H.B.C. taking umbrage here and Canada sulking there, and the Office in the middle. Britain passed the 'Rupert's Land Act' in 1868, which merely prepared legal machinery by which control of the west could be regained by Britain and turned over to Canada once H.B.C.'s claims had been satisfactorily met. Canada then found that, while H.B.C. was quite willing to relinquish its political power, it sought adequate compensation for the loss of its legal ownership of the land in Rupert's Land. The governor of H.B.C. outlined his definition of 'adequate': £1,000,000 cash, and ownership of all existing posts and 6,000 acres around each, and guarantees of earlier land grants made (to settlers) by H.B.C., and the right to continue the fur trade, including no duties on furs exported

[1] See page 63. In this takeover, the H.B.C. Committee had sold their shares to a financial organization called the International Financial Society, representing the Northwest Transit Company, which had wanted to erect a telegraph line into the west but had been blocked by H.B.C. The change had very little effect on the operations of the H.B.C. in Canada. Nor did the telegraph arrive in the west until some years later.

or goods imported. Canada issued a flat rejection. The Colonial Office murmured soothing words, and talked with H.B.C. about reducing the land demands. The Canadian negotiators emitted vague threats to annex the west without making terms with H.B.C. H.B.C. replied by suggesting that the west become a Crown Colony. Finally the harassed Colonial Secretary, aware at all times of the looming American presence, suggested a settlement of £300,000 cash and a varying amount of land around the posts as the basis of a compromise. As the two sides demurred, the Secretary threatened to send the whole question to the Privy Council for arbitration. The ultimatum brought H.B.C. and Canada together: the price and the land grant were agreed, Britain arranged a loan to Canada to cover the £300,000 compensation, and the actual transfer of control began.

Canada passed an 'Act for the Temporary Government of Rupert's Land and the North-Western Territory when united with Canada', which among other things provided for the appointment of a Lieutenant-Governor through whom Canada's western policies would be executed. H.B.C., in turn, signed a Deed of Surrender. Then, in late 1869, both sides awaited the formal Order in Council from Britain that would complete the transfer.

Hindsight affords many joys, among them the smug pleasure of watching leaders of the past fall into avoidable errors. To Canada and H.B.C., the transfer was a simple deal in real estate – though a fairly stirring one. It made the tiny new Dominion of Canada into a giant, territorially speaking; and it reduced the mighty H.B.C., after 200 years, to a mere trading company. (The Company's licence to trade had not been altered by the transfer.) But, while most of the negotiators had been vaguely aware of the importance of these developments, not one seems to have concerned himself with the intense trauma that the transfer produced among the people of the west. It seems almost as if none of the negotiators remembered that there *were* people in the west. But in 1869, before the last steps of the transfer could be taken, Canada and H.B.C. and Britain were sharply reminded of the presence of humanity along the Red River, when the trauma produced its rebellious reaction among the métis of the settlement.

.   .   .   .   .

The métis had been aware of certain danger signals, in terms of Canada's interest in the west, for years before Confederation. A Canadian takeover of Red River, they knew, would mean a large influx of Canadian settlers. As the dominant majority in Red River, the métis feared for the loss of their position and influence. The French Catholics (British métis were a minority among the mixed-bloods of the settlement) feared for their language, religion and culture under the impact of a horde of Anglo-Saxon Protestants.[1] The métis farmers, either squatters or working land granted to them by H.B.C., feared for their titles to the land if H.B.C. power was removed. The wandering métis buffalo hunters feared for their livelihood if extensive settlement drove the herds farther afield. And every one of these justifiable fears was exacerbated by the statements and actions of a new force in Red River life – a nucleus of new-comers from Ontario, calling themselves the 'Canadian Party', or 'Canada Firsters'. They gathered around a man named Dr John Christian Schultz.

Schultz's arrival in Red River in 1860 (as a merchant and general trader, not as a physician) ended the peace that had prevailed since the métis gained the freedom of the fur trade. He became the rallying point of all Canadian newcomers who hoped to see Red River as an extension of Ontario. Shortly Schultz took over the settlement's newspaper, the *Nor'wester* (later he turned its editorship over to another and ran the paper more discreetly) to propagandize energetically against H.B.C. and for annexation. From his outpourings the métis got a good idea of what would be in store for them when Ontarians began to pour into Red River. As the *Nor'wester* put it, 'the indolent and careless . . . will fall back before the march of a superior intelligence'. The métis, well aware of the Ontarians' racial and religious bigotry, knew who was meant.

The stresses mounted after Confederation, and during the negotiations with H.B.C. Schultz began provocatively to fly a British flag with letters spelling CANADA stitched across it. Other members of his entourage kept up the propaganda broadsides. Then in 1868 this tension diminished in the face of

[1] French Canada shared these fears: throughout the negotiations with H.B.C., Quebec had struggled in vain to have Red River admitted as a province to Confederation, which would have allowed some self-deter-mination, and preserved *la vie française*.

an emergency: grasshoppers once again gnawed the settlement bare. Help came from H.B.C., Britain, the U.S.A. and Canada. But Canada's assistance took the form of subsidizing a road (along the route surveyed by Dawson[1]) from Red River east to Lake of the Woods. It was a necessary road, and served as 'make-work' relief for Red River's economy; but it brought in with it a rowdy group of Canadian workers, who soon found fellowship among the Canada Firsters. Some of the newcomers decided to stay, and proceeded greedily to stake out huge tracts of land, while crowing publicly about the fortunes they would make on land deals. So the métis got a further foretaste of the nature of Ontarian settlement. They received yet more from one Charles Mair.

Mair, a clerk with the road-building company, had literary pretensions: he also had a small involvement with the west, being a protégé of William McDougall, editor of the Toronto *North American*, strong advocate of Canadian annexation of the west, and one of the negotiators with H.B.C. over the transfer. Shortly after arriving in Red River, Mair wrote a series of letters to his brother in Perth, Ontario; the local paper printed them; the Toronto *Globe* reprinted them. Presumably Mair had never expected such a wide dissemination of his spiteful, distorted views – for the *Globe* found its way to Red River, and the settlers read the letters.

They read:

> Many wealthy people here are married to half-breed women, who, having no coat of arms but a 'totem' to look back to, make up for this deficiency by biting at the backs of their 'white' sisters.

And more:

> The half-breeds are the only people here who are starving [after the grasshopper plague] . . . and it is their own fault, they won't farm. . . . As for the farmers: Scotch, English and French, not one of them requires relief. . . .

These were slanderous, racist lies. And Mair did not go unscathed. The wife of a leading citizen, Mrs A. G. B. Bannatyne (who was not métis), seeing Mair enter the Bannatyne general store, took down a horsewhip from the wall and whipped Mair out of the store and down the street. He was then ordered out

[1] See page 62.

of Red River by the furious citizenry. (Later he returned – after making a public apology – and promptly became a leading figure in Schultz's party.)

The progress of the negotiations towards their conclusion in 1869 sparked further resentment, for no one at Red River had been or was being officially informed of the impending transfer.[1] What news came to the settlement arrived by means of eastern newspapers, weeks out of date. Not even William Mactavish, the governor of Red River, had received any word from his H.B.C. masters; the métis were further out of touch. Fear and suspicion mushroomed: even the English-speaking Red Riverites, who had never been unduly disturbed by the Canadian party, became uneasy. It had always rankled with them that Red River had no real representative government. But at least the H.B.C. Governor, and the Council of Assiniboia, ruled by sufferance if not by suffrage. (They would have found it impossible to force an unpopular measure on to the people, and they knew it.) Now strangers were coming from Ottawa to rule – strangers who probably knew nothing of western conditions. (These realistic suspicions were to be justified.) It was intolerable. Had anyone asked, he would have found that the British Red Riverites hoped that the settlement would become a Crown Colony, with its own elected assembly responsible to the British Parliament and the Queen. But no one was interested in their preferences. They had been neither consulted nor informed when H.B.C. was sold, in 1863, to the International Financial Society – and the settlers sold with it, 'like dumb, driven cattle', as the *Nor'wester* said. Now they were to be sold again, the same way. But this time the métis, at least, did not remain dumb and would not be driven.

In late 1869 Canada sent a survey party to carve Red River into lots. The métis objected, understandably: Canada planned to divide the land in the Ontario and U.S.A. way, square townships composed of square sections. The Red Riverites farmed the old Quebec way, in 'river lots', which would never

---

[1] Joseph Howe, Secretary of State for the Provinces, did pay a quick visit to Red River in 1869, just before the crisis. But while he was sage enough to avoid all contact with Schultz and the Canadian party, he also made no effort to reach the métis. He talked privately with Mactavish and the Council, and then left – having made no public statements, and apparently unaware of the extent of the unrest.

fit into an Ontario-style township. Again the métis feared for their land titles, and so a group of them, unarmed but adamant, met the surveyors and stopped the survey. They also warned that if the survey was begun again, before there had been some word from Canada about safeguarding métis rights, it would be halted by force. The ultimatum was delivered by Louis Riel.

The leader of the Red River Rebellion, as it is called, was the son of a Red River métis leader who has appeared in this narrative before, and a French-Canadian woman who was the daughter of the first white woman to live in the west. Riel, born in 1844 in St Boniface, one of the most populous French parishes on the Red, had been educated in the College of Montreal, and then worked for a while in St Paul. As unrest increased on Red River, he returned in 1868 to join and then to lead the métis' resistance.

It must be clear that he did not rouse the métis to rebellion. Their resentment had already aroused them, just as their highly developed sense of community united them for concerted action. Riel, as leader, served to channel and focus their rebelliousness. He became their leader because he was educated, so could talk their enemies' language; because he was superbly eloquent, so could rally and encourage; because he was the son of a métis leader, so was committed to their aims; and because he was there. Riel has been painted in many colours: G. F. G. Stanley, his biographer, calls him inexperienced, vain and totalitarian, but believes he was a sincere patriot; W. L. Morton, Manitoba's greatest historian, describes him as impetuous, and speaks of an instability of character. Alexander Begg, a Red Riverite who was present during the troubles, insists he was an honest man. So, at this time, he seems to have been: an honest man with an honest cause, clever but by no means a tactical genius, making serious blunders under stress, fighting a losing battle as best he could.

By the time the ultimatum had been delivered to the surveyors, Red River had heard (at second hand) that its governor was to be William McDougall – the pro-annexation Toronto newspaper owner, federal Minister of Works, one of the negotiators with H.B.C. His Ministry controlled the survey and the road-building, and thus was associated in Red River minds with the Canada First interlopers and the land-grabbing road gangs – as well as with Charles Mair. The métis knew that McDougall had no first-hand knowledge of the west. Nor did many of the Canadians appointed to serve as his advisory council (though, to be fair, the council included some respected Red Riverites as well). As the unkindest cut, both Governor and Council had been appointed and were on their way to the settlement *before* the transfer was officially complete. So the métis determined to stop them.

A few days after halting the survey, a group met in a private home and formed a 'Comité National des Métis', with one John Bruce as figurehead president, and Louis Riel as secretary. The next day about forty armed métis rode south to the Rivière Sale, where they erected a barricade across the road from Minnesota which McDougall would take. At the same time they sent a note to McDougall, forbidding him to enter the west '*sans une permission spéciale de ce Comité*'.

The various separable groups in Red River reacted to these steps in more or less predictable ways. Schultz and the Canadian party hotly accused the métis of treason. (Legally, they were wrong. The métis' action was a *resistance*, not a rebellion. Sovereignty in Red River was still at that time held by the British Crown, since the transfer was not complete. The Canadian authorities had as yet no power in the west – and the métis were seeking to resist and prevent their assumption of power.) The Kildonan and other Scots communities remained cautiously neutral, sympathizing with the French métis but not siding with them. Governor Mactavish and the H.B.C. were understanding and sympathetic but officially could not sanction the resistance. The Americans were delighted, seeing a chance that Red River anti-Canadianism might produce pro-Americanism, and that the ripe plum might yet fall. The Catholic Church came out strongly in favour of the métis: indeed, several priests took an active part in Riel's progress, especially one Père Ritchot, whom some of the métis called '*l'esprit dirigeante des métis*'. The Council of Assiniboia termed the resistance outrageous, and sought – in vain – to prevent it.

In this divided land Riel moved smoothly towards consolidating his position. The discipline of the buffalo hunters' councils prevailed throughout the métis ranks: Riel's men even swore an oath not to drink liquor during the resistance, and apparently kept it. While some of the several hundred resisters guarded the road to the south, scouting over the prairie in case

McDougall evaded the barricade, Riel led a force of armed men to take command of Fort Garry – to 'protect' it, as he told the Fort's H.B.C. owners. The latter offered no resistance, and Riel had thus peaceably gained a highly defensible and well-supplied base of operations. Now he was firmly in control.

Extending a hand of amity to the other settlers, he issued a 'Public Notice to the Inhabitants of Rupert's Land' aimed especially at the British communities, inviting them to send representatives to meet with the Comité. The delegates duly arrived, but remained non-committal, stating at the meeting that the proper course would have been to allow McDougall to enter and hear the métis' objections. Riel, pointing out that such *faits accomplis* were often irreversible, claimed that the resistance would ensure that the métis' objections would be listened to. He then presented his plan: to form a provisional government in Red River which could negotiate with Canada. He sought only negotiation, not violence. But the British settlers felt that the formation of such a government, within a land ruled by the Crown, would be treason; and the meeting ended in stalemate.

Now the crisis was truly upon them. December 1, 1869, the date on which Rupert's Land would be officially made over to Canada, had arrived. McDougall was moving north from Minnesota. The governor-to-be apparently heard for the first time of the resistance only upon reaching Pembina. There he paused, and sent an aide to the barricade to talk to the métis. With the aide went a military member of the entourage, one Captain Cameron, who tried to bluster the barricade down by ordering the métis (as Alexander Begg describes it) to 'clear away that blawsted fence and let him pass; nor did he think it worthwhile to drop his eye-glass in the excitement.' But neither soft words nor ruling-class arrogance prevailed: the aide and the captain were escorted back to Pembina under métis guns.

Mactavish advised McDougall to go back to Canada and wait, but the expansive governor – whom Begg calls 'overbearing, distant and unpleasant' – insisted on staying and getting things under control. Worse, on December 1 he issued a provocative and pompous declaration, with many invocations of Her Majesty, that he was now the sole authority in Red River, on behalf of the Dominion of Canada.

Unfortunately for his self-importance, he was not. For Canada, hearing the news of the resistance, had decided not to accept the transfer just yet, preferring to let H.B.C. and the Crown clean up the mess before taking over. Since the métis were not in arms against Britain, but against Canada, a delay in Canada's assumption of power might permit a peaceable solution. The news of the delay reached McDougall after the proclamation had been made, and neatly jerked the rug from under him.

The delay also worsened Riel's position, since it replaced Red River authority in H.B.C. hands, and made the resistance – technically – an insurrection. But the métis were already far past considerations of legality. From Fort Garry they issued a List of Rights, setting out their demands for a representative legislature to balance the power of governor and council, and for guarantees of the continuance of their language, religion, and 'customs and usages'. The reasonableness of the List, and of its tone, reinforced the growing sympathy for the French among the English-speaking neutrals.

McDougall replied by trying to raise an armed force to crush the resistance. But the British Red Riverites failed to respond: only the Canada Firsters rallied to the call. Their action was doubly foolish: McDougall had no authority to resort to force, and the Canadians were vastly outnumbered. In the end it was a near-farcical conflict. About 600 métis gathered at Fort Garry in the face of the Canadian threat; and the Canadians, about seventy of them, set out to achieve their avowed end of crushing Riel by the strategy of barricading themselves in a warehouse. Riel surrounded the building, posted cannon outside, and gave them an ultimatum. The Canadians laid down their arms, and marched meekly off to imprisonment – as hostages – in the fort.

Riel then strengthened his position further by issuing a 'Declaration' (both sides were greatly given to grandiose documents) asserting the formation of a provisional government, of which he was elected president. The new government's flag reportedly bore a fleur-de-lis and a shamrock on a white background – the shamrock being (according to Begg) in honour of one W. B. O'Donoghue, an Irishman with Fenian inclinations who had risen to some prominence among the insurgents. Riel at this time also suppressed the Schultzite newspaper, the

Nor'wester, along with a paper named the *Red River Pioneer* which had never fully got into production. Finally, he took over H.B.C.'s accounts and funds at Fort Garry. Meanwhile, McDougall returned east, having been sharply reprimanded by Ottawa for his precipitate actions.

More diplomacy-by-proclamation followed, but temperate spirits were in charge. Britain spoke soothingly of 'misunderstandings' and 'peaceful negotiations'; Canada sent a Catholic dignitary and a respected French officer to Red River to mollify the métis. Riel listened to them courteously, but knew they had no authority from Ottawa to negotiate. He knew the same of a third emissary, from John A. Macdonald – the resourceful H.B.C. man and politician Donald A. Smith.[1] Because Smith had firmly refused to recognize Riel's government, he had been kept under wraps in Fort Garry. But he still managed some back-door persuasion, having been empowered by Macdonald to spread assurances and money on the troubled waters. Soon a few French began having Smith-inspired doubts about the new newspaper, the *New Nation*, set up by an American group with Riel's approval and tending to voice strong pro-U.S.A. sentiments. (Riel himself did not advocate that Red River join the United States, but he apparently did not object to this view being propagandized.)

Worried by these developments, Riel asserted himself. He evicted from the Fort a party of French métis who had never wholly favoured his methods; he put Governor Mactavish and his doctor (the Governor was ill during most of the crisis) under 'house arrest'; and he began to demand oaths of allegiance to the provisional government from all his followers. But eventually pressure from the other Red Riverites forced him to relent, and

[1] This man will figure prominently in many great events of the west, and so deserves an introduction. An immigrant from Scotland, with good connections, Smith had joined H.B.C. upon his arrival in Canada, and served in backwoods posts for many years, mainly in Labrador. He swiftly rose to the position of a Chief Trader, then a Chief Factor of the Labrador region – during which time his canny stock market dealings laid the foundations of his great personal wealth. In the 1860s he was General Manager of H.B.C.'s Eastern Division (based in Montreal) and was tipped as the next Governor of H.B.C. in Canada. Somehow Smith's experience in Labrador and Montreal bestowed on him the reputation of being an authority on the west – for which reason Macdonald turned to him during the Red River resistance.

to permit Smith to address a public meeting. The meeting proved to be the turning point. Smith, no great orator but vastly shrewd and calculating, read to the crowd from official documents designed to reassure the métis. Among the documents was a letter from Joseph Howe to McDougall, dated some weeks earlier, which read in part:

> You will be in a position to assure the residents of the North West Territories –
> 1. That all their civil and religious liberties will be sacredly respected.
> 2. That all their properties, rights and privileges of every kind, as enjoyed under the government of the Hudson's Bay Company, will be continued.
> 3. That in granting titles to land now occupied by the settlers, the most liberal policy will be pursued. . . .
> 8. That . . . the Government of Canada will be prepared to submit a measure to Parliament, granting a liberal constitution. . . .

So the meeting broke up with cheering, and the French and English Red Riverites met again, as a 'Convention'. They seemed wholly confident in Smith's assurance 'that on entering Confederation, they would be secured in the possession of all rights, privileges, and immunities enjoyed by British subjects in other parts of the Dominion'.

Riel, however, remained dubious – partly, perhaps, because he felt power slipping away from him, and partly because Smith had provided reassurance when he and his métis had been fighting for guarantees. So he tried to forestall the new mood: he suggested that Red River be admitted to Confederation as a *province*, not as a territory ruled by Ottawa. The Convention rejected this idea, and also turned down Riel's proposal that the transfer of Rupert's Land be renegotiated by Canada with his provisional government. Riel fought on, challenging Smith to admit that he had no real power to guarantee the métis' rights. Smith adroitly evaded the question by revealing a new concession: Canada had invited a delegation from Red River to come to Ottawa for talks.

The Convention accepted joyously. Then Riel desperately sought to convince its members that a new provisional government must be formed. The British settlers (prompted by Mactavish, who recommended a peace-keeping gesture) agreed: the new government was quickly formed, with Riel again as president. From that point – in February 1870 – the united settlement might have progressed smoothly to peace. But, sadly, the Canadian party was abroad again.

Some of the Schultzites had been released from prison, after promising to behave and swearing allegiance to the provisional government. Others had escaped – including Schultz himself, who got away in classical style, prying open a window with tools smuggled to him by his wife, and climbing down a rope improvised with strips of buffalo robe from his bed coverings. Riel swore to shoot him if he was recaptured, but remained calm enough to release more prisoners. At about the time that the last batch was going free, news came that the Canadian escapees had gathered a force of about sixty men, at Portage la Prairie, to assault the fort and free the prisoners. The force was joined by a few hundred settlers who objected to Riel's high-handed imprisonments, and by a few Indians whom Schultz had induced to come along.

The attackers moved on the Fort, mustering at Kildonan, the old Scots 'parish' at the Forks. There the Canadians captured a young métis whom they believed to be close to Riel (though Riel later denied him). They took him as a hostage, but shortly the captive broke away from them. In his flight he attacked and killed a prominent Kildonan Scot named Sutherland. The furious Canadians pursued him, recaptured him, and in the struggle the métis was badly injured. Within a short while he was dead.

These first casualties of the resistance shocked the settlers who had come to help the Canadians. They began to regret their recruitment, began to see that any further killings – which a siege of the Fort would certainly cause – would split Red River, irreparably, into French and English camps and drown the peace in a welter of race hatred. Many decided to go no further. Many more decided the same when a message came from Riel, stating that all the Schultzite prisoners had been freed, pleading for peace between French and British. The plea won them over. Suddenly the Canadians found that only their original nucleus remained – sixty against Riel's many hundreds and the stout walls of the fort. They left Kildonan – and as they passed the fort, apparently on their way back to Portage, the métis sallied out and arrested them without a struggle.

But now that the Canadian hotheads had precipitated a new crisis, Riel too succumbed to hotheadedness. He decided to prove that his government had teeth. Among the new group of prisoners was an Irishman named Thomas Scott, an Ontario Orangeman who had been Riel's prisoner before, and who – like many other Orangemen in the Schultz faction – had always been violently outspoken in his hatred for Riel and the French métis. Riel chose him – for no good reason – to serve as a warning to other would-be counter-insurrectionists. Scott was tried for his part in the abortive siege, and condemned to death. He was shot in early March.

No one at the time could guess at the reaction that this unnecessary death would produce. Instead, the new provisional government went quietly on with its business – selecting delegates to visit Ottawa. They chose Père Ritchot, a respected judge named John Black, and a settler named Alfred Scott (no relation to Thomas). And the government took a vital decision, virtually forced upon them by Riel (whose power was once again rock-steady). They decided to request Ottawa to admit the Red River Settlement into Confederation as a province. A revised List of Rights spelled it out:

1. That the Territories, heretofore known as Rupert's Land and the North-West, shall not enter into the Confederation of the Dominion of Canada, except as a Province, to be styled and known as the Province of Assiniboia, and with all the rights and privileges common to the different Provinces of the Dominion.

Other items sought guarantees of the settlers' land titles and way of life, of the provincial legislature's sovereignty over local matters, and of protection for the French language and customs in the new province. Thus armed, the delegates set out for Ottawa – and found themselves in the midst of a maelstrom of protest.

Schultz and his cohorts had reached Ontario earlier. There they had transformed the mild wave of shock that had rippled through Canada, as a result of Scott's death, into a frenzied demand for forceful action against the métis 'murderers'. (Schultz had whipped up the storm by sponsoring, or at least not denying, stories that Scott had been viciously butchered, tortured, and allowed to suffer for days.) The Liberal opposition in Parliament, dominated by Orange Ontario, scored political points by maintaining that Macdonald should not see the delegates. Ritchot and Alfred Scott were actually arrested on an Ottawa street (on a warrant sworn out by Thomas Scott's brother), but were released for lack of evidence. Quebec produced apologists for the métis, and the old animosities flared again. Against this atmosphere of opportunism and acrimony, John A. Macdonald began talks – discreetly – with the Red River delegation.

The talks themselves proved amicable and brief. Out of them came a settlement that incorporated many of the features of the final List of Rights (except for some of Riel's more exorbitant financial demands). Above all, Red River's desire for provincehood was accepted.

Shortly afterwards Macdonald brought a bill into Parliament providing for the acceptance of a piece of the west into Confederation: a comparatively small piece of about 11,000 square miles. The bill seemed designed to warm Red River hearts. It set aside 1,400,000 acres as a special provenance for the métis (to be looked at further below). It provided safeguards for the French language and the Catholic religion. It ordained a provincial government composed of an elected Legislative Assembly, an appointed Council (functioning like a ministerial cabinet), and a Lieutenant-Governor. It provided for a cash grant and an annual subsidy to shore up the initial development of the provincial economy. And, finally, it broke away from the British North America Act of 1867 by retaining all unoccupied territory as *dominion* lands, under federal control.

Because of this last measure, a special Imperial Act was required from the British Parliament. But in the meantime – in spite of some opposition from McDougall – Canada passed the bill in July 1870. The Red River Settlement and environs had been reborn as the first western province, Manitoba.[1]

Peace might then have fallen on Red River. But another provision of the Manitoba Act, designed largely to appease Ontario's thirst for punishment of the rebels, sent a military expedition struggling for weeks across the rock and muskeg north of the Lakes to 'restore order' in the new province. Of

[1] Said to mean 'spirit strait' in Cree, 'lake of the prairie' in Assiniboine. The name showed a desire for a fresh start: 'Assiniboia' had too many sombre associations, from the Selkirk days of suffering to the Riel days of violence.

84

Voyageurs shooting rapids in a freight canoe

The Earl of Selkirk

A drawing of some early Red River settlers, including French (holding the rifle), Swiss (in the peaked cap) and Scots (in the tam o'shanter, seated and smoking)

Fort Victoria, painted in 1846, showing the Hudson's Bay Company's steamer S.S. *Beaver* in the foreground

Fort Garry (the upper fort) in the 1840s, with Red River carts and an
Indian tepee in foreground

Métis in the wild and dangerous buffalo hunt

Part of the Cariboo Road, along the cliffs over the Fraser River. Note that part of the road is supported by pilings, and part (right) by interlocking ballast-filled cribbing

A Cariboo miner in the 1860s

A Plains Indian family. Notice the European clothing and rifle, but also the traditional tepee

Fort Carlton, on the North Saskatchewan River, sketched in 1872

The North-West Mounted Police, on parade at their Regina headquarters, 1883

A detachment of North-West Mounted Police at Fort Pitt (Saskatchewan), 1884. The bearded sword-carrying officer at the right is Inspector Dickens, son of the English novelist

A drawing of Main Street, Winnipeg, in the 1870s

Father Albert
Lacombe, O.M.I.

course order had been restored long before they arrived. Red River's own Bishop Taché, arriving rather too late from a trip to Rome, assured Riel that Canada would issue a general amnesty: and Riel and his followers quietly proceeded to disband their forces. Then the soldiers arrived. Their commander, Colonel Wolseley, was a reasonable man, but many Ontarians in the force were not. They openly avowed their intention of seeking 'revenge' for Scott's execution. In the face of such threats, and in the absence of an amnesty, Riel and the other métis leaders went into hiding.

Persecutions began. The soldiers treated the métis with rough contempt, and the remnants of the Canadian party imitated them. The métis, resentful and bitter, fought back, for the situation was exactly what they had feared from a Canadian takeover. Fights, beatings, near-riots broke out daily. Neither Wolseley nor the new Lieutenant-Governor – a fair-minded Nova Scotian named A. G. Archibald – could put a stop to the furore. Incident piled on incident, as more Canadians came: civilians now, some of them settlers, some merchants, some land speculators. In a particular case, a crowd of Ontarians chased a young métis into the river and hurled stones at him as he swam away. Reportedly, a stone struck him on the head. In any event, the boy drowned.

In another case, a band of métis had established themselves on good land – their share of that 1,400,000 acres – near a stream called the Rivière aux Ilets de Bois. Planning to farm *and* hunt, they left the land and moved on to the prairie after the buffalo. When they returned, they found a group of Ontarians had jumped their claim and settled on their land. The furious métis were at the point of driving off the trespassers by force, but Governor Archibald persuaded them that violence, with the soldiers on hand, would be disastrous for them and for all Red River métis. So the band concluded that their only alternative was to leave the area, to go as far away from Canadians as possible. They moved west, into the empty prairie – while the Ontario land-grabbers, as a final insult, renamed the little stream 'the Boyne'.

Many more métis were to take the trails into the deep west. The government of Canada had – of its own volition, for Riel had not demanded it – provided the huge 'reserve' of land for the métis, but administrative difficulties and delays in surveying had stalled the actual allocation. At first the land grant had been intended for métis *families* (at one time taken to mean unmarried children in 1870), to ensure them their share of Manitoba. Later the interpretation was extended to include heads of families. But, in the meantime, Ottawa issued 'scrip' to the métis on the basis of which they could select their allotted land. Pieces of paper meant little to many of the less settled métis – and these, too, were the most disturbed by the persecutions. So a great number of métis sold their scrip and moved to areas in the Territories – areas such as the Qu'Appelle valley, or along the North Saskatchewan river[1] – to take up the old life of wandering buffalo hunters. And the métis' distaste for the Ontarians was not lessened by the dealings between the buyers of the scrip and the often naïve sellers: speculators and confidence men acquired title to vast tracts of Manitoba for trifling amounts, even a bottle of whisky.

The widespread métis exodus from Red River would have dangerous repercussions, farther west, some fifteen years later. At the time it and the persecutions had effect enough. The métis leaders could not remain inactive while their people were being mistreated; moreover, they felt (given the shrill rage that still prevailed in Ontario) they would have to wait a long time for an amnesty. They came out of hiding and returned, quietly, to Red River – first Riel, then Ambrose Lepine (who had presided over the Court that had condemned Scott) and the Fenian sympathizer O'Donoghue.

The latter urged Riel to seek help – up to and including a request for annexation – from the U.S.A. Riel, remaining loyal to Britain, refused; so O'Donoghue went off on his own to rally the American Fenians. Red River trembled at the rumour that the terrible Fenians were marching. But the attack, when it came, was fine Irish music-hall farce.

O'Donoghue had been turned away by almost everyone: even Fenian leaders in New York had given up any wild ideas of invading Canada. But he fell in with a kindred spirit, a man named O'Neill whom even the Fenians had disowned, and together they rounded up a raggle-taggle crew of toughs. In October 1871 this party rushed across the border from Pembina, attacked an H.B.C. fort – which proved to be unoccupied – and took possession of it.

[1] See Chapters 6 and 9.

86

Apparently they expected the French métis to rise and join them. But Riel had meanwhile met with Archibald and assured him that the métis wanted only peace – and the governor had publicly shaken Riel's hand and promised him temporary immunity from arrest. So the Fenians were left out on a very fragile limb. Almost immediately after they had made their fine foray against the empty fort, a detachment of U.S. troops came over from Pembina and led them home again.

Ontario, of course, objected to Archibald's dealings with Riel, and the now blazing controversy over the amnesty question burned even hotter. Macdonald, using a reliable technique, paid Riel and Lepine $1,000 to stay out of Manitoba until the temperature dropped, while in Ottawa he made a fine show of regret at the flight of the rebel leaders. So the matter continued – for over three years. Petitions flew to Ottawa, from Red River, from vengeful Ontario and watchful Quebec. Manitoba, favouring an amnesty, expressed its views clearly by electing Riel as one of their representatives to the federal Parliament. Of course he never took his seat. But, elected a second time, he once slipped into Ottawa and signed the members' register in the House of Commons.

In 1874 the controversy reached its peak. The Ontario Orangemen in Parliament, led by another new M.P. – Dr Schultz, still Riel's nemesis – sponsored a vote that expelled Riel from the House. At about the same time Ambrose Lepine was captured, tried, convicted of murder, and sentenced to death.

As petitions multiplied, and the conflict deepened, Canada's Governor-General, Lord Dufferin, stepped in and on his own responsibility commuted the sentence. He had sought to relieve Macdonald's ministers of the onus of such a decision; but many people, on both sides of the controversy, felt he had overstepped his constitutional powers. The debate over this and related questions, broad or trivial, went on and on. Finally, however, in the tortuous manner of parliaments, a decision was reached. In 1875 an amnesty was granted to the Red River rebels.

It was a full amnesty for everyone involved, except for three leaders. Riel and Lepine received their pardon on condition that they remained 'in banishment', outside Canada, for five years. Two years later O'Donoghue (who had been arrested after the Fenian débâcle) was included in the five-year exile.

With this decision the afterbirth of Manitoba's emergence had finally been cleared away.

Already the new province was becoming a magnet for settlers. But the growth of settlement in the 1870s and after must be left for later chapters: here it will be enough to look briefly at the existing settled areas, as they were when Manitoba was created.

In 1870, according to R. G. MacBeth (a Presbyterian minister in Red River), the settlement held exactly 11,963 inhabitants. At the risk of a statistical overload, the figure can be broken down, still following MacBeth. The population was composed of 5,700 French métis; 4,000 English-speaking métis; 1,500 whites; and about 575 Indians. The white segment divided into about 750 native-born Red Riverites; 290 Canadians; 240 immigrants from Scotland; 125 from England; 70 from America; 47 from Ireland; and a scattering of other nationalities including 15 French from France. In terms of religion, the Catholics numbered 6,250, the Protestants 5,700.[1]

The various separate communities had gathered themselves, Hargrave says, 'in a long line of isolated houses along the banks of the rivers, in no place stretching back any distance on the prairie'. The British settlers lived mostly north of the Forks, the French mostly south. This linear development of the settlement necessitated a rather astonishing number of churches. Ten Anglican (C. of E.) churches were strung out along the upper Red and the north side of the Assiniboine, with three Presbyterian churches among them. The Presbyterians and the Methodists also had 'preaching stations' spotted westwards to Portage la Prairie. The Roman Catholics were served by seven churches along the lower Red and the south bank of the Assiniboine. The Church of England parishes each contained at least one small day school; the Catholics had a sizeable school, an orphanage and a convent in St Boniface. More will be made later of religious and missionary activity in the west, but it should be added here that two bishops reigned in Red River: the Anglican Bishop of Rupert's Land,

[1] J. J. Hargrave provides an extension to these figures. In 1871, he says, there were 12,800 Manitobans, and the French métis population had passed 6,000. The province's growth rate would increase more dramatically in the next few years.

who governed the missionaries scattered across the emptiness (including one who was ministering to the Yukon, 3,000 miles away), and the Catholic Bishop of St Boniface, who oversaw the same immense diocese.

Newcomers after 1870 found land where they could along lesser waterways, or settled farther west along the Assiniboine where the riverbanks were still empty. But a good many, who had not come as farmers, gravitated to the newly born hamlet of Winnipeg. Its beginnings date from the start of the 'free trade' in furs, when local traders and merchants from the U.S.A. set up warehouses for their goods, and then stores as well, under the shadow of H.B.C.'s Fort Garry. The collection of ramshackle log or frame buildings, with one or two solid houses, was at first called McDermotsville after its leading citizen, an Irish settler-turned-trader named Andrew McDermot, who with his son-in-law, A. G. B. Bannatyne, erected Winnipeg's first buildings. Soon the town's shops were thriving, and challenging the Fort as the settlement's focal point. (A few years later it would ruthlessly demolish the Fort as an obstacle to its growth.) By 1870, as Colonel Wolseley saw it, the village held 'about fifty houses in all; there are a few stores, but grogshops are the principal feature of the place. . . .'

Rev. George Bryce, a leading early historian of the province, describes Winnipeg in 1871 as 'an unsightly . . . village of log houses, of not more than 300 people'. Rev. George Young, the first Methodist missionary in the west, paints a clearer picture of the village as he saw it in 1868:

. . . what a sorry scene was presented by that long-thought-of town of Winnipeg on the day we entered it! What a mass of soft, black, slippery and sticky Red River mud was everywhere spread out before us! Streets with neither sidewalks nor crossings, with now and again a good-sized pit of mire for the traveller to avoid or flounder through as best he could; a few small stores with poor goods and high prices . . . a few passable dwellings with 'no rooms to let', nor space for boarders. . . .

Young adds that in 1868 the population could not have been more than 100. In the 1890s, however, when Young was writing, Winnipeg held almost 40,000 people.

Early in its life Winnipeg became conscious – or self-conscious – of its great potential future as the gateway to the west. It was determined that the gate's hinges would not be found rusty. In 1871 the prairie path that had been graced with the name 'Main Street' was properly surveyed, graded, and furnished with one or two culverts (but no sidewalks). It was a symptom of the magnificent optimism that prevailed. Yet the optimists were justified: Winnipeg and Manitoba were on the threshold of great things. Opportunity-seekers of every kind were settling into the village like flies on honey. Alexander Begg lists the new businesses and small industries springing up overnight, and every night, in 1871: butchers and bakers and cabinet-makers, insurance companies, lawyers (a Quarterly Court had begun sessions) and of course a brewery. Newspapers began operations: the *News Letter*, the *Manitoban*, a French-language journal called *Le Métis*. In late 1871 the long-awaited telegraph link between Ontario and Manitoba was opened; in the same year Winnipeg acquired its own school, and became the site for the west's first essay in higher learning, Manitoba College.

By 1873 Winnipeg's certainty of future greatness demanded some manifestation in the present. The 2,200 residents clamoured for incorporation as a city – passing grandly over the intermediate stage of 'town'. The provincial legislature discussed the idea, but due to some procedural technicality the Speaker had to rule the debate out of order, and incorporation was postponed. Proof of the Winnipeggers' strong feelings on the subject came when the Speaker, the following night, was attacked by a mob, beaten senseless, and tarred and feathered. At the next parliamentary session, needless to say, no further delay arose: the city of Winnipeg was incorporated in 1874. Its name had created some argument: some wanted it to be renamed Selkirk, others advocated Garry, a few suggested Assiniboia. But its early residents had dropped 'McDermotsville' in favour of Winnipeg, after the lake, and the name remained.

If Winnipeg had its roots in commerce, Manitoba's only other settlement in the 1870s, Portage la Prairie, was an offspring of religion.[1] In 1851 a pioneering Church of England minister named Andrew Cochrane (or Cockran) travelled some sixty miles west of the Forks to Christianize the Indians of the

[1] From 1870 onwards, the progress of civilization across the prairies was pushed forward by religion, by missionaries, as much as by any other single factor. See Chapter 6.

Assiniboine and Qu'Appelle areas. Where he built his mission (a log church with a spire and a log school) a settlement grew up – on land purchased from the Indians, at a spot which had been a favourite portaging place of the fur traders.

Incidentally, Cochrane had earlier founded the Scots parish of St Andrew's on the upper Red, as well as an Indian settlement called St Peter's, where the Red runs into Lake Winnipeg. An indefatigable giant of a man, to whom Manitoba owes much, Cochrane ruled Portage la Prairie as a patriarch until his death in 1865.

Portage's spiritual beginnings soon gave way to a progress more turbulent than even Red River's. The Red Riverites, having grown up together as a settlement, seemed to maintain almost effortlessly as much law and order as frontier living required. Sheriffs and constables existed, but like the Council of Assiniboia they wielded their authority on sufferance, and had in fact little to do. But Portage was outside the Selkirk 'District of Assiniboia', an island unto itself – and so became rather wilder. After Cochrane's death the village was dominated by the Schultzite Canadian party, who seemed bent on stirring up trouble, with anti-H.B.C. (and anti-métis) agitation.

In the early 1860s, for instance, the Canada Firsters had decided to break away from the (very loose) H.B.C. governance, and set up their own 'Republic of Manitoba', appealing to the Crown for recognition. It was the first time the name had been used; but it was not otherwise important, even as political gestures go. The Republic grew shaky when a citizen accused the president of dipping into the treasury for drinking money; it toppled completely after a sharp word from the Colonial Office.

A streak of lawlessness runs through the early history of Portage, and many of the more violent tales centre on a family of Ontarians, the McLeans, who had arrived in 1862. John McLean, the head of the family, seems to have taken over as local patriarch after Cochrane's death. When the 'Republic's' president arrested the complaining citizen for 'treason', it was John McLean who put a stop to the farcical trial and hastened the Republic's collapse. When a ne'er-do-well métis roamed at large waving a rifle at any whites, it was John McLean who shot it out with him in true Wild West fashion – though it was John's son Alex, joining the gunfight, who killed the métis.

(When Alex was brought to trial over the killing, the McLeans and friends, armed, filled the courtroom while others waited outside with horses – in case the verdict went against Alex and he needed an escape route. In fact, he was acquitted.)

McLean was one of the first settlers to take up land near Portage: and so he became an unofficial welcoming committee and land agent for other newcomers, especially Canadians. Typically, this powerful and individualistic pioneer paid no attention to Indian claims to land, so he found himself fighting a running war with the Indians. It never grew particularly dangerous: the Indians stole cattle, burned fields, and threatened to burn his house and kill his family, but the threats were not carried out. The closest McLean came to real danger was one time when two armed Indians hid in ambush, apparently to waylay two of the McLean children. A neighbour saw them, and told John. McLean disguised himself – by dressing in top hat and tails – and boldly rode up to the ambush. By the time he was near enough for the Indians to penetrate the disguise, it was too late: McLean fell upon them, singlehanded and barehanded, and in a furious fight disarmed them and put them to rout.

When not engaging in wild and woolly adventures, the McLeans and their neighbours got on with the job of frontier farming. Then the Manitoba Act brought them into the ambit of the first western province; and when treaties were concluded, by Canada, with the Indians in the early 1870s, peace settled on Portage la Prairie. Soon the banks of the Assiniboine between Portage and Winnipeg had filled up, and settlers searched for land farther west, to avoid crowding. In 1870 a Scot from Ontario named Kenneth McKenzie had been helped by McLean to find land near Rat Creek, which made him briefly the most westerly farmer in the province. A few years later the Department of Agriculture, compiling a booklet called 'Information for Intending Emigrants', obtained some statements from McKenzie which made excellent advertising copy.

In his answers McKenzie said that he had carved a farm of about 200 acres out of virgin prairie, ploughing the thick sod to reveal a rich alluvial soil, sowing two bushels of wheat to the acre and reaping about thirty or forty. He added that sowing could usually begin after mid-April, and that summer growth was more rapid than in Ontario soil. Generally, his remarks to incoming settlers set the tone for all such immigration pamphlets in succeeding years:

> I think few countries in the world are superior to ours for agricultural purposes, and although the winter is hard and long, cattle if provided for thrive well. . . . Let everyone come and judge for himself. I have seen people newly arrived from the old country grumble for a time, and afterwards you could not induce them to go back. . . . We have a large increase this year, principally from Canada. . . . All the land round here, say from 30 miles west . . . to say 25 miles east is rapidly filling up, especially this summer, but plenty is to be had all the way westward to the Rocky Mountains.

Plenty, indeed, all the way westwards. But the filling-up process was to take considerably longer, and require rather more preparation, than this optimistic statement would lead one to believe. Canada had realized that the process would be neither as smooth nor as speedy as the American rolling back of the frontier, and had realized that settlement would need stimulation and help. In 1871 an immigration conference had been held in Ottawa, and Manitoba's attorney-general, Henry Clarke, one of the delegates, reported glowingly:

> . . . the Government at Ottawa expressed the most serious determination to make Manitoba and the North West Territories the chief object and charge in all their plans and disbursements in matters connected with immigration.

But expressions of determination had to be translated, sometime soon, into expensive action. Clarke's report had begun with an account of his progress eastwards: over the newly completed Dawson Road from Winnipeg, by a series of steamboats over eastern Manitoba's lakes and rivers, with wagon journeys at the portages, steamships again on the Lakes, then an Ontario railway to Toronto and thence to Ottawa. Complicated enough for a lone traveller, the route became virtually impossible for settlers loaded down with possessions, provisions, farm implements and other bulky baggage. So many headed west through the U.S.A., south of the Lakes – and many succumbed to the salesmanship of U.S. immigration agents, who sold them land and made them Americans.

Transport was the key to the opening of the west – transport from Ontario over that wild *terra incognita* north of the Lakes, which would avoid the American salesmanship as well as the crushing American duties on goods and freight passing through the U.S.A. And in 1871 the dominion was aflame with an idea, vision or dream that would solve the need for transport – except that the dream was almost as startling, and rather more unlikely of accomplishment, than Confederation itself.

The Canadians, with their tiny, impoverished dominion, and their vast hinterland, were dreaming of throwing a railway from Ontario across those thousands of empty miles of forest, swamp, prairie and mountains all the way to the Pacific coast. This newly independent nation, barely out of the colonial cradle, with a population of only 4,000,000 and a total annual revenue of not more than $20,000,000, was dreaming of constructing a transcontinental railway that would be two-thirds longer than any other single line then existing in the world. And in this dream it was being encouraged and importuned by the isolated colony of British Columbia.

5

The Far and Golden West

Beyond the granite curtain of the Rocky Mountains, the second western settlement had gone grandly on its own individualistic way, acquiring a pioneer history that in no way resembled that of the prairie frontier. Chapter 3 tells of the Royal Charter of 1849 that gave H.B.C. a clear title to Vancouver Island, and that made Fort Victoria the site of a colonial venture. The charter had specified that H.B.C. sell land to colonists 'at a reasonable price', and that it prove to Britain upon demand that a suitable settlement had been established. (Britain also reserved the right, when the H.B.C. trading licence came up for renewal, to buy the island back if she felt the settlement did not measure up to the ideal of a British colony.) But H.B.C. had adopted a curiously restrictionist view of colonization: it priced the land at one pound an acre, and told would-be buyers that for every 100 acres three families (or five single men) had to be placed on the land – at the *buyer's* expense.

The Company's declared reasons for these tight rulings exhibited a nice brand of doublethink. Other colonies, H.B.C. stated, suffered from unrestricted settlement, 'no regard being had to the character, means, or views of the immigrants'. How much better it would be to set up rigid conditions that would

> have the effect of introducing a just proportion of labour and capital, and also of preventing the ingress of squatters, paupers, and land speculators.

But of course, the statement continued, H.B.C. could not be said to be imposing a discriminatory immigration policy.

> The principle of selection, without the invidiousness of its direct application, is thus indirectly adopted.

So Victoria was born with the snobbery that has since become (for outsiders) basic in her traditions.

As it happened, H.B.C. discriminated rather too much. As a critic of H.B.C. policy, James Edward Fitzgerald, wrote in 1849, any British emigrant yearning for the Pacific coast could find 'as much land as you please . . . 20 miles just across the Straits [in Oregon], for a dollar an acre'. In fact it soon became clear that H.B.C., with its monopolistic instincts, had intended to limit colonization and keep the island for itself. Its subsidiary, the Puget Sound Agricultural Company (mentioned in Chapter 3), was moved to farmlands around Victoria, and H.B.C. employees (or retired employees) formed the total population of the 'colony'. A. Waddington, a historian writing in 1858, summed up the prevailing attitude:

> The truth is, the Company did not wish for colonists. Not that it refused to sell ground; on the contrary, any settler might go and choose it, when it was measured out to him and he paid for it. But . . . there was nobody but the Company to sell to or trade with. . . .

And, he might have added, there was the Puget Sound Company and the Oregon farmers as competitors in this limited market.

H.B.C. did, however, bring out new blood for its colony, not relying entirely on former fur traders to populate the Pacific coast. The Puget Sound Co. had been set up as four model farms, hopefully resembling the estates of British gentry. To oversee the farms, H.B.C. imported 'gentlemen bailiffs', who, with their families, established a tight little aristocracy on the island. One of these transplanted country squires, a Captain Langford, formed a focal point for leisure-class activities, thanks to his five daughters, who acted like magnets on visiting naval officers and other young bloods. Dinner parties, riding parties, shooting parties, socials and balls emanated from the gracious Langford home – while the cost of these functions was charged to H.B.C. Such was Victoria's wild frontier.

By about 1851, the colony of Vancouver Island had attracted exactly *one* immigrant colonist – and one who rather turned back on the Company its statement about 'regard being had to the character' of immigrants. He was Captain W. Colquhoun Grant, an enthusiastic young man (in his twenties) whom some thought dashing and others thought flighty. He began his colonial career by missing the boat that was to take him to Victoria; he ran out of money en route; and after quarrelling with and dismissing four of the eight men he had brought with him, he was deserted by the others. On the Island, he found it necessary to take up land some twenty miles from Victoria – for nearer land belonged to H.B.C. Extravagant and imprudent, he found himself unable to meet his debts, and so sold up his land and returned to England. There he read a paper to the Royal Geographic Society about the Island, in which he complained that aside from himself and his men

> not a single other independent colonist has come out from the Old Country to settle in the Island; all the other individuals who have taken up land have been in the employ of the Company, and brought out to the country at its expense.

He was entirely right – yet by 1851 there were a few Islanders who were able to proclaim independence. Earlier, deposits of coal had been found on the Island: at the northern end, where H.B.C. built Fort Rupert to exploit the mines, and then closer to Victoria, at the bountiful deposits of Nanaimo. Miners were brought over – mostly from Scotland and Staffordshire – to dig the coal. A Scots family named Muir seemed to be the natural leaders of the contingent, and shortly – when their contracts expired – turned to leading an anti-H.B.C. agitation. The Muirs gained their freedom in time to buy Captain Grant's land, and used their freedom to clamour for responsible government on the Island.

Till then the colony's government had been laughable. The charter which gave H.B.C. the land also specified that the colony was to have a governor and 'certain powers of local self-government' – namely, an appointed council and in time an elected assembly. So in 1849 a governor duly arrived – a sad man named Blanshard, who had wanted to be a colonial governor so badly he served without salary. Blanshard had found no gubernatorial mansion, but a patch of worthless, rocky ground which he had had to develop and build a house on, at his own expense. Furthermore, he was a governor with no one to govern – except Captain Grant, briefly – for he had no authority over H.B.C. employees. Within a year he had despondently resigned (though he had to wait months for his

97

resignation to reach London and its acceptance to return). With some clever lobbying H.B.C. convinced the Colonial Office that his successor should be a man with some experience of the area – i.e. an H.B.C. man. So James Douglas, H.B.C.'s Chief Factor west of the mountains, became governor of Vancouver Island.

Events were to prove him an excellent choice, but in 1851 the Muirs, and other Islanders who had extricated themselves from H.B.C., had their doubts. They presented Blanshard (who retained the position while he remained on the Island, waiting for a ship home) with a petition:

> We, the undersigned inhabitants of Vancouver Island . . . beg to express in the most emphatical and plainest manner our assurance that impartial decisions cannot be expected from a governor who is not only a member of the Company . . . but is also charged as their chief agent . . . in this island and the adjacent coasts.
>
> . . . we respectfully beg your Excellency to consider that we, and we alone, represent the interests of the Island as a free and independent British colony, for we constitute the whole body of independent settlers, all the other inhabitants being, in some way or other, connected with and controlled by the Hudson's Bay Company. . . . And we further allege . . . that the untoward influences to which we have adverted above are likely, if entirely unguarded against, not only to prevent any increase of free and independent colonists in the Island, but positively to decrease their present numbers.

The petition, which concluded by asking that a legislative council be appointed, was signed by fifteen persons, six of them Muirs.

Blanshard did in fact appoint a council, as his last official act, but it somewhat denied the spirit of the petition. The councillors were three: two retired H.B.C. men and the Chief Factor himself. Within months Douglas had succeeded to the governorship, apparently finalizing the Company's absolute power in Vancouver Island.

But the colonists, independent and otherwise, found that Douglas was actively interested in colonization, and had even naïvely believed, at one time, that H.B.C. shared this interest. As governor, he devoted himself to the colony's needs. He oversaw the construction of roads in and around Victoria, of schools, even of small but thriving local industry – mainly a sawmill, taking advantage of the Island's luxurious forests. To pay for these improvements – since he was unable to impose taxes (Britain insisted that only an elected assembly could take this step) – he imposed a liquor licence. The Islanders – now numbering about 1,000, including some 600 children – rose in wrath against this high-handedness, and demanded that before any further drastic measures were enacted a representative government should be formed. Douglas gave way, and in 1856 elections were held. But property qualifications for candidates (no one could stand who owned less than £300 worth of freehold land) and for voters (no one could vote who owned less than twenty acres) put the electoral power into a very few hands. In fact, forty property holders elected seven men. In some districts nomination meant automatic election, for each held only one qualified voter.

Nevertheless, the assembly thus formed was the very first elected governmental body in the west. And, though all the representatives had been H.B.C. men at some time, three o them were strongly opposed to the Company's restrictive practices, while the others hastily sought to prove they were not Company puppets. They presented, potentially, some sizeable obstacles to Douglas's devoted planning of the Island's future.

External tensions added to his headaches. The 1,000 colonists shared the Island with some 30,000 Indians – and, like most of the tribes west of the mountains, the Island tribes did not suffer the white presence gladly. H.B.C. struggled to maintain its western reputation of friendly relations with the Indians, but was frustrated time and again by outbreaks – a petty theft here, a killing there. The settlers at Victoria had less trouble than the other, smaller outposts – i.e. at the mining establishments – where the whites remained behind stockaded forts and kept guns to hand. Douglas made a point of pursuing, trying and punishing any Indian who broke a law – especially any who killed a white. (In 1853, for instance, he organized a company of volunteer militia who, aided by the navy, tracked down an Indian murderer and brought him back for a full-dress trial by jury.) The Indians, in spite of themselves, came to be impressed by the fact that Douglas's justice seemed both swift and fair, and did *not* (as on the American coast) take the form of vengeful attacks on an Indian criminal's innocent tribesmen.

To add further weight to Douglas's burden, the Crimean

War was fought in the 1850s, which – with Russian Alaska in the north – kept the colony on edge. And American land-hunger still rumbled south of the Island: a group of miners from the U.S., wandering (whether by design or accident) on to the Queen Charlotte Islands, north of Vancouver Island, precipitated a flurry of diplomatic protests from Britain. And trouble was brewing over San Juan Island, and the ambiguous route of the boundary,[1] on Victoria's very doorstep.

So Douglas had more than his share of preoccupations. But all of these became only petty problems when 1857 brought two new and far-reaching developments to the colony. First, the Select Committee appointed to consider Company operations in the west[2] began taking hard looks at the organization of the colony and the transmontane fur trade. Second, a few small deposits of gold were found on the mainland, along the Thompson river.

The Committee recommended that H.B.C. rule of the Island be terminated – i.e. that Britain buy back the Island, and assume whole and direct control of the colony. This move alone would have blown a fair-sized wind of change through Victoria. The gold finds brought a hurricane. When gold was found on the Fraser river as well as the Thompson, the whole Pacific coast came down with gold fever. Vancouver Islanders – settlers, H.B.C. employees, even seamen from visiting ships – streamed across to the mainland. By early 1858 the news had reached California, where the leftover population from the great gold rush of 1849 swarmed north to the Fraser. Indian troubles in Oregon meant that they swarmed by steamer, and therefore landed in Victoria. By the middle of 1858 people were flocking in from eastern Canada, from Britain, Europe and Asia. Between May 15 and June 1, according to Margaret Ormsby, historian of British Columbia, some 10,000 men went prospecting up the Fraser. In the wake of the gold-mining thousands came the merchants and caterers, the speculators and camp followers, attracted like vultures to carrion by the news of sudden wealth. All of them landed at Victoria, whether passing through or settling in. Under their impact the quiet little provincial centre shuddered, and began to grow.

By far the majority of the newcomers, whether miners or

[1] See p. 51 and also p. 116.
[2] See p. 59.

parasites, were Americans. The Victoria *Gazette*, the colony's first newspaper, was founded by Americans; U.S. merchants set up shop by the hundreds; Wells-Fargo moved an express office in; American steamers, jamming in twice their legal passenger load, sailed into Victoria daily with more gold-seekers. And while the colony's 'gentry' curled their lips at the new buildings thrown up in their dozens, overnight, and at the miners' rowdy shanty town on the fringe of Victoria, Douglas and other leaders worried about a more serious threat to the colony's welfare: the old bugbear of manifest destiny. If the Americans gained too much control over the local economy, and carved out – as miners and squatters – too many land claims on the mainland, it might be a short step to annexation. So Douglas, instead, took a short and bold step: he proclaimed that the mainland goldfields were Crown property, and miners would need licences (obtainable from him) to work them. In one stroke he had asserted British rule, provided a means of controlling the miners, and created a new source of revenue.

Actually Douglas had no authority over the mainland, except as Chief Factor of H.B.C. But no one else had even that much authority – and Douglas could not wait for instructions from London. Things were moving too quickly. And it was just as well that someone did take command, for the miners had brought with them their violent hatred and contempt for the Indian, and chose to vent it on a band of Indians who were themselves finding gold on the upper Fraser. The Indians struck back, and a few dead Americans came floating down the river. Douglas and some volunteers rushed to the scene, but the miners had by that time driven the Indians off. Peace was restored, but when Douglas returned to the Island he left law officers behind him in the mining camps.

Soon Douglas received a commendation from Britain for his swift action, and a request that he continue to wield an *ex officio* authority over the mainland until some legal provisions could be drawn up. But Britain did not approve of his attempt to protect H.B.C.'s profits by barring all other merchants and traders from the Fraser. The Colonial Office pointed out sharply that H.B.C.'s exclusive licence extended only to the trade with the Indians, and had nothing to do with ordinary commerce. In fact, as Douglas guessed, this reprimand foreshadowed the end of H.B.C.'s monopoly west of the mountains. To make the most of the gold rush, the Colonial Office had decided to withdraw H.B.C.'s exclusive licence and to permit free trade. It had also decided to transform the mainland into a Crown Colony, ruled by a governor who for five years would hold sole dictatorial powers. Vancouver Island, still owned by H.B.C.,[1] would remain a separate colony – at least in principle. In fact, the new mainland colony would be governed by James Douglas, who (though he would resign as Chief Factor of H.B.C.) would remain at the same time the governor of the Island.

The new colony was christened British Columbia – a name reportedly chosen by the old Queen herself, which seems plausible considering its stuffy imperial dullness. Its area lay between the Rockies and the Pacific, extending northwards from the 49th parallel to the Peace River, near the 56th parallel. The colony contained a few small fur-trading posts, a few rough trails, a great many wild Indians and about 30,000 wilder gold miners. Douglas and his officials – including Judge Matthew B. Begbie, a fierce bulwark of law and order – had their work cut out.

Peace-keeping became their top priority, since the new population of British Columbia included some of the most dangerous (and wanted) criminals of California. In California, vigilante committees and lynch law had prevailed, and miners carried revolvers and bowie knives as a matter of course. They carried them to British Columbia as well. But most found that in the new gold rush the weapons were unnecessary. Douglas had organized a police force, and had placed at least one constable (and/or a law officer called a Gold Commissioner) in each camp; and he made a point of catching and punishing wrongdoers speedily and justly. Some of the Americans, Douglas reported, had 'a degree of confidence in the sterling uprightness and integrity of Englishmen which they do not entertain for their own countrymen'. Taking advantage of this awe for British power, Douglas requested and got a detachment of soldiers. But as usual he had more than one purpose. The soldiers were Royal Engineers, who were to help build as well as police the colony.

Soon, then, the fur-trade forts and mining camps along the

[1] Though the Select Committee's recommendation had been accepted, complex negotiations over the price delayed the restoration of the Island's lands to British ownership until 1867.

Fraser and its tributaries turned into towns; the land was surveyed, divided into lots and sold to the merchants and the miners. In this way squatters were forestalled and more revenue brought in. And so shack towns were born into boom times: Yale and Hope, on the lower Fraser; Lytton and Lillooet and others farther up the river, beyond the navigable stretch. And a brand-new town was to be created as the mainland centre. Douglas chose for its site the plateau where the first Fort Langley had stood,[1] but the Royal Engineers' commanding officer, Colonel Moody, rejected the plateau as strategically indefensible, and picked a spot nearer the river's mouth. There, in 1859, his men began felling trees and uprooting stumps, and in the same year the first buildings were erected. (Needless to say, the governor still resided on the Island, and administered the mainland from that vantage point – a fact that was resented by the new British Columbians.)

Incorporated in 1860, the new capital was first called Queens-borough, but again Queen Victoria intervened, exchanging the prosaic colonial name for another, considerably worse: New Westminster.[2]

By the end of 1859 the Fraser and its tributaries had made many men rich, and the gold pouring into British Columbian and Victorian banks had set both colonies on their financial feet. Then news came from the interior that some intrepid souls had scrambled farther up the Fraser river, as far as Lake Cariboo. Some had stayed to prospect on the banks of the lake; others had pushed on, along the Quesnel river or the Thompson, or the multifarious creeks running into the larger waterways. All had found gold, voluminously. The news electrified the two colonies: miners working the Fraser, together with new arrivals, began trekking northwards in increasing numbers.

Then in 1861 word came that prospectors on Antler Creek were taking out some $10,000 worth of gold *a day* – with the other creeks not far behind. If gold on the Fraser had produced a rush, gold in the Cariboo region in 1862 produced a frenzied, frantic stampede.

.   .   .   .   .

[1] See p. 51.
[2] By 1864 it held only 200–300 people, and exhibited a rather untidy clutter of buildings surrounded by the rubble from the clearing process – which caused some critics to call it the 'imperial stump-field'.

Cariboo was far to the north, in the wilds of the region that Simon Fraser had called New Caledonia, and almost inaccessible except to the experienced woodsmen of the fur trade. Matthew Macfie describes the area as 'studded with mountains closely packed together. . . . Tremendous masses, tumbled and irregular in character, with summits from 6,000 to 7,000 feet above the level of the sea. . . .' The gold-seekers faced scores of miles of steep, densely forested inclines, rocky gorges and precipices, with only occasional flimsy rope-and-pole bridges, left by Indians, to show that humans had ever passed that way before. Many died on that northward stampede – but not many turned back, spurred as they were by the gold-dazzle. Obviously, if Cariboo were to be properly exploited, transportation was essential. Earlier, the miners on the Fraser had been provided with routes by British Columbia: a trail barely good enough for mules had been hacked out along Harrison Lake north to Lillooet, and another trail joined Yale to Lytton, where the Fraser forked with the Thompson. But crude pack trails would not have served for Cariboo. The distance was greater, so the packs would be larger. And most of the creeks were being mined by deep diggings, demanding heavy equipment as well as provisions in the supply trains. Douglas saw that a wagon road would be necessary.

The government, the Royal Engineers, private contractors and the miners themselves combined to build that road – as remarkable an engineering feat as any new and struggling colony ever undertook. Douglas permitted no halfway measures: he demanded a highway eighteen feet wide for almost all of its 400-mile length.

Parts of the road ran through relatively passable land on the banks of the Fraser, where the only problems were steep grades and thick stands of British Columbia's giant fir trees. But elsewhere the Fraser's path narrowed into deep gorges or canyons; and there the Royal Engineers, tackling the worst stretches, had to string the road along the side of the sheer cliffs, blasting the granite to make a ledge on which to smooth the roadway, erecting supports of log pilings, or cribbing ballasted with rock, in order to edge the road around the flank of a mountain. North of Yale, a private contractor named Joseph Trutch achieved the near-impossible by hurling a strong and attractive suspension bridge across the Fraser. And all this was accomplished while the roughest of bush trails provided the only supply routes for the builders. Trutch, for instance, found the trails too poor to carry the heavy cable he needed. But, true to the engineering tradition which never says 'impossible', he had *wire* brought in, in batches small enough to traverse the trail, and his men wound it into cable on the spot.

By the spring of 1864 the great highway was completed, up to the riotous mining town called Barkerville. The total cost had been about $1,000,000; British Columbia alone had incurred a debt of £100,000. (Private contractors were paid in cash or bonds or – more often – with the right to levy tolls on their sections of the road.) But the value of the Cariboo Road far outweighed its cost. In 1863 alone the *official* figure for Cariboo's output of gold had been given as $4,000,000 – and most authorities were sure that the amount of gold that by-passed the official tally would at least have doubled that figure.

As the new road provided easy access and vastly cheaper freight rates, the swarms of gold-seekers multiplied past counting. Many tales are told of the amateurs and greenhorns who faced enormous hardships in the hope of making their fortune: among the most dramatic of the stories was that of the 'over-landers', men, women and children from eastern Canada who crossed the continent in 1862.

They had travelled (in several parties) in reasonable comfort from Canada, down through the U.S.A., then up to Red River, where they were provisioned with pemmican and the notorious Red River flour. Then they loaded themselves on to Red River carts, and proceeded across the prairies – meeting only relatively mild hardships, such as heavily rutted trails, or no trails at all, or the delicate operation of crossing rivers with carts and animals.

After pausing for a brief rest at Fort Edmonton, they advanced towards the mountains. Their way grew more danger-ous, along steep, rocky trails, often blocked by fallen trees or the rubble of avalanches, sometimes dwindling into a danger-ously narrow ledge on the side of a sheer cliff. They plodded on, making only about ten miles a day, their provisions running short and supplemented with whatever game they came across. Finally they reached the upper Fraser, at a point where the river was only a few feet wide.

By then autumn was well advanced, and snow was imminent. The party decided to split up. Some would challenge the river; the rest would strike southwards on land, planning – if they failed to reach Cariboo before the snow – to build huts and live off the land for the winter. The river party promptly built rafts, loaded them, and (farther down the river) launched them. They had had no idea of the nature of the upper Fraser. But with the immense, unbelievable luck of beginners and tenderfeet, most of them survived the torrential rapids, the whirlpools and jagged rocks, which met them within a few miles and lasted many miles more. Some, however, had employed canoes; inexpert, most of these had been lost and drowned in the icy waters. But the majority floated down, exhausted but intact, through Fort George and then on to Cariboo.

The remaining overlanders made less spectacular progress. They hacked their way through the overgrown forest, along a barely visible trail pointed out by an Indian guide, until they reached the North Thompson river. Then they, too, built rafts and took to the water and ran headlong into foaming rapids and rocks. Their craft were overturned, their possessions lost; men, women and children were hurled – freezing, provision-less, often injured – on to the banks, or swept away by the current to drown. Eventually the survivors left the horrors of the river, regrouped, and followed another vague trail. But this soon petered out; and for the final 100 miles of their journey the group forced its way through totally virgin forest, each with only a mouthful of pemmican and flour a day to sustain them. (Earlier, one of their number had apparently developed an allergy to pemmican, and had had to continue the march on nothing but a few handfuls of dry flour. His raft overturned on the Thompson, only a few yards from shore; weakened by malnutrition, he drowned.)

Finally the remaining overlanders emerged from the bush near Fort Kamloops. They found themselves in a potato field, and stopped to gorge on raw potatoes before staggering on to the fort. In Kamloops came the coda to their adventure. The party included a Mr Schubert (a German immigrant), with his Irish-born wife and three young children. All had survived the 3,000-mile journey, the forest, the hunger, even the moment when their raft had shattered into kindling on the rocks of the

Thompson. Shortly after the arrival at Kamloops, Mrs Schubert went calmly to bed and gave birth, without complication, to her fourth child, a healthy girl.

Great wealth came out of the Cariboo in the early 1860s, but few men became more than temporarily rich. The deposits and veins of gold proved freakishly unreliable: yielding thousands of dollars a day, then stopping as if chopped off with an axe. The gold's whereabouts was equally unpredictable: nuggets might be lying around on sandbars, requiring shallow diggings at most; or they might be in a stratum of gravel many feet below ground. As for unreliability, a group of Welshmen had dug to bedrock in 1864 and taken out 90 ounces of gold in the first few days. The usual pack of speculators descended, offering to buy the claim; one of the partners sold his share for $18,000. But when the new owners went to work they found that the gold was so widely scattered they could barely cover the cost of digging it. Yet deep diggings continued, the miners remembering how they had laughed at Billy Barker, in Cariboo's early days, when he sank a fifty-foot shaft through the blue clay of the Fraser canyon; and had stopped laughing when he struck gravel that paid five dollars a pan. They had named Barkerville after him, and it had become the wide-open centre of the Cariboo.

But even if a claim paid well and proved reliable, too many other hands were reaching out for the gold. Gamblers, prostitutes, saloon-keepers and confidence men had followed the miners – even before the Cariboo Road existed – to set up shop in the shanty towns and camps. Speculators and claim jumpers seemed to fall from the skies when a strike was made; thieves followed newly rich miners through the wilderness on their way back to civilization. Merchants profiteered: potatoes sold at ninety dollars a hundredweight, flour at three hundred dollars a barrel, boots at fifty dollars a pair. Then too, if a miner who had struck it rich managed to avoid all these traps and temptations, he was still likely to follow the archetypal pattern that western folklore loves to dwell on: throwing all his wealth away in an orgy of wild celebration. A story is told of a miner who staggered into a Barkerville saloon with $40,000 in nuggets, and got rid of it all in one incredible night – treating the packed saloon to bottles and cases of drink, including champagne at fifty dollars a bottle, and ending the evening by smashing the huge bar mirror with his last handful of nuggets. The next day he went to work for a mining company, and remained an employee from then on.

Other more fabulous characters also lost everything, if less suddenly. 'Dutch Bill' Dietz, discoverer of Williams Creek, the richest of all the Cariboo creeks, was within a few years living off charity in Victoria. The great Billy Barker spent his fortune on a widow from Victoria who promptly left him when there was no more to spend; he worked for a while as a cook for a road gang, and died a pauper, in 1894, in a Victoria Old Men's Home. John A. 'Cariboo' Cameron, the most legendary miner of them all, left British Columbia in 1863 with $150,000, and everyone was sure that he would stay rich for life. But a series of foolish investments drained his money away in a few years. He went back to Cariboo, hoping to repeat his luck, but died there in 1888, penniless.

If anyone stayed rich in British Columbia it was the upright citizens of the boom towns – representing all the commercial interests that preyed on the miner. They and the colony with them rode a crest of prosperity through the early 1860s. Smug in its success, the colony even expanded its area: a group of prospectors, probing northwards, had spilled over the boundary line to do a little digging – enough so that in 1863 British Columbia was able to annex the land to her north and extend herself up to the 60th parallel (still the boundary today). Towns were expanding as well – not only the mushrooming shanty towns of Cariboo, but the 'civilized' centres on the coast. New Westminster had incorporated itself as a city in 1860, almost before the paint was dry on its first buildings, and faced its future with a self-confident ambition that startled Governor Douglas. The circumstances, however, proved to be against it. Even at its mouth the Fraser was not navigable by all ships or at all times of the year – which hampered the flow of commerce. Also, Governor Douglas had imposed some stringent customs duties to help defray the cost of road building and other public works. On the other hand, Victoria had the perfect seaport of Esquimalt only a few miles away; and it had earlier been declared a free port, free of duties and tariffs and other hindrances. So New Westminster's dreams of becoming a commercial magnet and thriving seaport were thwarted by Victoria, as that city would be years later by Vancouver.

In the 1860s, however, nothing was thwarting Victoria. Incorporated as a city in 1862, its population was estimated at about 5,000, with transients adding several thousands more. New buildings sprang up constantly, no longer frame and canvas as in the early days of the gold rush, but solid wood and plaster, or more solid brick. The roads were macadamized, and had wooden sidewalks. In the mid-1860s the city boasted a fire department, a police department (with jail), a hospital, a library, five breweries, four daily newspapers, two banks, and one theatre. There were six Protestant churches, including two Anglican, one Catholic church, and a synagogue. The numerous schools included several *élite* private colleges nurturing the offspring of the Island aristocracy. To complete the picture, an alphabetical list of trades and professions in the city (compiled by Matthew Macfie in 1865) includes the following: Architects, 4; Bakers, 23; Barristers, 5; Billiard Halls, 17; Clothiers, 11; Dentist, 1; Estate Agents, 18; Grocers, 39; Gunsmiths, 2; Innkeepers, 11; Photographers, 4; Plumber, 1; Restaurateurs, 22; Tailors, 16; Undertaker, 1.

Oddly enough, no mention is made in this list of a doctor. But then, given the nature of a frontier doctor's usual duties, the dentist and the undertaker might have shared them. Then again, the list does not dwell upon the 85-odd licensed saloons in the city, nor upon the added attractions of gambling-rooms and brothels which most of the saloons supplied.

By the mid-1860s the old guard of Victorian society had become outnumbered by new residents, with different ideas of the good life. Leading citizens now led by virtue of their money, not their 'gentle birth'. As Governor Douglas said, 'business is now the sole occupation of all classes, and social meetings are now rarely heard of and Country rides are something beyond the aim of even the most ambitious pleasure hunters'. Mercantilism had replaced agriculture; the Island's landed gentry had been shouldered aside by the *nouveaux riches* of the gold boom. The old colonial dream of 'keeping out the riff-raff' was long abandoned. The floating population of Victoria included not only all classes but a good many races and colours as well.

About 400 Negroes had come up in the late 1850s from

109

California – where they had suffered the usual discrimination[1] – after an exploratory party had visited the city, and reported favourably that the Governor had welcomed them, land was available, and they would be able to claim the rights of British subjects once they had stayed seven years and become naturalized. But of course actual conditions were far from ideal. The Negroes met prejudice in Victoria as they did anywhere: they were barred from local clubs and organizations, there were complaints (and sometimes fights) over their admission to bars and theatres. At the same time the Negroes demanded and asserted their rights under British rule: they had, after all, come to the colony to escape discrimination.

Aside from occasional individual clashes, no cases have been recorded of serious mob violence or other forms of organized racism. When the whites took concerted action, it was usually in the form of appeals to authority. In one instance, related by Macfie, the white congregation of an unnamed church complained about Negroes sitting wherever they chose, rather than in a segregated block. The clergyman rebuked them for this unChristian attitude; most of the whites then withdrew from his church. And, to his surprise, so did many of the Negroes. At the same time, a new church had opened – the minister of which had announced that no segregation would be allowed in his establishment. He, too, was astonished to find that he had no congregation of any colour. It seemed that the whites were worshipping elsewhere, and the Negroes – enjoying the unfamiliar pleasure of making white men uncomfortable by sitting next to them – followed the whites to continue the game. So both preachers of integration and brotherhood were left with nearly empty churches.

Interestingly, the controversy over seating arrangements apparently aroused no more violence than some rude letters in the newspapers about the Negroes' 'odour', and some even ruder replies from Negroes. It is possible that the Negroes met no communal violence because they themselves did not live

[1] Negroes could not give evidence in a California court against whites; nor could they attend white schools. They were bullied and maltreated, with no hope of redress, all over the California goldfields. When the state introduced a bill banning further Negro immigration to California, and requiring resident Negroes to register and be *licensed*, the Negro community thought of emigration. But only a scattered few followed the first 400, for the bill was never passed.

as a community: to avoid a ghetto, and perhaps to further the game of making whites uncomfortable, their homes were scattered throughout the city. It is also possible (or so one would like to think) that the Negro volunteer rifle corps, which Macfie calls 'efficient' and 'highly creditable', showed the white Islanders that the Negroes were no *helpless* minority. The corps had been formed when Negroes were not allowed into the corresponding white corps; regrettably, the governor eventually disbanded the Negro corps, terming it an illegal armed body, while the white riflemen remained.

For the Chinese, the second racial minority for whom the Pacific coast was truly foreign, peace did not come so easily. A few hundred scattered Negroes seemed to Victoria to be a far different threat from a few hundred Chinese who might be the advance guard of hundreds of thousands. When the first few Chinese disembarked in 1858, the scare stories sprang up at once. The 'Yellow Peril', it was said, would overwhelm the whites; fear spread that the Chinese would introduce drugs, gambling, and all manner of vice to the colony (which, in actuality, would have been like performing introductions between old friends). Above all, worry spread that the Chinese would work for little money, and so steal jobs from whites; and that they would rob the colony's economy by sending their earnings home.

By 1864, according to F. G. Howay, there were about two thousand Chinese in both colonies. Some lived in the towns, engaged in what seems to be their traditional North American occupations: laundering and restaurant-owning. Others mined gold, avoiding the populous Barkerville area of Cariboo, and working in the wake of the gold-rush advance. These gleaned a small but steady living from areas where miners had skimmed off the cream and then rushed off up the Fraser after another rumour. A few Chinese, making enough money, set up shops to import Chinese food and other specialities. The Chinese chose to live in separate areas of the towns, in separate camps in the mining areas. They lived peacefully, caused no trouble, got in no one's way, worked incredibly hard – Macfie terms them the most 'industrious and law-abiding class . . . in these dependencies' – and were thoroughly resented and hated by almost everyone.

On one occasion, in 1858 – before Cariboo, when only a

few hundred Chinese had arrived in the colony – a boat approached Fort Hope on the Fraser, intending to deposit some Chinese gold-seekers. A group of Californian miners swarmed down to the jetty and forbade the Chinese to land, threatening them and the boat's owner with violence. An H.B.C. official, one Donald McLean, was present with his son. Enraged at the arrogance of the miners, the McLeans drew revolvers and held the mob off, pointing out (not entirely accurately) that Hope was H.B.C. territory, and they as H.B.C. representatives would see to it that whoever wished to land there *would* land. The miners backed down, and the Chinese quietly disembarked. On other occasions, however, they found no protectors. A resident of Victoria in the 1860s, Edgar Fawcett, recalls in his reminiscences an item from the *Gazette* of August 1858:

> A Chinaman was found shot dead with five bullets in his body. He was on his way to a spring to fetch a bucket of water, and had to pass a camp of miners. Further comment unnecessary.

By the newspaper's tone, such outbreaks seem to have been all too familiar. Yet apparently they also remained fairly isolated – as long as the heyday of Cariboo gave the miners and colonists too much else to think about. Later, as will be seen, the Chinese were to become victims of wholesale and concerted governmental discrimination, and mob violence.

As the 1860s progressed, the Fraser's wealth of gold diminished. Cariboo's output hit its peak in 1862–3; by 1864 miners with foresight knew it was petering out. A year later, the main outflow of gold came from 'placer' mining, where gravel from diggings was washed and separated from gold in a costly construction of troughs and sluices. The equipment necessary to garner paying quantities of gold was beyond the resources of most individuals: mining companies took over in Cariboo. In 1865, therefore, the usual spring migration of gold-seekers simply did not occur. And the commercial interests of the colonies, having stocked up as usual for the expected thousands, found themselves without customers. Economic collapse struck: private banks failed, investment dropped sharply, speculators with debts vanished over the border, and merchant followed merchant into bankruptcy.

The mainland's recession was slightly alleviated in 1865 by a small gold rush to the Kootenay region (the southeast corner of the province). Although these diggings were mostly worked by Americans, who brought in supplies from Idaho and sent gold out the same way, some of the gravy spilled over on to New Westminster. Another minor rush occurred at the Columbia river's 'Big Bend' – where the river swings majestically around a mountain range, changing direction from northwest to nearly due south. These new finds gave the mainland another boost, since the Big Bend was accessible from the Fraser region. The Island, however, felt no effects from these finds of gold; Victoria became an economic disaster area.

The recession forced a reappraisal, and brought about a radical change in the political structure of the two colonies. It brought about their union, a logical culmination of their political history.

From its earliest days, in 1858, British Columbia had always resented the fact that it was ruled by a governor who resided on the Island, and who had never appointed a legislative council or made any gestures towards elections. (Douglas had allowed Judge Begbie and Colonel Moody to serve as 'unofficial advisers' in British Columbian affairs, but no stretching of the term could have made them into a council.) Petitions fell like snow on the British Colonial Secretary's desk, complaining that the mainland had been forced into the position of a poor relation, and demanding for it some voice in its own government. Mainland newspapers – John Robson's *British Columbian* and the *British Colonist* of Amor De Cosmos[1] – added to the clamour. In 1863 Britain paid attention. The five years of Douglas's autocracy, allowed by the British Columbia Act, expired in that year.

The Colonial Office had hoped then to unite the two colonies, but British Columbia objected. In the end, the two were further separated: each acquired its own governor. Each was also to be permitted a legislative council, of which some members would be elected. More representative government, Britain

[1] A Nova Scotian, born William Smith, who changed his name while in California to avoid confusion at the post office, and became the multilingual 'Lover of the Universe'. Flamboyant, fiery, a reformist in politics, he became a powerful political force in B.C., eventually a federal M.P. and provincial premier.

decided, could wait until the colonies were convalescing from their bout of gold fever.

Douglas was induced to retire. He had done undeniably great work: the Cariboo Road and the general keeping of the peace would alone have made his régime memorable. But his bold financial methods – probably necessary to open up the colonies – had incurred debts, which worried the cautious clerks of the Colonial Office. Also, his administration could be fairly accused of a certain measure of high-handedness, paternalism, and nepotism – which had won him, as with all autocrats, benevolent or otherwise, many enemies. So the old governor, who had virtually created the colonies on the Pacific, received a knighthood as his golden handshake, and two lesser men replaced him.

The mainland received Governor Seymour – described by one historian as a 'well-meaning, easy-going mediocrity' – and the Island received Governor Kennedy. Both arrived in 1864 full of ambition and optimism – in time to watch the bottom fall out of Cariboo. Both, also, ran foul of the crafty politicians and vested interests of their councils. The Island councillors demanded that they become a ministerial council (or cabinet), to share some executive power, and proved obstructionist on vital bills – principally money bills. While this power game was being played, the Island's economy tottered more and more desperately.

Now, under some quiet urgings from London, the two colonies reconsidered their union. At first the Island sought to impose stringent conditions, demanding a federal union in which it would retain some autonomy, and also demanding that Victoria be the capital of the united colony. The mainland, on the other hand, pointed out that the Island was in no position to make demands. Kootenay and Big Bend had preserved British Columbia from all-out disaster (as was seen above), and the mainland simply did not need union as much as the Island. Eventually, the long-standing animosities were set aside by more important realities: in the economic troubles, the continuing competition for trade between Victoria and New Westminster could be disastrous. British Columbia, being less desperate than the Island, found itself in the position of dictating terms – and in 1866 proceeded to do so.

In London, when agreement had been reached, a bill was

rushed through Parliament to enact the union – which turned out to be more of an ingestion. Vancouver Island was to be subsumed or incorporated into the new colony of British Columbia, with Governor Seymour and council in charge. The difficult decision of siting the capital was put off till a later date, though Seymour made it clear that he favoured New Westminster. Rancour between mainland and Island did not diminish.

Nor, for that matter, did the financial troubles – for the debts remained, trade continued to decline, and the latest gold rushes soon fizzled out. Various groups began presenting alternatives to the colony. Some insisted that British Columbia soldier on, perhaps with a little boost in the form of a British loan. (Britain was unwilling.) Others noted that California seemed to thrive whatever the state of its goldfields, and recommended applying to the U.S.A. for statehood. (The U.S.A. would have been delighted.) Still others, after July 1, 1867, urged the colony to seek admission into Confederation, as a province of Canada.

The Dominion was definitely interested, for John A. Macdonald's dream of a transcontinental nation had caught many eastern imaginations. But, in British Columbia, the Island opposed the idea, and by this time the Island had become a powerful voice in the council. It displayed its power when in early 1867 the council overrode Seymour and declared Victoria the capital of the colony. The following year, living up to the mainland's description of it as 'despotic', the council postponed the discussion of Confederation indefinitely.

But the idea came to life again in a very few years. The colony spent those years retrenching, seeking new and reliable ways to regain prosperity. With the population having stabilized at about 15,000 (only about 8,000 of whom were on the mainland), agricultural settlement seemed to be the answer. But settlement came slowly to British Columbia – as it always had. Douglas had written in 1859 that the colony 'has no farming class, the population being almost entirely composed of miners and merchants'. He had repeated the complaint in 1861, and was echoed by Vancouver Island's surveyor-general, J. D. Pemberton: '. . . in neither [colony] have we, as yet, any farming population worth mentioning'. And Matthew Macfie, in 1865, showed the situation unchanged, remarking that 'there is no branch of industry more strikingly neglected in this colony' than agriculture.

After the gold finally ran out, some new farming settlements appeared, mainly along the Fraser, in the delta regions, where a few former miners or freighters or other leftovers from Cariboo had decided to make their homes. Again, a few turned to raising stock elsewhere on the mainland (for instance, near Kamloops), while others found work with the embryonic lumber or fishing industries. But these developments remained small-scale. Immigration to British Columbia gravitated to the towns where a living was more likely to be made.

So the economic situation did not improve, and it became clear to the most chauvinistic British Columbians that the colony's horizons needed widening. More colonists came to be attracted to the Confederation idea: the undiminished British-ness of the colony kept the pro-American propagandists in a very small minority. Especially when the Britishers grew more vocal during the trouble called the 'San Juan dispute'.

Remember that the Treaty of Washington in 1846 had left ambiguity regarding the exact line of the International Bound-ary, as it curved through a small and not particularly valuable group of islands south of Vancouver Island. Three channels through the group each qualified for the 'said channel'[1] vaguely specified by the treaty. Britain chose to interpret the treaty so as to give her possession of San Juan island; America, however, claimed San Juan as well. Diplomatic notes flew back and forth through the 1850s; a Boundary Commission appointed in 1856 failed to reach a decision. Then the dispute led to an inter-national incident – because of the death of a pig.

An American squatter on San Juan shot a pig that belonged to the H.B.C. establishment on the Island. H.B.C. threatened to take him off the Island, forcefully, and have him tried at Victoria. An American general who had been waiting for an opportunity of any kind – even a quarrel over a pig – landed an armed force on San Juan. Britain responded by sending a warship to hover menacingly offshore.

But the collision did not occur. Britain had no intention of provoking the U.S.A. over pigs, or islands, or even colonies; and President Buchanan rescued the situation by proposing

[1] See p. 51.

116

joint military occupation of San Juan while negotiations got under way. The Civil War then interrupted the talks, but afterwards – to settle the dispute once and for all – the German Emperor was called in to arbitrate. Eventually his decision was announced: San Juan and the other islands were to be American.

Few Americans, indeed, saw any reason why the rest of the British territories west of the mountains should not follow San Juan. In 1868, before the Emperor's decree,[1] resolutions had been passed in the U.S. Senate which included a statement of the price America would pay for the Canadian west: $6,000,000 to H.B.C. for Rupert's Land and the western Territories, $2,000,000 to cover British Columbia's debts. At about the same time a U.S. Senate Committee, considering the need for a railway to the Pacific across the northern states, minced no words about the effect such a line would have on Canada:

> The line of the North Pacific . . . when built will drain the agricultural products of the rich Saskatchewan and Red River districts east of the mountains, and the gold country . . . west of the mountains. . . . The opening by us first of a North Pacific railroad seals the destiny of the British possessions west of the 91st meridian. They will become so strongly Americanized in interests and feelings that . . . their annexation will be but a question of time.

And President Grant, hinting openly that Canada might give up some land in reparation for American damages suffered during the Civil War (the 'Alabama Claims'), made it clear that he felt Canada's absorption by the U.S.A. to be inevitable.

In the face of these pressures from the south, Canada had exerted every possible pressure to bring British Columbia into Confederation. And slowly British Columbians had become willing, even eager. After 1869 Canada's territory extended westwards to lap at the foothills; in the same year Governor Seymour died, and his replacement, Anthony Musgrave, proved to be an ardent Confederationist. Balked at first by powerful pro-American interests on the Island, Musgrave had by 1870 wheedled and persuaded most of the colonials into line. His breakthrough came when one of his toughest opponents, Dr J. Helmcken, altered his anti-Confederation stand – no longer rejecting the idea outright, but instead stating on what *terms*

[1] And before H.B.C.'s transfer of the west to Canada.

British Columbia should join the Dominion. It is necessary to admire the man's impeccable pragmatism:

> No union between this Colony and Canada can permanently exist, unless it be to the material and pecuniary advantage of this Colony to remain in the union. . . . Therefore no union on account of love need be looked for. The only bond of union outside of force – and force the Dominion has not – will be the material advantage of the country and the pecuniary benefit of the inhabitants.

So now everyone knew where they stood. British Columbia, aware that it was being courted, wanted a good price – not so high that it would be abandoned to its American suitor, but still satisfactorily high. From then it was a straightforward process of deciding on the terms to be demanded, and of delegates (one of whom was Helmcken) going to Ottawa to demand them.

Canada welcomed the British Columbians warmly, and surprised them by the readiness with which it acceded to their demands – even improving on them. So negotiations proceeded smoothly in the early summer of 1871. Canada agreed to take over the colony's debts, and to pay the province-to-be a sizeable cash subsidy. The strategic naval base on Vancouver Island, at Esquimalt, would stay; and the colony was allowed to retain the right to decide when it was ready for full representative government.

Above all, in terms of Helmcken's 'material advantage', Canada made a momentous promise – perhaps not realizing just how momentous. British Columbia had wanted the Dominion to end its isolation by building a wagon road across the Rockies, and by beginning work within a few years on a railway linking the east with the Pacific. Canada, in a burst of expansive optimism, went further. It gallantly undertook to begin that long-dreamed-of transcontinental railway within two years – and to *complete* it within ten.

So the second western province entered Confederation in July 1871, bringing with it Canada's commitment to realize the vision of a fantastic railway spanning 3,000 and more miles of emptiness, finishing the work that the fur traders had begun of opening the west to settlement.

6

The Great Lone Land

While Manitoba and British Columbia were being elevated
to provincehood, the prairie and parkland that lay between
them remained a nearly untrammelled emptiness. Two hundred
years exactly after the formation of the Company of Adventurers, the Plains Indians still pursued vast herds of buffalo
over the oceanic grasslands, which were interrupted only by
scattered islets of métis and fur-trade settlements. But, just as
H.B.C. no longer owned the west, so its employees were no
longer the sole white occupants. In the mid-nineteenth century
the Indians came to know another kind of white man: the
missionary.

The Catholics had been the first to arrive in the west. In the
old days of French–English rivalry, Jesuits had travelled from
New France in the *voyageurs'* canoes, ministering to the trading
posts and to a few Indian camps. Later, an Irish priest named
Bourke had been the first clergyman in Red River, under
Lord Selkirk's tolerant Protestant aegis. But Bourke, according
to his contemporaries, exhibited considerable 'eccentricity' – a
pleasant euphemism hiding we know not what transgressions.
He returned to Britain, and the Bishop of Quebec – whose
diocese included all the known area of British North America –
sent two priests to Red River. Fathers Provencher and Dumou-
lin arrived in 1818, in time to soothe Red River tempers after
the Seven Oaks massacre, and established the first permanent
mission in western Canada.

Their central parish became St Boniface, just south of Fort
Garry (Winnipeg); and Provencher in 1820 became Bishop
of St Boniface. Throughout the 1820s and 1830s he sent
priests into the interior, establishing missions at many Indian
gathering places within Manitoba's present boundaries: on

the Assiniboine some thirty miles from Fort Garry; on Rainy Lake, and elsewhere. In the 1840s the Church of Rome finally penetrated the great lone land, when Father Thibault travelled to Fort Edmonton and, a few miles west of the fort, built the mission of Lac Ste Anne.

The Church of England, in the person of Rev. John West, came to Red River in 1820, and also concerned itself with Manitoba missions. Andrew Cochrane's foundation of Portage la Prairie will be remembered from Chapter 4. The Anglicans also sent lay catechists to the wild forests of what is now northern Manitoba. One of them, Henry Budd, who was himself an Indian, set up a mission in the vicinity of the present town of Le Pas; and in the 1850s he began work in the Territories,[1] where his mission, at a spot on the North Saskatchewan river called Nepowewin, formed the beginnings of the present town of Nipawin. Other catechists preached to the Woods Crees at Cumberland Lake, Lac la Ronge, and similar tribal meeting places in the northern forests. But the Anglicans apparently concentrated their main missionary drive, and their ordained ministers, in the far northwest – the true north, Athabasca and Peace River and the Yukon. Their permanent missions came late to the prairies – not until the 1870s. By that time the Methodists had stolen a march on them, their smooth-running missionary machine taking the lead in prairie Protestantism. From the ranks of the Methodists and the Catholics, then, came most of the grand missionary figures, the devoted and far-seeing men who prepared the Indians for the shock of losing their prairie freedom with the colonization to come.

This is no place for an argument about the value, in principle, of the missionary idea. One could take the view that the 'opiate' of religion lulled the Indians into a state of mind in which they were more easily robbed of their birthright, and given nothing (of this world, anyway) in return. Or there is the view that the missionaries were the true heroes of the west – that by Christianizing the Indians they smoothed their inevitable transition from lords of the land to unwanted residents of reservations. Both of these views depend on one's accepting that the missionaries were widely successful in their work. Of course, statistics of baptisms performed could be impressive – as long as one was convinced that backsliders were few, and that the Indians were

[1] The unsettled land between Manitoba and B.C. See note on p. 4.

aware of the meaning of the baptismal sacrament. But these matters are not tallied in the records. In the end the question remains open. It is certainly true that sometimes the missionaries were not taken as seriously, perhaps, as they took themselves. (Before the visit of a Church of England minister to the Qu'Appelle region, in the late 1850s, the Indians of the region sent a message to the bishop saying that 'if the great praying father did not intend to send any rum, the sooner he took his praying man away from the Qu'Appelle Lakes the better for him'.)

Nevertheless, it is equally certain that most Indians treated most missionaries with respect – while giving their devotion, religious or just emotional, to the exceptional few. The respect and devotion worked both ways, in many cases, and so the Indians had valuable friends and advocates to plead their cause. Finally, however, the missionaries may be justified by the fact that, whatever their denomination, they were men of peace. And peace (as will be seen) was a commodity urgently needed in the Northwest Territories.

For better or for worse, then, the missionaries formed an advance guard for settlement, contributing no small effort to pacifying the west before its occupation. Thanks partly to them, no settlers would roll into the Canadian west with fingers on triggers, totally ignorant of Indian ways and indifferent to Indian life or death, and collide violently with the proud tribes of the plains. In Canada's west, on the whole, good Indians would not be equated with dead ones, but with Christian Indians on reservations. And while romantics might miss, in Canadian history, the glorious futility of the American Indian risings, and might claim that Christianity and reservations are fates worse than death, it is doubtful whether many Indians would agree.

The first Methodists in the west set up a central mission at Norway House (a major H.B.C. way-station in northern Manitoba) and sent Rev. R. T. Rundle to establish himself at Fort Edmonton and peripatetically convert the north-west. The leader of the Methodist incursion and superintendent of the Norway House mission was Rev. James Evans, the unhappy genius who guided the Indians to literacy.

Evans wanted to give his nomadic converts some concrete

manifestation of their new religion, to carry with them on their wanderings. Yet Indian hunters struggling for survival had little time or energy to spend on the effort of learning to read English. Especially when reading was itself, as an act, new to them – for like other Canadian Indians the Crees had no written language. From this quandary came Evans's great creation. He perceived that the spoken Cree language is syllabic – and that it is comparatively simple, containing few basic syllables. So he constructed (in 1841) a written language in which simple symbols represented syllabic sounds, and which could be learned in a matter of days.

The language itself is a marvel. He took four vowel sounds (ā, ē, oo, ah) and eight basic initial consonants; combining these, he invented thirty-six simple characters to represent the syllables. With the addition of eight characters for *final* consonant sounds, and the convention of a dot over a character to vary the length of a vowel, he could write virtually anything that could be said in Cree, and a good deal that could not.

As one example: matching the consonant 'p' with the four vowels gives the following characters and their syllabic sounds: V (pā), Λ (pē), > (poo), and < (pǎ). So 'papa' would be written << in Cree. The frequently used name of Jesus was written, in the first line of the first English hymn translated by Evans, thus: ∩ b ⌐ which syllabically sounds like chē/sǎ/s (cheesahs).

The Indians, delighted with their new skill, wanted more and more to read. So Evans supplied them – by *printing*, in the wilderness. He carved type out of wood at first, but later used lead from tea chests cast in clay moulds; he made ink out of soot and fish oil; and he took that northern standby, birch bark, as his paper. With these implements he printed hymns and prayers and extracts from the Bible, and his converts carried them to teach their tribesmen to read, and to spread the Word. Everyone used the language from then on for dealings with the Indians, in every religion and in quite secular matters; and Indians and Eskimos of the northwest continue to read Evans's 'birch bark talk' today.

Evans himself, unfortunately, clashed with H.B.C. over the proper observance of the Lord's Day. His converts observed a day of rest, which slowed the Company's fur shipments.

Somehow the missionary found himself victimized by trumped-up charges of immorality: Indian women, obviously bribed, testified against him in an H.B.C. court. At the same time, a shooting accident resulted in the death of an Indian at Evans's hands. The dead man's tribe absolved Evans of guilt, and even adopted him as a tribesman; a British court cleared him of the false charges. But the misery of these experiences, and the hardship of his frontier life, had wrecked his health: he died, aged forty-five, in 1846. Perhaps because of the disgrace that attached itself to his name, he never received the recognition he deserved for his great gift to the Indians. Its value cannot be overestimated, for it opened a way of communication and understanding between Indians and whites.

In 1860 Rev. George McDougall came to Norway House as the new superintendent, and dispatched Methodism over the prairies. At times McDougall went out himself, spending months with the Indians; later he shared this duty with his son John, who was to become one of the west's best-loved missionaries and a central figure in the settlement of Alberta. The McDougalls held the respect and trust of both Blackfoot and Crees, and moved freely among them even when they were at war. During the late 1860s, when the two great Plains tribes were constantly at each other's throats, a marauding band of Blackfoot killed the great Cree chief Masketoon. Bent on vengeance, the Crees organized a giant expedition which would have launched the tribal war to end all tribal war, probably drawing other tribes into the conflict. But John McDougall went to the Cree chiefs, Sweetgrass and Big Bear, risking his own scalp to talk them into peace. Apparently he succeeded, for the full-scale war feared throughout the west did not begin – though the enmity and the petty raiding continued. Later, John McDougall lent his enormous influence to smooth the negotiations with the Indians towards the treaties – and even helped to conclude some inter-tribal treaties, as between the Bloods and Assiniboines in 1872.

And always the paths of the Protestant missionaries crossed with those of the Catholics. In the 1840s a new missionary order, the Oblates of Mary Immaculate,[1] sent their first two representatives, one of whom, Père Taché, was to become the

[1] The Oblates order was formed in France in 1816, and the first Oblates to come west were French-Canadians.

Bishop of St Boniface in the days of Riel. The Oblates' numbers increased, their work spread: they moved into the north, building missions on Lesser Slave Lake, at Ile à la Crosse in northern Saskatchewan, and later on Lake Athabasca; they even penetrated the Arctic Circle.

In 1852 came the best-known and most effective Oblate of all, Father Albert Lacombe, whom later writers romantically call 'the black-robed *voyageur*', but whom the Indians more aptly called 'the man of good heart'. Lacombe, soon as fluent in the Indian languages as any of the missionaries, provided another bridge over the abyss between Blackfoot and Cree. He set up his base some miles from Fort Edmonton, which stood on the firing line, the boundary between the two great tribes. Lacombe called his mission St Albert; from there he set out on his wanderings, living with the Indians, preaching to them (he devised a pictorial, almost hieroglyphic, representation of the idea of grace and redemption, and it had a great success with the Indians), and urging peace.

Lacombe, like the McDougalls, risked his life in many ways to bring about intertribal peace. During one battle, while Crees were attacking a Blackfoot camp Lacombe was visiting, the missionary strode out into the thick of battle, shouting to both sides to lay down their arms. But the firing was too heavy and he was not heard; instead, he was felled by a ricochet. The Blackfoot screamed that 'Good Heart' had been killed; the Crees, protesting that they had not known he was there, stopped fighting and withdrew.

In fact Lacombe was only slightly injured, and lived to reverse the process another time, when a Blackfoot expedition surrounded Fort Edmonton itself. They were not fighting the whites, but trying to take from the Fort a group of Crees on whom they sought vengeance for a raid. Lacombe walked out of the fort and approached the Blackfoot, calling out in their language that they must not attack, that the whites and the Blackfoot must not fight. While he was trying to placate them, it is said, a trigger-happy defender in the fort nearly shot him, hearing the Indian language but not clearly seeing the speaker. Eventually Lacombe's counsel prevailed, and the Blackfoot launched no attack on Fort Edmonton.

Such adventures on the firing line were the rarest, if the most memorable, activities of the missionaries. They spent more normal days preaching and baptizing, teaching in schools they had set up for the Indian children, tending the Indian sick in crude hospitals, and trying – as best they could and however slightly – to alter the nomadic ways of the Indians and prepare them for the inevitable future. Usually this preparation took the form of lessons in agriculture, though few of the wild proud hunters took to farming with alacrity. But the missionaries persevered, and small but creditable agricultural settlements eventually began to spring up around the missions – Indian settlements that served to bring at least a few Indians closer to the white man's ways, and to prove, if anyone still doubted it, the fertility of the land.

Out of these missionary efforts came the nuclei of some of the Territories' earliest settlements. Fur traders had tilled some ground around their posts, especially at the great 'crossroads' forts of the trade such as Fort Edmonton, Fort Carlton and Norway House. When the missionaries came, and the Indians began their farms, the transformation from trading post to settlement was hastened. In many cases, a few white farmers – perhaps H.B.C. employees, or the missionaries themselves – added to the effect. Such was the case with Fort Edmonton when it was visited in 1866 by those transcontinental wanderers, Lord Milton and Dr Cheadle.[1] They described St Albert as a colony of some twenty houses, with a church, school and nunnery (the Sisters of Charity, or Grey Nuns, had come west in 1844) and commented on its 'several very respectable farms, with rich corn-fields, large bands of horses, and herds of fat cattle. . . . Altogether this little settlement was the most flourishing community we had seen since leaving Red River. . . .' Also, the McDougalls had built a Methodist mission at Edmonton, and had begun homesteading there as well. By 1870 there were seven separate homesteads staked out beside the H.B.C.-owned land at Edmonton, each with a full complement of log houses and farm buildings. The fort had become a village.

Another premier settlement in the early days of the Territories arose from Presbyterian missionary activity. Oddly, the Presbyterians were late in coming to the west. Some say that H.B.C. had been against too many Protestant variations, which might confuse the Indians. Certainly the Scots Red Riverites had clamoured long and loudly enough to indicate that the

[1] Two young curious Englishmen, the first tourists in the west.

delay was due to factors other than a lack of missionary zeal. In fact, they had to make do with Anglicanism until 1851 – over thirty years after Red River's founding – when Rev. John Black arrived. Eventually the Presbyterians joined in the missionary drive. A minister of the Presbyterian church in Red River, James Nisbet, gathered a few pioneers in 1866 and set out to build a mission on the northern fringe of the prairies. The small group, including three children – one the Nisbets' – travelled overland in Red River carts until they reached the North Saskatchewan, then floated downstream on rafts until they landed at their place of settlement: near an H.B.C. post at an important Indian meeting place. The spot had woods on one side of the river and prairie on the other, a useful place for wintering and finding game. (A small community of métis had earlier for this reason settled a mile or two downriver.

The Presbyterians loyally named the place Prince Albert, in irrelevant honour of the Royal Consort, and erected the usual log houses and church. (The church still stands, now both a museum and a museum-piece in the city of Prince Albert.) Within a few yards the colony had expanded, as more Red Riverites, encouraged by the Nisbets' success, came out to find free land for homesteads.

So the missionaries not only prepared the way for settlers but did some actual settling of their own – and continued to do so. (John McDougall and his brother David were the first farmers to bring cattle into the incredibly rich grazing lands of Alberta, where ranching – as a later chapter will show – became a thriving industry.) But by the late 1860s and early 1870s the men of God began to fear that the pacifying effects of missions and farms had failed. Other white men who had come recently to the west had managed to counteract much of the missionaries' work – and in the process had raised the terrible threat of an all-out Indian war against the white man.

Too many changes had been taking place in the west all at once, and most of them involved hardship or death for the Indians. But for some time these changes had remained well south of the border, where the onrush of American settlement bore down upon the Indian like a bulldozer clearing the wilderness. There, treaties were made, but were also blandly broken, or ignored, in the clamour for land. Indian agents were appointed, but many were ex-Army officers with little know-ledge of and less sympathy for Indians – and many, also, were eminently corruptible. Opposing these flimsy bastions of law and justice were the rugged-individualist settlers, always ready to exchange a plough for a gun, always believing in a genocidal 'final solution' of the Indian problem. And there were the profiteers, too, outright swindlers who exploited the Indian's legal *naiveté* and cheated him out of his land.

In the long run the swindlers proved the worst of all. They sought buffalo hides, which had become increasingly valuable, for robes and for leather. In exchange they provided the Indians with whatever they wanted – which usually turned out to be liquor, sometimes guns. So, in the aftermath of the Civil War, when thousands of footloose and battle-calloused men were turned out into the west, anxious to make their fortunes, the vicious and ultimately disastrous Montana whisky trade was created.

The troubles in America had at first only tangential effects on the Canadian west. The Blackfoot, who claimed Montana as their hunting ground as well as Alberta, were disturbed by the spread of settlement to that territory (Montana gained territorial status in 1864). The Plains Crees were disturbed when the Minnesota Sioux, in the 1860s, retreated from their bloody rising to find sanctuary in Manitoba.[1] The Crees were further upset when the Blackfoot, first to be in contact with American traders, began obtaining the new and deadly repeat-ing rifles. Indians of all tribes realized that such weapons would mean more buffalo killed, and faster – which could lead to a dangerous depletion of their dietary staple.

Then the great trauma of the century – H.B.C.'s surrender in 1869 of its long-held lands to the unknown quantity, Canada – affected the Indians as it did all westerners. They feared that law and order would vanish from the west – for H.B.C. was no longer master, yet there was no visible sign of Canada's authority. They also (like Riel's métis) feared the settlers. The Indians had seen, in America, what heavy settlement meant to them: they had seen the indiscriminate slaughter of buffalo, partly because – as some Americans made clear – exterminating buffalo meant exterminating troublesome Indians. They had heard the tales of Indian camps wiped out to the last child

[1] See p. 57.

simply because a few braves had stolen a few horses: for horse-stealing was a common everyday occupation, almost a sport, among the Indians, but was the ultimate sin to the American westerners. They heard, also, of the infamous Massacre of the Marias – in 1870 – when a detachment of U.S. cavalry, on a punitive expedition against a band of Blackfoot raiders, had devastated a Blackfoot camp in Montana, killing more than 100 men, women and children before realizing that they had attacked a different, totally innocent band.[1]

In Canada, Indian unrest was exacerbated in 1870 when another threat, another kind of sudden death, swept the prairie camps: a smallpox epidemic. Captain W. F. Butler (sent out by Lieutenant-Governor Archibald of Manitoba to check on Indians and disease) was among the contemporary authorities who gave some credence to the rumour that the epidemic was purposefully caused: by American traders selling or giving infected clothes and blankets to Blackfoot in order to avenge a comrade's murder. But such revenge would seem rather too subtle and long-range for these violent men. They would have preferred guns – as others of their kind did, later, in the Cypress Hills. A more likely theory suggests that infected clothing discarded by white men was picked up, unknowingly, by Indians. At any rate, as always, the scourge spread with the speed of a blizzard through the Indian encampments. Chiefs led their bands out into empty wilderness to avoid contact, but often went too late, took the disease with them, and died far from human aid. The missionaries again came into their own: Père Lacombe exhausted himself moving from camp to camp in a frenzied attempt to tend the sick and comfort the dying. Young John McDougall contracted the disease, but shook it off in time to help his father among the stricken Indians. (Two of George McDougall's daughters, and a third adopted Indian daughter, died in the epidemic.) Altogether, John McDougall estimated, 3,500 Indians died of smallpox –

[1] In fact, the field day that the press had with exaggerated accounts of that error – as if such horror needed exaggeration – led to a healthy reorganization of U.S. official attitudes. Indian Affairs were taken out of the jurisdiction of the War Department and turned over to the Department of the Interior, and new qualifications were demanded for Indian agents. But the changes were too little and came too late to save the American frontier from the terrible wars of the '70s – including the Sioux rising when Custer died.

and according to another rough estimate the entire Plains Indian population (Blackfoot, Cree, Assiniboine) numbered by then only about 26,000.

For some Indians, the scourge completed – or anyway speeded – the process of demoralization begun by the violent changes sweeping over the plains. But it snapped others, especially the Blackfoot, into action: perhaps to propitiate their gods, as George McDougall conjectured; perhaps to seek revenge on the white man for having brought his vile diseases among them. In small and vicious raiding parties, the Blackfoot took to the warpath – marauding, stealing, burning, murdering. And both the demoralization and the violence were given an added stimulus in 1870 and after: for then the American whisky traders, seeking new and easier markets as the U.S.A. belatedly began to clamp down on the illegal trade, moved their operational bases into Canada's unprotected west.

With careless arrogance they spread over the southern prairies, building forts that flew the Stars and Stripes, bringing their wares to the few settlements that were available. Missionaries and H.B.C. men at the settlements did their best to remonstrate with the traders, but they had no legal authority – nor had anyone else, and the whisky men knew it. The trade went on.

It was a foul business. The stuff they traded was the vilest of liquor, first extensively cut with water and then given strength – for the Indians liked to be burnt by their firewater – by various appalling additives, anything from tobacco juice and red ink through tabasco to even vitriol. Indians often died of drinking it, and then the strength of the traders' forts might be tested by a short and furious siege. The liquor killed Indians, too, in other ways: drunk, they froze on the plains in winter, they murdered each other in savage quarrels, they were shot by the traders when trying to steal more. It undoubtedly aggravated the cruelty of many intertribal battles at this time. Certainly it contributed indirectly, for the traders handed over liquor for buffalo hides – which made competition for hunting territory even more avid (and which, incidentally, began to wreak havoc on the great herds).

In late 1870 the Blackfoot and Crees collided on the plains (near the site of the present city of Lethbridge, Alberta) in what is often called the last great Indian battle in western Canada. It began when some Crees came upon an undefended camp of Piegan women and children (the men being off on a hunt), and gleefully attacked and slaughtered them. Of course the Blackfoot rode in revenge. When they caught up with the Crees, the battle raged for long and bloody hours; many of the warriors, in the end, ran out of ammunition and reverted to knives and tomahawks. Several hundred were killed on both sides, until finally the Cree defence broke and they fled, to give the Blackfoot the victory. The fight seemingly took a good deal out of each side, for later an edgy peace was concluded between these traditional enemies.

In the following years, however, the west was generally far from peace. The marauding Blackfoot still struck at vulnerable parties of whites; other tribes grew sullen and bitter in the aftermath of the smallpox epidemic and the growing strength of the whisky traders. Canada had proved powerless to expel the American corrupters from the prairies: the Indians began to indicate that *they* might undertake the job, and rid their lands of all other whites while they were at it. War drums sounded from the Indian camps: traders, missionaries and other whites waited fearfully for the terror to begin.

But somewhat earlier the Canadian Government had become aware of the imminent danger, and of the need for law in the Territories. Ottawa's awareness culminated in a decision that effectively forestalled the general Indian rising that the west had feared. The Canadian Adjutant-General travelled to the Territories on what a modern bureaucrat would call a fact-finding mission. He found numerous facts, all of them frightening, about the whisky trade and the Indian threat. His report recommended that a military force be sent out, and established in posts scattered strategically across the west. But the politicians, especially John A. Macdonald, were unwilling to send soldiers – who might spark off an international conflict and cause further excesses of American manifest destiny. Instead, Macdonald and his advisers devised an idea which produced one of Canada's greatest sources of romantic legend, tradition, and tourist attraction: a mounted police force. They would function like cavalry, but would be under civil control and so less likely to upset the U.S.A.

As Macdonald presented to Parliament, in 1873, a bill that would create the force, the whisky traders themselves provided an incident, a horror, which fired the indignation of the country and prevented all argument (if there had been plans for any) about the proposed police. Few of the violent episodes in western history have so many contradictory accounts as the Cypress Hills Massacre.[1] But the bare bones of the story, at least, have been fairly well substantiated.

Aside from the whisky traders, Canada's Indian territory had been invaded by groups of Americans who were called 'wolfers': they killed wolves, coyotes and other animals for the skins, using the ugly trick of poisoning buffalo carcasses. The Indians objected to this practice, for the poison killed their dogs, and the wolfers killed too many buffalo. So the Indians tended to kill wolfers. At one time, because too many of their number were being killed in skirmishes, the wolfers demanded that the whisky traders stop giving the Indians repeating rifles. When the traders ignored them, the wolfers staged an abortive attack on the well-defended stockades of a traders' fort. Violence was breeding violence in every direction.

Sometimes, of course, the Indians merely harassed their enemies with the enjoyable game of horse-stealing. In this way one group of wolfers, travelling in early 1872 towards Fort Benton, Montana (the centre of the whisky trade as of most other activities on America's northern plains), had a few horses stolen overnight. The group went on to the fort, gathered some local hard-cases and gun-happy plainsmen – about a dozen in all – and set out in pursuit of the Indian thieves. They lost the trail, but pressed on, and eventually came to a small whisky-trade post in the Cypress Hills, where they paused. There they hoped to rediscover the trail of their horses, or at least to hear word of the thieves.

At this point the story becomes garbled. One account says that a band of Assiniboines (camped nearby) brought in one of the stolen horses, claiming to have found it: but the horse

[1] It occurred within a group of forested hills which rear up – to 4,000 feet at their highest – out of the flat treeless prairie on the Alberta–Saskatchewan border, near the U.S. boundary. The Hills were a favourite gathering place for Indian, métis and white hunters or travellers – a refuge from the open barrenness of the plain. Of course, no cypress grows so far north: but early French explorers had glorified the local jackpine with the name *cypres*, which the British retained.

wandered off again, which led the Americans to believe that it had been stolen again, by the Assiniboines, and that they were also the original thieves. Another version says that the Assiniboines had simply come in to trade, and that the wolfers had somehow convinced themselves that these Indians were the thieves. But Paul F. Sharp, the American historian, provides the most believable untangling of the various stories. He first makes it clear that, in the Cypress Hills, hatred between Indians and white whisky traders had been building to a violent climax for months (as it had elsewhere). And, he says, it was a stolen horse belonging to a local whisky trader – *not* to a wolfer – that touched off the explosion.

Apparently the trader stormed over to the Assiniboine camp to regain his horse, accompanied by the Fort Benton boys – who went along to help, but who may *not* have believed that these Indians were their quarry. It was the entrance into the camp of these armed and belligerent whites which brought about the showdown.

By this time, it seems, the Indians were drunk, and greeted the whites with insolence and threats. No one knows who fired first; some say that after exchanging insults and challenges both sides began firing at about the same time. The whites took up strategic positions from which they could rake the exposed camp. Panicky and disorganized at first, the Indians rallied and charged three times, but were beaten off with severe losses. Then they took cover, and continued the gunfight until it was clear the whites were not to be dislodged.

Finally the Indians retreated. Some of the whites, over-bold, pursued them, and one was killed – the only white casualty. Estimates of the Indian dead range from thirty to eighty, but the lower number is likely nearer the truth. The Americans then wrecked the camp, placed their dead comrade in a hut and burned it (to protect his body from mutilation), and left. (Paul Sharp says they went off to take up the chase again of the original horse-thieves.) Rumours later accused them of perpetrating atrocities on the Indian dead, and on two Indian women taken prisoner, but these tales can perhaps be discounted. The Americans were hardbitten men, ready with a gun, but were not the homicidal maniacs they were thought to be by outraged easterners. Nor were the Indians entirely innocent: they were known – to James McKay, a Scots métis and member of Manitoba's council – to be expert and incorrigible horse-thieves.

And yet the fact remains that the Indians were mostly drunk and incapable – enough to allow their attackers to move unscathed from shouting in the open to firing from cover – while the whites were not. The conflict may have *become* a battle, once the Indians organized themselves to fight; but at first, while the whites were firing into the confused, chaotic camp, it was a murderous slaughter.

Very soon after news of the massacre reached the east, Macdonald's bill became law, and the North-West Mounted Police came into existence. Shortly a group of 150 recruits travelled to Winnipeg for a hasty training programme. It seems a near absurdity, now, to think of such a handful of men policing the vast expanses of the prairie. Nor was the apparent absurdity lessened when the first Commissioner, G. A. French, asked the government for more men, and received another 150. (By 1910 their numbers had only doubled again to 600.) Of course, they were mostly seasoned veterans of the British or Canadian Army – but each one would have many thousands of square miles to oversee, and no amount of experience could lend them wings.

Yet it can be seen to have been the only way. *Authority*, not more violence, was needed in the west. An army might have had a salutary effect on the whisky traders, but would have been wasted on such opposition; while Canada knew that an entire army would do no good if the threat of a Plains Indians rising became a reality. (After all, the U.S. Army had created as many Indian crises as it had solved.) But if Canada sent to the west a handful of men, acting with firm authority but visibly concerned with being just and fair-minded and tolerant, the Indians might well respond – as most had always responded to the manifestations of British law and order. (The N.W.M.P.'s scarlet tunics were devised to remind the Indian of the British soldiers whom generally he admired.)

So into the valley of death, as it were, rode the 300.

Their goal was the central region of the whisky trade, which was dominated by the infamous Fort Whoop-Up. (Other whisky forts included Fort Stand-Off, Fort Slide-Out and the comparatively prosaic Fort Kipp.) Whoop-Up, within a few miles of the present site of Lethbridge, had been built flimsily

133

in 1870; but after it had been burned that year by a band of Indians enraged at being refused more drink, it was rebuilt as a solidly stockaded and armed fort, with small narrow windows through which the trade went on. The fortification ensured that the Indians kept their murders among themselves: even so, about fifty whites had been killed around the place in the early 1870s.

The Mounties had a map based on the Palliser expedition, and had directions to Fort Whoop-Up supplied by the Adjutant-General. They marched on a southern trail which had been laid down by the Boundary Commission (the Canadian–American survey party who in 1872–3 had located the exact line of the International Boundary). Part of the police cavalcade was detached and sent northwest to Edmonton: with this detachment went men and animals who succumbed early to the rigours of prairie travel.

Rigours there were, indeed, and historians of the R.C.M.P. (as it now is) have made the most of the Great March. Water was scarce, for waterholes were rendered mucky and questionable by the buffalo herds which wallowed in them; the prairie sun blazed down on the white cork helmets (stetsons came much later); fuel was shoddy (no wood, only buffalo dung); food, mainly pemmican at first but fresh meat when they reached the buffalo country, was monotonous and inadequate. The men suffered, and plodded on; their huge wagon train – carrying heavy material such as guns and ammunition, agricultural implements, and so on – often spread out four miles long. Their route took them 400 miles along the border, then another 300 to the Bow River (where they thought Fort Whoop-Up stood). Northwards, the separate detachment under Inspector Jarvis struggled for eighty-eight days through thick mud on the trail's deep ruts, building corduroy roads over marshy ground, bridging rivers or crossing them on rafts. The oxen grew weak and slowed down progress, the horses collapsed and died: there are stories of men actually carrying horses for miles.

Yet, with all the undeniable hardships that they faced, the impression remains that the N.W.M.P. were less prepared than they might have been for the western actuality. Perhaps in modern terms the march was heroic; but men of that time felt otherwise. Some time later, when Inspector Jarvis was reliving the story in conversation with Rev. John McDougall, the reverend exasperatedly provided the inspector with some perspective on the matter – and in the process provided an evocative picture of prairie life at the time:

> Nine or ten miles north of Edmonton there dwells, when at home, a French half-breed who, when the spring comes, will load his carts with his winter's trade and catch of furs and pemmican, and, with his wife and children, will take the trail you came by, crossing all the streams you crossed. In due time he will reach Fort Garry; then he will sell his furs and robes, and purchase his fresh supply of goods and articles of trade, load these on to his carts, turn his face westward, recross all the streams, now at their highest, reach his home north of Edmonton, put up several stacks of hay, fix up his winter quarters, mend his carts and harness, and having carefully stored his goods, he and his family, with the same horses and carts, will cross the Saskatchewan and travel out from two to three hundred miles on to the plains . . . run buffalo, stand on guard day and night, make many bales of meat, make many bags of pemmican, and finally . . . return over the long journey to their home north of Edmonton. And still, it is not yet winter; and thus this native has travelled about three times the distance you and your party did . . . and they had no government behind them, and what they have done is a common occurrence in this Western country.

So, it is reported (by McDougall), the inspector was abashed. In fairness, however, it must be remembered that in 1875 the N.W.M.P. were very much amateur plainsmen – and therefore their march acquired a tinge more heroism than if they had been seasoned. And further, it is to their credit that within months the Mounties had become professionals, and in the process had changed the face of the west.

At the end of their march they arrived at the Bow River, only to find that they had been misled, and that Fort Whoop-Up was elsewhere, on another river. They camped to rest, and a detachment rode south, to Fort Benton, to get supplies and tell their troubles to Ottawa by telegram. As well as supplies they acquired the services of one Jerry Potts, a Scots-Piegan métis – one of the greatest plainsmen at large. (As a youth he had trailed, caught and killed a Blackfoot who had murdered his father; his courage and stamina were renowned, among Indians as well as whites; he had fought with the Blackfoot in the last great Indian battle already described, and, legend says, emerged from the fray with a head-wound, an arrow through his body, and nineteen Cree scalps.)

With Potts's guidance the N.W.M.P. found Fort Whoop-Up, and with it anti-climax. The whisky traders, forewarned, had vanished (back across the border, as it turned out). The police pulled down the American flag, for want of anything else to do. Riding on, they chose a site on which to build their Fort Macleod, named after the justly famous Assistant Commissioner who was setting the standard for Mounted Police action and attitude at this time.

The action then began in earnest. Most of the traders had crept out of the country, but the police found and arrested one, slower than the others, named Bond. Other police searched for the perpetrators of the Cypress Hills Massacre; when some of these were found, in Montana, an extradition trial was held that led to considerable bad feeling across the border. The suspects were acquitted, and remained in the U.S.A., due to conflicting and dubious evidence on the part of 'witnesses'. The Chief Justice who conducted the trial did so with exemplary scrupulousness, but could not find proof of guilt – and in his summing up declared his belief, rightly, that neither Indians nor whites were the true villains of the case, but the vicious liquor trade that had created its circumstances. At least, though, the Mounties had made the effort – and this, it seems, helped to impress the Indians.

N.W.M.P. relations with the Indians developed well. Crowfoot, the head chief of the Blackfoot Confederacy, visited Fort Macleod and came away reassured that law and justice had arrived at last. Another later incident helped to strengthen the Indians' respect for the Mounties. Superintendent Walsh (after whom Fort Walsh in the Cypress Hills was named), with one constable, was visiting a large encampment of American Sioux. (The Sioux were now moving into Canada in large communities, to escape post-Custer reprisals from the U.S. Army.) An Indian rode in telling of a successful horse-theft he had committed, and Walsh – surrounded by about 10,000 potentially hostile Indians – promptly put him under arrest. The thief, too astonished to do anything but back down, assured Walsh that he had just been boasting, that he had only found some horses and would certainly make sure their owners regained them. Walsh then released him with an admonition. Both the courage and the magnanimity had their effect, and contributed to the creation of that charisma which for so long enabled the Mounties' mere *presence* to keep the peace. This quickly grown reputation paved the way for the finest achievement, in those early years, of the N.W.M.P.: the patient, tactful and equitable negotiation of treaties with the plains tribes. Treaties had already been signed with many Manitoba bands – from Selkirk's treaty in 1817 to the Lake Winnipeg treaty with the Crees in 1875. In 1876, through the offices of the Mounties and the Northwest Territories Council, a major treaty was concluded at Fort Carlton with the Woods and Plains Crees of Saskatchewan. Then in 1877 the mighty Blackfoot Confederacy treated with the white man.

The Blackfoot treaty might be glanced at as fairly representative of the plains treaties. It called for the Indians to cede their ancestral rights to their territory, while retaining hunting rights on unsettled tracts. It allotted reservations, enough land to give one square mile to each family of five (with larger or smaller areas in proportion to different-sized families). Each Indian man, woman and child received twelve dollars at the time of signature, and the tribes also received various gifts – including a few rifles, agricultural tools, clothing, food and trinkets. And treaty money was arranged to be paid annually – twenty-five dollars for chiefs, fifteen for lesser chiefs, and five for every other individual. Also, schools and teachers were promised, and the basis of herds for cattle raising.

The signatories were Crowfoot, of course, along with thirty-four chiefs and councillors from the Blackfoot, Blood and Piegan tribes; Commissioner Macleod and Lieutenant-Governor Laird (of Manitoba and the Northwest Territories) for the whites. Witnesses' names provided some symbolic satisfaction: they were representatives of H.B.C., the N.W.M.P., and the Christian Church (John McDougall signed, but Père Lacombe, regrettably, was ill and could not be present) – in other words, the three great spearheads of the invasion of settlers that was then in the offing.

The treaty was quite an accomplishment. Only a few years earlier the Blackfoot had been fingering their rifles and talking about white scalps. Yet the great rising had never materialized. The arrival of the N.W.M.P., and the overnight departure of the whisky traders, had given the most bloodthirsty Indians pause, but it had not removed all the causes of Indian unrest. In particular, it was obvious by 1877 that the buffalo was in imminent danger of extinction. At the same time a new threat had emerged to the Blackfoot hunting grounds: the Sioux nation was settling firmly into the Canadian west, Sitting Bull himself having crossed the border early in 1877. Now they as well as the Crees would compete with the Blackfoot for the dwindling herds – and the Blackfoot answer to competition had always been war. In the light of these circumstances, no praise can be too great for the handful of police and missionaries who pacified the Blackfoot and made the treaty possible.[1]

Not all the Plains Indians, however, could be brought to the council table to talk treaty. Some bands, within the tribes, remained mistrustful – and among these was the Cree chief, Big Bear. His passive resistance was later to change, in 1885, into uprising and war. But that event was far in the future. And this narrative has already jumped too far ahead in time, perhaps leaving the false impression that the Mounties' arrival and the Indian troubles were the only momentous events in the west during the 1870s. They were not. That decade, in fact, saw the first true beginnings made in the opening of the west, of which the Indian treaties were only a part. Those ten years saw the first wave, small but significant, of organized immigration to the prairie farmlands. And they saw a beginning, patchy but promising, made on the transcontinental railway.

[1] It must also be added that the task would have been considerably harder, perhaps impossible, without those ideal intermediaries, the métis. Jerry Potts, for instance, a trusted confidante of Crowfoot and the Blackfoot chiefs, acted as a diplomatic emissary as well as interpreter and guide for the N.W.M.P. Other métis living in Blackfoot country exercised their influence in the same way.

7

Railway Building

Canada began work on her grand dream of a railway with admirable promptness. Ceremonially, on the very day that British Columbia officially joined Confederation, exploratory surveys got under way in the forests of the new province's mainland. In the east, the railway's engineer-in-chief, Sandford Fleming, grouped his 800 men into divisions (Eastern, Prairie and Mountain) and set them searching for a practicable route. It was to be a long, hard search.

The railway, it was soon decided, would set out westward from a point in Ontario called Mattawa – a town somewhat east of Ottawa and north of Toronto. (This eastern terminus would later be altered.) The line would have to fight its way through the murderous terrain of the Pre-Cambrian Shield north of the Great Lakes: then, crossing the prairies, it would require pathways through the Rockies, then through the Selkirk and Gold ranges, and finally through the Coast range to a yet-to-be-named Pacific terminus.

Above Lake Superior, the engineers knew, the line must run as near as possible to the shore, in order to link up with water-borne traffic. But should the track be placed on the lakeshore itself, or could a better path be found farther into the interior? The final choice would be the lesser of two evils, for, as Fleming said in a characteristic understatement, the whole area 'was not favourable for railway construction'. One of his articulate surveyors, J. H. E. Secretan, working in the Lake Nipigon region, managed to be more descriptive about the interior landscape:

> The country assigned to us was most uninteresting, consisting . . . of a series of muskegs occasionally intersected by high rocky ridges; the timber was small scrub spruce of a most funereal

aspect with long pendant weepers of black crepe – no birds, no beasts, no fish. . . . Millions of poisonous black flies by day and mosquitoes by night. . . . We were no doubt the first human bipeds that had ever traversed that God-forsaken country – although perhaps we didn't fully realize the honour and glory of all this at that time.

Another surveyor, J. H. Rowan, provided a brusque picture of the forbidding lakeshore:

> The greater part of the country explored was of the most barren and rugged description, traversed by high ranges of hills of primitive rock from which every vestige of vegetation had been removed by fire, and quite impracticable for a Railway.

By 1874 Fleming had found three possible routes through the Shield. One passed north of Lake Nipigon, requiring a fairly long branch line to reach Lake Superior; the other two passed south of Nipigon, each curving down to touch Lake Superior at different points. So Rowan's dismissal of the lakeshore prevailed; and Fleming himself eventually dismissed the north-of-Nipigon way, which narrowed the choice to two.

In the same year – three years after British Columbia's entry into the Dominion, one year after a start should have been made (according to the terms of entry) on railway *construction* – nothing more than a similar narrowing of choices had been achieved in the far west. Two likely passes through the Rockies – the Howse and the Yellowhead – had been found, which linked with suitable routes through the province; two likely termini were being discussed as well. Bute Inlet had the advantage of being easy to reach from the available mountain passes; Burrard Inlet, farther south, by the mouth of the Fraser, had a better natural harbour. Various permutations of routes linking one of the termini to one of the passes had been worked out by 1874, and Fleming had tentatively decided to advocate the Yellowhead Pass and Burrard Inlet. Argument, of course, raged. No rails were going to pass through British Columbia without trouble: steep gradients, many bridges, cuttings and tunnels appeared in every proposed route. It would all be desperately expensive, in time as well as money – and probably in human life as well.

The British Columbian and Lake Superior surveys had already proved costly in these ways. North of the Lakes, a survey party of two whites and five Indians had been burned to death in 1871 when trapped by a forest fire. Four surveyors had drowned the next year when their boat overturned on the Ottawa river. Three more died in 1872 when a Lake Superior steamer sank. Many others narrowly missed death: J. H. E. Secretan's party ran out of provisions when the supply centre failed it, and was forced to walk for days through the wilderness living on nothing but rose hips and water. (All its members reached safety.) In the mountains snowstorms, avalanches and narrow trails over abysses wreaked havoc among the survey parties, but miraculously none of the frequent accidents was fatal – to humans. (Eighty-six pack animals were killed in one winter's exploring.)

The hazards of mountain surveying are depicted by Secretan, again, who had been transferred to the Mountain Division:

> . . . many a time I was slung up with a line under my armpits, laboriously trying to find room for the tripod of a transit on a narrow ledge of projecting rock often many hundred feet above the foaming whirling white waters of the stream below.

Sandford Fleming, himself a remarkable engineer, seemed able to inspire his men to immense labour and some heroism. Unfortunately, decisions about the railway in general were not to be taken strictly on engineering grounds. From the outset the railway acquired an overlay of politics. The politicians used it as a road to power, in their various ways: while a very few risked their careers to further it, the majority hedged and delayed and finagled, sought ways to obstruct it or to profit by it. Even by the late 1870s, no real progress had been made and the whole great concept itself had come near to being buried in a political morass of indecision, ineptness and irresponsibility.

Shortly after British Columbia's entry had been ratified by Parliament, the Conservative government of Sir John A. Macdonald decided to let out the job of building a Pacific railway to private capital – which would be supported by generous land grants and cash subsidies. Groups of businessmen, many of them Americans, immediately began jostling one another in the rush to bid.

The American interests came extensively from the groups

that had built the continent-spanning Union Pacific (completed in the late 1860s), and that were in the 1870s thinking in terms of the Northern Pacific. (The latter proposal, presenting a serious threat to the Canadian transcontinental idea, had undergone various financial shake-ups which had held it back.) The railway tycoon Jay Cooke, involved in the Northern Pacific, was a leading light in a syndicate formed by a Montreal shipping millionaire named Sir Hugh Allan. They called themselves the Canada Pacific Railway Company, and sought the contract. They were opposed by a Canadian group which had heavy backing from the powerful Grand Trunk Railway,[1] and was headed by a friend of Macdonald's, D. L. Macpherson.

Macdonald found that the Hugh Allan bid was clearly the better. But he had always promised that the Pacific line would be all-Canadian: '. . . we will see that Canadian interests are fully protected, and that no American ring will be allowed to get control. . . .' He escaped the dilemma by strongly recommending that the two companies shake off their American influences and amalgamate to do the job. Both companies seemed dubious – but Allan proved devious as well. He announced that he would accept the amalgamation if he remained president and retained a controlling interest. By this he implied that in other respects he would live up to the bargain; but apparently he had no intention of sloughing off his American associates. Macpherson suspected as much, and balked at the merger proposal. None of Macdonald's blandishments could speed the settlement. Yet speed, for him, was necessary: he was facing an election, and needed a satisfactory railway decision for his campaign.

Allan, meanwhile, began dipping into politics. He found a weak spot in Macdonald's ageing colleague, Sir George Etienne Cartier, offered financial and propagandist help in Cartier's own campaign, and soon had the tired old politician under his thumb. From this vantage point he applied pressure on the Conservatives, alternating it with temptation: promises of ample campaign funds. Macdonald, with his party short of money, wavered and then accepted. (He still believed in Allan's good faith.) By the time he had won the election, he was trapped

[1] The Grand Trunk, built in the 1850s, linked Ontario and Quebec. It ran a network of profitable lines through Ontario, and had extensions into major U.S. cities on the Great Lakes.

by Allan's contributions of more than $100,000. Only then did he find that Allan's American associates had never been dropped.

Instead, they manifested themselves as possessors of some indiscreet correspondence between Macdonald and Allan, regarding funds, and let it be known that if they were pushed out in the cold without suitable compensation the correspondence would be made public. But Macdonald had no time to decide what action to take over the blackmail: for the Liberals had, by devious means, obtained some of the correspondence for themselves. They promptly published it, and the Pacific Scandal of 1873 erupted.

So the prime mover of Confederation, the great John A., had been caught promising the moon to a railway magnate in return for sordid money. Or so it seemed. And because the magnate was American-influenced, Macdonald's sin seemed magnified. So he fell, far and hard. As he toppled, certain of his political associates hastily deserted him – prominent among whom was Donald A. Smith. Aside from being the M.P. for the Manitoban constituency of Selkirk, Smith (who was introduced in Chapter 4) also held a seat in the Manitoba provincial legislature, and had risen to the top Canadian position in the Hudson's Bay Company. (Other M.P.s had called him the member for H.B.C.) He was no demagogue, but a political and financial expert at profitable deals. He operated in terms of self-interest, H.B.C. interest, and the interest of his constituents: but if these realms ever clashed, it was not self-interest that he dropped first. Smith had also been on the board of Allan's Canada Pacific Railway Company – and it is unimaginable that he had not known of Allan's back-room dealings with the Americans.

Yet, in a speech rich with unction, he professed to the House that he had not known, and could not have been a party to the enterprise had he known, and was shocked at those whose lack of honour could permit them, and so on. It was widely rumoured that Macdonald went over and struck him after that speech, but in fact the ex-Prime Minister was too busy with his sinking ship to bother with deserters. So Smith saved himself from the Tory wreck, and from the wreck of the Pacific railway idea. (Later he will be found back on the bandwagon, devoted in every way to the cause of the railway.)

In the end it was neither Macdonald nor Allan who suffered most from the scandal, but the railway. It had been dangerously delayed; now it was soiled as well, a dubious venture. So with Macdonald's resignation the plans for the railway fell into the doldrums. The new Prime Minister, Alexander Mackenzie, was a cautious, unimaginative leader, who was facing national economic troubles as the 1873 depression spread up from the U.S.A. It was no time to throw money away on visions.

Mackenzie at last concluded that a rail-and-water route to the Pacific would suffice. It would avoid the need for costly construction north of the Lakes: the railway could run in the west, but steamers could carry the traffic across the Lakes into the east. Mackenzie also decided that the government would build the project as a public enterprise.

But the government was in no hurry. While the depression, tariff troubles with the U.S.A., and inexperienced Liberal cabinet ministers posed knotty problems, the albatross of the railway could wait. As a gesture and nothing more (a gesture to keep British Columbia happy), Mackenzie instructed Sandford Fleming to make further surveys. Fleming did his duty. He sent men to explore the Pacific coast for other possible terminal points, and for mountain passes and land routes across the province. More groups ran exploratory surveys for possible branch lines in Ontario; others occupied themselves with trial surveys of possible routes on the prairies. This unproductive, niggling work went on through 1875 and 1876, into 1877. Yet the basic routes remained (Yellowhead to Burrard Inlet in British Columbia, and south of Nipigon in the Shield), having been more or less decided earlier.

As Mackenzie hesitated, British Columbia grew restive. Three of the ten years allowed for completion had passed, and there was nothing to show for it. The province had received no immediate benefits from the project, and was notably impatient regarding talk of long-range benefits. So it demanded reassurance. In reply Mackenzie sent a special envoy empowered to negotiate with British Columbia for a *relaxation* of the terms of entry.

The envoy offered the tempting bribe of a promise to build, immediately, a special railway on Vancouver Island between Esquimalt and Nanaimo. But the gambit failed. The mainland, predictably, rose in fury at the idea of such favouritism; and the Island suspected that it might lose its share of the trans-continental line if it accepted this sop. So the envoy returned to Ottawa, bearing with him some black threats from British Columbia concerning the possibility of secession. Then in January 1876, the province petitioned the Queen for relief of its grievances, and in the document repeated the threat to secede.

The Colonial Secretary came to the rescue, as arbiter between Ottawa and the Pacific, and his diplomacy resulted in an agreement over new terms. Canada promised to determine finally the route of the railway; to build immediately a wagon road along the route, into British Columbia, to serve until the track was laid; and to spend at least $2,000,000 a year on construction. In return British Columbia extended the deadline for completion to December 31, 1890.

While Mackenzie's record as a railway builder justifiably failed to impress the British Columbians, he had done slightly more than sponsor futile surveys. In June 1875 at Fort William (on the western 'head' of Lake Superior) the first sod was turned to mark the beginning of main-line construction. It might have been a memorable historic moment, had it been anything more than a merely ceremonial – and qualified – first step. Some months earlier, construction had begun on another portion of the Pacific railway – the true first step. This initial portion was only to be a *branch* line: but branches take on prominence when a main trunk does not yet exist.

The arrangements that produced the branch line may not be compared to the events leading to the Pacific Scandal, but they were not entirely above board. First, however, some background to this new development.

The state of Minnesota, in the 1860s, had begun work on an 85-mile-long railway running north from St Paul, aimed at attracting settlers to the area and transporting them there. The line, called the St Paul & Pacific, was financed by bonds held by Dutch bankers, and was for a while a subsidiary of the U.S.A.'s Northern Pacific. But when the latter's financial problems halted the progress of its main line, it also (in 1873) halted the St Paul & Pacific – and the Dutch bondholders wanted out.

The situation then came to the attention of Donald A.

Smith, now a close confidant of Mackenzie's. Smith's interest was shared by one J. J. Hill – a Canadian-born businessman who ran a steamship company on the Red River out of St Paul – and Hill's partner, Norman W. Kittson, who has appeared in this narrative before.[1] Smith also approached a cousin of his: George Stephen, a Montreal financier and president of the Bank of Montreal. Stephen as well quickly saw the potential value of the St Paul & Pacific. Using his Bank of Montreal credit, he, Smith, Hill and Kittson formed a syndicate and acquired control of the line, in its incomplete state. As they saw to its completion, they renamed it the St Paul, Minneapolis and Manitoba Railroad – which made their intentions clear. By that time the reason for their interest in the little railway had also become clear: Mackenzie's government had constructed that trunkless branch line from Winnipeg to Pembina on the U.S. border.

The object of the Pembina branch, ostensibly, was to provide for eventual railway access to Winnipeg, the west's jumping-off place. Once some American railway reached Pembina (so ran the government's thinking), a route would be available for transporting into Winnipeg, by rail, construction materials for the Canadian transcontinental. Also, the Pembina branch would provide a valuable commercial link between Winnipeg and the east.

These were reasonably acceptable explanations for beginning Canada's Pacific line with a branch line. But they did not tell the whole story. J. M. Gibbon, the historian of the Canadian Pacific Railway, implies that the construction of the Pembina branch might be traced back to Smith's influence over Mackenzie. Indeed, in 1872 a financial group including Smith and Stephen had applied to the Canadian Parliament for a charter to place a railway line along that very route, from Winnipeg to Pembina. (Obviously they had wanted the line in order to form a profitable link with the St Paul & Pacific, work on which was then still advancing.) But their application had been refused, on the grounds that the line they sought would compete with the proposed Canadian transcontinental. Yet within a few years Mackenzie himself had sponsored the construction of the same line to Pembina, as part of the larger project. Clearly Smith had had a hand in that decision, which would make his

[1] See p. 54.

group's railway (the St Paul Minneapolis and Manitoba) immensely more valuable.

So far, of course, nothing underhanded had occurred – except, perhaps, Smith's using his political influence to further one of his private financial projects. But the interests of his province had been furthered as well: Manitoba's isolation was ended for ever, and its prosperity was assured as the gathering place for the builders of the Pacific line, and as the main railway outlet of the west. Then, however, came a more discreditable step, which slightly tarnished the golden future that the Pembina branch promised to Winnipeg. Mackenzie had a bill passed in Parliament that enabled the government to *let* the Pembina branch on a long-term lease.

Only George Stephen's name was mentioned as a likely lessee. But everyone knew that the lessees would be Stephen's syndicate, of which that leading *eminence grise* in Mackenzie's government, Donald A. Smith, was a prominent member. In short, it was said, Mackenzie was about to turn over to private interests the first piece of Canada's national railway. Naturally, John A. Macdonald, still scarred from the Pacific Scandal and Smith's desertion, made the most of the situation. Unfortunately for Mackenzie, that year (1878) was an election year.

Macdonald, barnstorming brilliantly, gained forgiveness for his earlier lapse from grace, and used the Pembina-branch deal, and the general delay and fumbling over the railway, as efficacious clubs with which to beat the government. Needless to say, he was swept back into power. (Curiously, his own Ontario constituency did not re-elect him, and he had to find hurriedly another safe seat – which turned out to be Victoria, B.C.) In the new and shining Macdonald era the Pacific railway assumed prime importance. Macdonald's heir apparent, Charles Tupper, became Minister of Works with responsibility for the railway. (One of his first acts was to disallow the leasing of the Pembina branch to the Stephen-Smith syndicate.) John A. himself, outside his duties as Prime Minister, took the newly created office of Minister of the Interior, with special responsibility for stimulating development and settlement in the west. The Tories were determined to allow no further delay in the railway project.

But delaying factors remained. Macdonald reverted to his original idea that the railway should be constructed by private enterprise, with government backing. But the continuing depression (which persisted until about 1880) frightened capital away from large and dubious projects. And the financial help which Canada sought from Britain, to provide the backing which Canada's laughable income could not hope to manage, did not seem to be forthcoming.

Finally the first hindrance was overcome. A few groups of financiers put in their bids to build the Pacific railway. And, in one of those remarkable turnabouts to which politics and finance seem given, the most likely contender for the prize appeared to be the syndicate headed by George Stephen, including Donald Smith, J. J. Hill, and Norman Kittson.

Macdonald favoured the Syndicate (as it was simply called) because it had diverged from the usual proposal of floating bond issues to finance the railway (and so pocketing a profit at the outset). Instead, Stephen had proposed that the Syndicate receive a cash subsidy to begin with, and a grant of land which could be sold as construction progressed. The sale would then pay for the costs of building, and bring in settlers to the west.

Macdonald swallowed whatever ill feeling he retained for Smith, and approved the deal. (Smith's name was left off the agreement – an act of political circumspection which annoyed Smith and fooled no one.) The terms on which the agreement was based came in pleasantly round numbers: the Syndicate would get a cash subsidy of $25,000,000, and a land grant of 25,000,000 acres.[1] So in late 1880 the contract was signed, and the Syndicate became the Canadian Pacific Railway Company.

Macdonald had completed his reversal: now the Liberals, former bed-fellows of Smith and Stephen, began theirs. They accused Macdonald of selling out to American interests (refer-

[1] Some of this acreage would come in a 'belt' along the route of the C.P.R.'s main line. But for much of its length the line would run through territory 'not fairly fit for settlement', as the contract put it. Hence the rest of the grant was made up of reserve lands elsewhere on the fertile prairies (mainly in the Territories). The railway-owned belt, along the route, would not be a solid block: the C.P.R. and the Dominion would take *alternate sections* (an idea borrowed from the U.S.A.) so that both would profit from land sales as the railway pumped up land values.

ring to the Syndicate's ownership of the St Paul Minneapolis and Manitoba, forgetting that all the principals in the Syndicate were Canadians, in spite of their financial involvements in the U.S.). Further, the Liberals staged a heroic attack on the subsidy, the land grant, and the rest of the contract – especially a clause that came to be known as the 'monopoly clause'. It had been included to protect the railway against incursions from the U.S.A.: it forbade, for a breathing space of twenty years, the construction of other lines between the C.P.R. line and the 49th parallel. The C.P.R. depended, for survival, on quickly settling the country and in this way *creating* the traffic which it would carry. In the early days it could stand no competition for the first sparse dribblings of that traffic. For the same reason, clauses in the contract allowed the C.P.R. total tax exemption, duty-free importation of materials, and almost *carte blanche* in the construction of its branch lines. To protect his railway company George Stephen had pressured the government into unusual magnanimity. The Liberal opposition foamed with rage.

Other less impotent enemies, however, began to chime into the anti-C.P.R. chorus. American railway interests and other U.S. financial groups opposed the Canadian project, which would destroy their hopes of draining off the Canadian prairies' wealth. Ontario's Grand Trunk Railway, feeling cheated of an interest in the Pacific line, and fearing the C.P.R.'s effect on the eastern monopoly of the G.T.R., added its voice – but spoke mainly to British ears. Both dwelt on the impossibility of the task that faced Stephen, on the shaky Canadian economy, and other bogeys. Both sought to balk Stephen's attempts, to gather investment in the C.P.R. before he had begun. Clearly Macdonald and Stephen were going to have to fight a multitude of obstacles and opponents for every inch of the C.P.R.'s transcontinental advance.

Under the aegis of George Stephen – whom D. G. Creighton calls 'the greatest creative genius in the whole history of Canadian finance' – the C.P.R. Company quickly showed that it would not be a cautious or short-sighted railway builder. As one of the first constructional decisions, the directors startled the nation by drastically altering the railway's projected route – bringing it well to the south.

149

Of course, the northerly route[1] proposed by Sandford Fleming and accepted for so many years, by government and public, still remained a better choice. Yellowhead Pass was the easiest natural path through the Rockies, and led to similarly practicable passes through the inner mountains. Also, the northern route crossed through parkland, where the immense fertility would have soon attracted abundant settlement. But these considerations no longer carried enough weight. The C.P.R. desperately needed to cut corners, for economy and speed: and a more southerly route would be shorter, and would avoid costly bridges over the rivers (including the South Saskatchewan) of the central plains. As further justification,[2] the new route would reinforce the monopoly clause, thoroughly blocking any American encroachment. (By 1880 the Northern Pacific had recovered, as had the U.S.A., from the depression, and its railhead had advanced as far as North Dakota. The C.P.R. feared its tentacles reaching up to, and perhaps into, the Territories.)

But even with these powerful arguments the decision might have been scotched, except that new information about the western prairies had been received. Earlier, thanks largely to Captain Palliser and Professor Hind, the southwest of the Territories was believed to be mostly arid and infertile, offering little opportunity for settlement. But a botanist named John Macoun, who had journeyed west with Sandford Fleming, showed fairly conclusively that far more land was arable than Palliser had realized. (Palliser, he claimed, saw the land in an exceptionally dry season, and when the gigantic herds of buffalo still grazed over it. By the late 1870s the herds had been

[1] From Fort William this route plan crossed the Red River at Selkirk, a town northeast of Winnipeg (and Donald Smith's home constituency), then proceeded between Lakes Winnipeg and Manitoba to the Swan River valley. It then veered due west, crossed the South Saskatchewan somewhat north of where Saskatoon now is, at a place now called Clark's Crossing (see page 172). Farther west it followed the south bank of the North Saskatchewan, through Battleford, through a spot across the river from Edmonton, then west to Yellowhead. Later, the Grand Trunk Pacific would adapt part of this plan to its own transcontinental purposes. See Chapter 11.

[2] The historian H. A. Innis offers yet another likely reason why the route was shifted. Donald Smith had not given up his position in the Hudson's Bay Company; and a more southerly route would keep the railway well away from H.B.C.'s stamping grounds in the fur forests.

enormously reduced.) When Macoun announced that the southern plain, 'although not everywhere suited for agriculture, possesses many fine tracts fit for the plough, and always good pasture', the C.P.R. was encouraged to take its radical decision.

And that decision involved more than a new route across the prairies. The C.P.R. scrapped the surveyed line north of Lake Superior, and set out to challenge the crags and muskegs of the lakeshore itself – again in the interests of a shorter line. And in British Columbia the surveyors were sent out once again, to find – if it was possible – more southerly routes through the mountains. If the passes were available, the C.P.R. would have a shorter line to the Fraser (through the rich land around Kamloops) and thence to Port Moody on Burrard Inlet. The news delighted British Columbians: the railway looked like being finished in less time even than optimists, in 1878, would have guessed. Only a few pessimists, in 1881, could foresee how much the new and speedier route was going to cost.

But the railwaymen ignored any gloomy prophecies, caught up in the heady joys of – at last – getting started. On the prairies, the line immediately west of Winnipeg was relocated and shortened; the initial clearing and grading, begun patchily in Mackenzie's time, was pushed ahead in that direction and east towards the lakehead. In British Columbia a brilliant young engineer named Andrew Onderdonk, who while still in his twenties had built up a notable reputation for achieving near-impossibilities of construction, took up contracts for parts of the proposed line. (He was later to take over nearly all the contracts for construction of the railway in that province.) Then, as the climax of the C.P.R.'s preparatory organization, Stephen hired a general manager – and in so doing transformed the story of the railway from a historical romance into an epic.

The epic hero, a bulky American named William Van Horne, had been a railway manager in the U.S. until J. J. Hill found him for the C.P.R. He was just the tonic the Canadian project needed. As a general manager, he combined the skills of a brilliant administrator with those of an exceptional engineer. He was tireless and ruthless; he drove his men like slaves, the way he drove himself. He was everywhere, with a fine concern for detail and an amazing grasp of the whole. Legends grew up about him within weeks of his arrival – and some were close to the truth. He was said to be able to play poker and drink all night and work hard all next day without any sign of weariness: it was rumoured that he *never* slept. Some employees claimed he could miraculously be in two places at once – and in this connection a tale can be told (though it occurred some years ahead of this narrative).

Van Horne, in his private car, was on one of his regular inspections of completed parts of the line north of Lake Superior. At a small station where the train was taking on water, he got out for a stroll – during which he overheard a message coming in on the station's telegraph. (He had begun his railway career as a telegraphist.) The message, just a chat between station operators, mentioned that some trainmen on an eastbound train were having a good time lounging around on cushions from the first-class car and playing poker. Van Horne waited until he had reached another station; then he telegraphed to a point at which the guilty trainmen were about to arrive, ordering them explicitly to return the cushions to the first-class coach and to stop playing poker in company time – but saying nothing about his source of information. The news spread – and the boss, from then on, was believed to be omniscient.

Van Horne arrived to take over the C.P.R.'s management in late 1881. The winter had barely ended when he began a fantastic drive. J. H. E. Secretan describes the first he heard of it, from the boss himself:

> . . . Van Horne sent for me and announced in a most autocratic manner that he wanted '*the shortest possible commercial line*' between Winnipeg and Vancouver, also that he intended to build *five hundred miles* that Summer, lay the track, and have trains running over it. . . . I doubted if he could possibly construct five hundred miles in a short Summer but he scowled at me fiercely, and . . . informed me that 'nothing was *impossible* and if I could show him the road that was all he wanted and if I *couldn't* he would have my scalp'.

So Secretan and the other engineers who were locating the line showed Van Horne the road he wanted. The manager promptly threw about 5,000 men, with 1,700 teams of horses and mules, into the westward effort on the prairies. Later in the season he put crews on night shift and laid track twenty-four hours a day. The surveyors managed to keep only a few weeks ahead of the graders; the track-layers followed on their heels.

J. M. Gibbon quotes a writer who worked on the construction crews that summer, describing the hectic process:

> In places the track was laid so rapidly that there was not time to set up camps. Large two-storey cars were built for the use of the men. In the upper storey the men slept, and in the lower they had their mess. Each car held . . . eighty men. These cars, together with the cooking, inspector's, and workshop cars, were permanent portions of the construction train, and were always left at the front. The rest of the train consisted of twenty-one flat cars (or trucks), and was backed up by the engine. . . .
>
> The sleepers or ties (laid 2,640 to a mile) were packed thirty-three to a car, and the rails (which were 30 feet long) were thirty pairs to a car. . . . The sleepers were loaded on to carts and . . . distributed, spaced, and lined well ahead of the track-layers. In order to unload the rails the train was backed up to the end of the track, and the rails were thrown off the cars, fifteen pairs on each side. The engine then drew off, and the fifteen pairs were loaded on to a trolley drawn by horses. . . . When the trolley reached the last laid rail, a pair of rails was dropped, gauged, and the trolley run forward over them. A gang followed to affix the fish-plates, and was in turn succeeded by the spikers. When the load was finished, the trolley was thrown off the rails to make place for another.

In this way the end of steel advanced, often at the record-breaking speed of 3 miles a day, across what is now southern Saskatchewan – more than 400 miles that summer. As well, Van Horne's crews built more than 100 miles of essential branch lines in Manitoba, which gave him his 500 prairie miles.[1]

In 1883 the work went on at nearly the same rate, though that year the mileage dropped: the crews were working in heavily rolling prairie, and preparation of the road-bed required more effort than it had on the level plains west of Winnipeg. Nevertheless, before the end of that season the railhead had reached the site of the present city of Calgary – within view of the Rocky Mountains. The prairies had been spanned: travellers could now move from Winnipeg to the mountains in a long day's train trip. But that had been the easiest part of the route. Van Horne's ingenuity and aggressive

---

[1] Critics complained that a railway built that fast could not possibly have been built well; but some years later Sandford Fleming travelled the line and, in an independent report, praised it without qualification.

energy would now be tried by the terrors of the mountains and, eastwards, by the cruel terrain of the lakeshore.

Of course, the advance of the railhead across the plains had not been trouble-free. The sheer extent of the task of supplying the crews – with construction materials as well as with food, fuel, and so on – had produced enormous organizational problems. But Van Horne thrived on pressure. Not even a flood of the unpredictable Red River held him up – though it inundated the Pembina branch line over which supplies and materials came. Trains were carrying their vital cargoes to Winnipeg across the flooded tracks before the water had wholly run off them. Then, in the second year of Van Horne's reign (it is the only word), a new crisis sprang up: a threat of an Indian rising.

It never came to a fight, but it was a near thing. In 1883 the end of steel had crossed the borders of a great Blackfoot reservation. And no one – neither the government nor the railway – had thought to tell the Blackfoot that compensation would be paid them for any lands taken over by the C.P.R. All the Indians saw was white man's steel on their land. They had held a council of war when the surveyor had gone through, but had decided to wait and see. Now they had seen. The white men had brazenly and arrogantly broken the promises of the treaty. So the young Blackfoot warriors clamoured for war, and their proud old chief, Crowfoot, did not discourage them.

Dramatically, at the last minute, the Blackfoot were halted by the intervention of the west's best-loved missionary, Father Lacombe. Lacombe hurried to Crowfoot, and convinced him that the whites meant no harm, and would certainly pay adequate compensation. Mollified, Crowfoot called off the planned rising. When Van Horne heard how close his men had been to an Indian war, and how Crowfoot's decision had prevented trouble, he presented the chief with a special lifetime pass on the C.P.R. which he, Van Horne, had designed.

Now the railhead was edging up the slopes of the Rockies. Van Horne had demanded a new pass through those mountains, and his surveyors had found one for him – the path of the Kicking Horse river. It was far from ideal, but was possible: though it would demand heavy grades and many tight curves, it would probably need no tunnelling. So Van Horne aimed his track-layers at the Kicking Horse Pass. Yet at the same time, typically, he had no evidence that there was any route at all through the Selkirks (the next great barrier after the Rockies) that would be near Kicking Horse. Again he ordered his men to forget the word impossible, and find a pass. Otherwise he would have had to send the track up the Columbia Valley and *around* the Selkirks, by means of the Big Bend. (But this route would still have been shorter than the original line through Yellowhead.)

Van Horne's luck held, however, when a dogged surveyor-explorer, Major Rogers, struggled up into the Selkirks and found the necessary pass, which was named after him. Again the route was barely possible, in terms of obstructions and gradients: but it was quite good enough.

By the end of 1883 the railhead had been pushed up to the summit of the Kicking Horse Pass, after a 'tote-road' had first been built on which materials and supplies were hauled up by wagon. Work stopped over the winter, except for the ground-work, especially cutting timber for ties. Then in spring the crews continued to hack their way through the Rockies. Now the progress was slow and arduous: heavy machinery for cutting through rock could not be brought up by the tote-road, and so the railway's path was carved out of the granite by manual labour – interrupted when sudden flooding of the Kicking Horse River made the supply road impassable, and much of the railway roadbed was overrun.

Beyond the summit the terrain did not improve: roaring mountain creeks feeding the river required bridges, and as it turned out a few tunnels were necessary after all. Morley Roberts, a literary Englishman who worked and tramped his way into interesting adventures all over the world, describes the work on the 'Mud Tunnel', through a hill beside the river:

There must have been a hundred or more men employed at this work, which was of a hazardous and dangerous character. The hill was being attacked on both sides at once, and at the west end, downstream, the tunnel was advanced to some distance, but at the east end, though there, too, the hole had been run into the hill, the work was to do over again, owing to the tunnel having 'caved' in, in spite of the huge timbers. The hill was composed of gravel on the top, then a thick stratum of extremely tenacious blue clay, and beneath that a bed of solid concrete [granite]. . . . We had to remove the immense mass of clay and gravel which

155

had come down when the 'cave' had occurred, and to cut back into the hill some distance. . . .

As the cut into the hill was now very deep, we worked on three 'benches'. The lowest and farthest out from the crest of the hill attacked the clay at the bottom; the next, twenty or thirty feet above us, cut into the loose gravel . . . and the highest gang above that again wheeled away the sand at the top and cleared out the stumps as they came to them. The highest gang worked in comparative safety; the next in some peril, as they had to look out for the rocks that might fall on their own bench and for those from the upper bench as well; but the lowest gang were in danger of their lives all the time, as from both benches above them came continually what rocks escaped the vigilance of those working over their heads.

On the other side of the mountains Andrew Onderdonk and his men were blasting, tunnelling and cutting their equally hazardous way towards the Gold Range – where Eagle Pass had been chosen as the meeting point of the two railheads. Onderdonk was building the line from Port Moody to Savona's Ferry (on Kamloops Lake) under a contract let by the government; now the C.P.R. gave him the contract for most of the remaining British Columbia mileage, from the Lake to Eagle Pass. (It turned out later that the government contract had contained inaccurate specifications, so Van Horne had to have much of that portion of the railway rebuilt – through no fault of Onderdonk's.)

Once again the Cariboo Road came into its own. The road was now some twenty years old, and was in a dangerous state of disrepair, thanks to time, weather and railway construction. But it was still the only means of access for materials and supplies, since both railway and road passed through the fearsome Fraser canyon. One old railway builder tells of the supply wagons fighting their way along its treacherous surface, in formations that 'usually consisted of two wagons, coupled together and drawn by nine yolk of oxen or teams of mules, the whole well over 100 feet long. It will be gathered what these meant going around curves'.

Naturally Onderdonk's few hundred miles demanded a disproportionate amount of work. In many places, in order to answer the C.P.R.'s need for speed, Onderdonk built temporary lines – sometimes using trestlework, where possible, instead of levelling or tunnelling – which would serve until increasing traffic required (and could pay for) a more permanent road. But the Pacific section was not shirking its job. In a letter to the Chief Engineer, Onderdonk indicated in a laconic 'bare facts' manner the kind of effort that was being made over an especially difficult five miles near Lytton:

> The nature of the work . . . was, in a great part, solid rock cuttings, rock slides of loose rock, large boulder cuttings and some heavy earthwork. . . . The solid rock cuts turned out very favourable, being hard on the exterior, but when opened, drilled easily and 'shot well' [blasted freely].

He went on to give some figures: 200,000 cubic yards of solid rock were shifted within those five miles, 90,000 of loose rock, and 400,000 of earth – aside from the rock and earth moving required for 400 feet of tunnel. Onderdonk added: 'The five miles above referred to is as heavy as any five miles . . . in British Columbia.'

Another source gives a less modest and more dramatic view of the British Columbia line:

> For nearly sixty miles from Yale to Lytton, the river has cut through this lofty range [the Coast Range], thousands of feet below the summit. Mountain spurs of granite rock, with perpendicular faces hundreds of feet in height, projected at short intervals along the entire passage. Between them are deep, lateral gorges, canyons and plunging cataracts. On this sixty miles of tunnels, rock work and bridges, the greatest portion of Mr Onderdonk's construction army of 7,000 men have been engaged since 1880. The loud roar of enormous discharges of giant powder has almost constantly reverberated among the mountains. Fifteen tunnels have been bored, one 1,600 feet in length, and millions of tons of rock blasted and rolled with the noise of an avalanche into the rushing, boiling Fraser; workmen have been suspended by ropes hundreds of feet down the perpendicular sides of the mountains to blast a foothold. . . . It is estimated that portions of this work have cost $300,000 to the mile.

Apparently, to hasten the progress of supplies, Onderdonk had a special steamer built to challenge the turbulent upper Fraser. The boat's hull was divided into many separate watertight compartments, so that she would not sink even if several holes were punched in her bottom. Against the Fraser's current the steamer advanced slowly, using not only her engines but a cable and steam winch to pull her through the rapids – and, at least once, 150 Chinese as well pulling on the cable.

In the east, progress had been satisfactory from the new Ontario terminus – the town of Callander, diplomatically equidistant from Toronto and Montreal. But north of Lake Superior Van Horne's engineers were facing an effort almost as Herculean as Onderdonk's: 10,000 men fought a slow and expensive battle through what Van Horne called 'two hundred miles of engineering impossibilities'. Gibbon relates that one particular mile contained enough difficult Pre-Cambrian Shield terrain to cost $700,000. They blasted the peaks of the granite ridges, and filled the muskeg's hollows between ridges. One patch of muskeg swallowed up the track seven times – and took three locomotives as well.

Van Horne met the problems head-on. As in British Columbia, supply routes were unreliable, except in summer when the lake transport could be used. So the engineers blasted out rough roads for winter supply wagons. But extra blasting used even more immense quantities of dynamite. To reduce a supply wagon's load and save time in the long run, Van Horne took the startling step of building a dynamite *factory* north of the Lake. When the need increased, he added two more factories. He also opened stone quarries in the area. To speed things further, he imported the first track-laying machine ever used in Canada. And for many miles of alternate rock and bog he replaced the 'blast-and-fill' technique with the erection of temporary trestles – from which trains could bring 'fill' to solidify the muskeg.

Yet even with these innovations and short cuts the eastern section was becoming a dangerous drain on the C.P.R.'s finances. And because of it there had arisen a new demand for utilizing American rail to take C.P.R. trains *south* of the Lakes, avoiding the expensive construction in northern Ontario. Advocates of the idea pointed out that U.S. lines already had links with Winnipeg through the St Paul, Minneapolis and Manitoba Railroad; much time and more money would be saved in the building of the transcontinental line. And, they added, the C.P.R.'s route north of the Lakes could be built later, when (or if) the volume of western traffic warranted it.

Not surprisingly, the C.P.R. board contained some noisy proponents of the U.S. detour: most especially J. J. Hill, now the dominant figure in the very railway (the St Paul, Minneapolis and Manitoba) which would most profit from the diversion. By this time Stephen had come firmly to agree with Macdonald that the C.P.R. must be all-Canadian, or else its value as a concrete form of Confederation would be ruined. And, strange to say, Van Horne – though an American – sided with Stephen in the boardroom battle against Hill.

Hill lost, and resigned from the C.P.R. board, going south to devote himself to expanding the St Paul line into a transcontinental rival, the Great Northern (which eventually swallowed up the Northern Pacific). Shortly afterwards Stephen and Smith gave up any further direct involvement with the St Paul line, though they retained their holdings 'so long at least as the policy of the company is not hostile to the C.P.R.'

Another more serious battle had arisen, initially, because of the decision to take the lakeshore route: with the Grand Trunk Railway. As has been seen, the G.T.R. originally had put in a bid to build the Pacific line, and resented its loss of the contract to Hugh Allan. Later, when Stephen's company was in its infancy, the G.T.R. had sought to restrict the Pacific line to the *west*, so that its powerful position in the east would not be threatened. The C.P.R., it had hoped, would stop at the Manitoba–U.S.A. border; traffic would pass south of the Lakes on American lines, and come up into Ontario on the Grand Trunk. But the plan had been rejected. And, what was worse, the C.P.R. had soon begun to stretch tendrils into G.T.R.-dominated Ontario. The G.T.R. had a near-monopoly on railway traffic to and from Montreal, and blocked the C.P.R.'s way into that city. But it could not prevent Stephen from securing leases to smaller Ontario and Quebec railways, which gave access to other large eastern centres. Instead, the G.T.R. (in concert with the Liberal party, with which it was closely associated) set out to obstruct Stephen's money-raising efforts – at a time when the C.P.R.'s finances were trembling towards disaster.

As the mountain and lakeshore construction bills came in, Stephen found that the C.P.R. was costing more than even pessimists had estimated. The money had to be found. Yet, according to the contract, the government subsidy and the land grant had both to be acquired by the C.P.R. in instalments, during the course of building as more miles of track were laid.

Stephen's other sources of working capital were reduced largely to sale of common stock – by no means lucrative, given the climate of opinion in which the railway was functioning – and any loans that could be raised. Through 1882 the C.P.R. had squeaked by, meeting their expenses only because Stephen exerted himself beyond measure to raise money – for instance, pressuring a land company to buy large blocks of C.P.R. land, rather than waiting for sales to settlers. And all the time Stephen's enemies were whispering: that Stephen was in league with speculators, that the lands were infertile, that the Indians were on the point of rising. Propaganda from what Stephen called Grand Trunk 'scribblers' in London hindered his efforts to dispose of more stock. So Stephen turned to U.S. financiers, and set up an intricate financial structure to provide the C.P.R. with working capital. But he had achieved only a temporary relief. Prosperity and boom times were once again beginning to fade at the end of 1883. One more C.P.R. crisis might bring ruin.

The crisis came soon. Van Horne had made his great march across the prairies, and his first assault on the mountains. The money had been drained away. The stock market was reacting badly, seldom favourable to C.P.R. holdings. Somehow Stephen had to create an atmosphere of confidence, in which he could dispose of more stock: he had to declare a special dividend. He had been declaring dividends throughout – but now he wanted the Canadian Government to display its confidence in the C.P.R. by guaranteeing part of the dividend for the next ten years.

Macdonald raised no objection, and the guarantee was given. But it had little effect on the stock market. The C.P.R.'s enemies were still abroad, vocal, and being heard. Macdonald was then forced to see that a few fragmentary shorings-up could not save the railway. Canada would have to provide concrete support in the form of hard cash. And there was little time. For the Northern Pacific had suddenly collapsed into ruin and bankruptcy, and railway shares everywhere had suffered in the stock-market backlash – the C.P.R. most of all. Creditors now haunted Stephen, enemies waited for the end. Stephen turned in desperation to Macdonald for a government loan of $22,000,000 – against a mortgage of the main line.

The enemies of the C.P.R. outdid themselves in their violent, hysterical attempts to discredit Macdonald and Stephen and forestall the rescue. But in a gruelling political battle, in Parliament and in back rooms – wheedling, soothing, reassuring, threatening, promising – Macdonald forced through a bill that ratified the loan. The creditors got their money, and the rails continued to be laid.

But rail-laying continued to be cruelly costly, especially the lakeshore line, which swallowed money like the muskeg swallowed tracks – even though it was by 1884 still being built piecemeal, not in a continuous line. The $22,000,000 dwindled and vanished, having bought a few more months and miles. Now the railway's completion was nearly within sight – but in 1884 the available sources of capital were again drying up, and a new crisis was approaching.

At the same time a wider crisis, beyond the C.P.R., was threatening the entire west.

8

And No One Came

Compounding the crisis, in 1885, in the C.P.R.'s finances, a feeling had begun to grow in political and financial circles that the optimism in the railway's future – and in the entire west's – had not been justified. The hoped-for waves of settlers, who alone would create the traffic that would make the railway profitable, had simply not materialized in the 1870s and early 1880s: at any rate, not in the numbers that had been anticipated.

Back in 1872, following up its grand public promises at the Immigration Conference[1] and elsewhere, Canada had formulated legislation to prepare the west for settlement. First of all, surveyors were sent out to divide up the land, as much as was practicable, in the Territories. They followed the American example: checker-boarding the land into townships, six miles square, each township containing thirty-six sections of 640 acres each. Every section was sliced again, into more manageable pieces, 160-acre quarter-sections.

As the surveys pushed ahead (mostly in Manitoba, where the incoming settlers would arrive first), Ottawa promulgated its Dominion Lands Act of 1872. It later went through a number of alterations and amendments, but its basic provisions can be extracted. The Act permitted a settler to take up a quarter-section of unoccupied[2] Dominion land and – upon

[1] See p. 93.

[2] Free homesteads could be established only on *even*-numbered sections. The odd numbers were otherwise reserved. Two odd sections in each township were to be sold, when needed, as an endowment for schools. One and three-quarters sections in each township (and an extra section in every fifth township) went as H.B.C. reserve land. In some areas, Indian (and métis) reserves claimed a share. Much of the remainder was set aside for the C.P.R., in the manner described on p. 148. So until the free-homestead policy was extended, much valuable land, ideal for settlers, was kept out of the hands of would-be homesteaders by being offered at varying prices for *sale*.

payment of a $10 registration fee – to work those 160 acres as a *free* homestead. After three years, he could file with a government Land Office a claim of ownership of the land, but then had to show proof that he had occupied and cultivated (i.e. 'improved') his homestead. A later amendment established a corollary of 'pre-emption': a homesteader could take an option to *buy* (pre-empt), within three years, a quarter-section of unoccupied land adjoining his homestead.

Also in 1872, the Dominion passed an Immigration and Colonization Act which set up various ways of attracting settlers to the west. A few agents were scattered abroad (in Britain mainly, but also some Continental cities), propaganda pamphlets were printed, a publicity campaign begun. Then Canada sat back and waited for its new westerners.

But optimism soon faded into disappointment. Farmers may have been emigrating from other countries, but they were showing no interest in Canada. Even a special Dominion attempt to stimulate immigration, through private enterprise, foundered miserably. Ottawa granted large blocks of unoccupied land to firms who proposed – as a speculation – to bring settlers in. Three such firms, aiming their propaganda respectively at Swiss, German and Scots emigrants, spent much money to no avail, and soon wound up operations. Another Dominion land grant was made, later, for 'repatriated' French-Canadians – farmers who had left crowded Quebec for the U.S.A., and who were to be tempted back to land near French areas in Manitoba. But only a few hundred repatriations were achieved.

In short, plans for populating the west had little success during the 1870s. Nor did they even *begin* to succeed until the 1880s, when the C.P.R. had stretched across the prairies. Too many obstacles, which have been described here before, continued to turn settlers away. The depression of the 1870s had its effect: few emigrants cared to tackle a totally wild and isolated country when prices were crippling and markets (for produce) depressed. A few seasons of drought, and grasshopper invasions, became as widely publicized (by rumour and word of mouth) as the Dominion's glowing advertisements. But, mainly, the transportation difficulties and the attractions of the U.S.A. (where free homestead land remained voluminously available) held up the settling of Canada's west. In fact, as will be seen, over twenty years would pass from the year of the

Immigration Act before the west would see the tidal wave of settlers that the Act had naïvely anticipated.

Nevertheless, this gloomy outline of early settlement should not be taken to mean that *no* immigrants arrived. A few undaunted groups or individuals found their way into Manitoba during the 1870s; a smaller few even dared the far reaches of the empty Territories during that decade. And more flocked along behind the C.P.R.'s 'end-of-steel', which left settlements like droppings as it advanced across the prairie. These early arrivals, their nature and their origins, deserve some close consideration.

The first group immigration into the west, which arrived in 1874 to settle in Manitoba, was a Mennonite community. Mennonitism is an offshoot of the radical wing of sixteenth-century Protestantism. Its doctrines include a denial of original sin and a rejection of the sacraments of baptism and communion – although adult converts were baptized as a symbol of their conversion. (Hence they were originally called Anabaptists.) They take no part in state affairs, especially refusing military service. The Anabaptists of the Netherlands (and later, as persecution scattered the movement, of other countries) were rallied during the Counter-Reformation by a Frisian named Menno Simons, from whom the name 'Mennoites', and then 'Mennonites', came to replace 'Anabaptists'. The movement continued to spread; then in the eighteenth century, Catherine II of Russia invited colonists to settle in what is now the Ukraine. The Mennonites, famous as skilled and thrifty farmers even then, answered her call – for she had promised them religious freedom and exemption from military service. But by the mid-nineteenth century the new Czar rescinded the exemption, which – along with a land shortage in their expanding communities – sent the Mennonites again looking for a home. They found it in the New World.

They investigated carefully before they moved, corresponding with the Canadian and U.S. governments, listening to agents sent by these governments, then in 1873 sending a delegation of their own to examine the prospects. In Canada, an Ontario Mennonite, Jacob Y. Shantz, something of a propagandist for the west, took the delegates to Manitoba. They were not especially impressed. Lack of transport, the presence of Indians and métis, the unpleasant effects of grasshoppers and drought and mosquitoes – these novelties upset them. But Canada had assured them of military exemption and religious freedom, to be guaranteed by legislation. This guarantee outweighed the drawbacks, and the delegation committed themselves to a Mennonite immigration.

The immigration, as E. K. Francis points out in his book on the Manitoba Mennonites, was not a gradual flow of settlers arriving a few at a time, but the organized removal of entire villages – a removal which saw some 7,500 new Manitobans take up land through the 1870s. (More Mennonites were later to settle in the Northwest Territories, as Chapter 10 will show.) The co-operative nature of the Mennonite colonies never showed to such advantage as in this emigration. Shantz looked after the newcomers as they landed, organizing passage for the earlier groups through the U.S.A. to Manitoba, preparing places for later groups that year to winter in Ontario. There they worked on Canadian farms, saving money and learning the language and the local farming ways. In Manitoba, the immigrants gathered in a camp set up by Shantz's organizers, and lived there for some time while the men built homes on the land, or went into Winnipeg for supplies, machinery, tools, and other necessities. (Many of the newcomers had capital from sale of their land in Russia; poorer families were looked after by the more well-to-do.)

But no group, however thrifty, could then have made that long and costly journey without some financial help from the Dominion government. The Mennonites received a loan of $100,000 (not without some complaints from M.P.s who professed to want immigrants who would fight for the country, if necessary). In return, of course, their spending in Winnipeg – and their importation of goods and livestock from the U.S.A. – restored considerable health to the Manitoban economy. But the Mennonites' greatest contribution to the west, worth many such loans, came simply from the way they settled, and especially *where* they settled.

They were the first western settlers to farm open prairie. Before, new settlers, in Manitoba or farther west, had always feared the empty plains and had huddled near rivers, lakes or creeks, to be sure of water and of wood for buildings, fuel, fences. But the Mennonites came from the steppes of the

Ukraine, and knew about open spaces. The blocks of land set aside for them by the government (the first was ten townships, then later grants brought the Mennonite total in 1876 to twenty-five townships, over half a million acres) had been chosen and surveyed by the Mennonites themselves. While the first or 'East' reserve (east of the Red River) contained some low-quality land, the later reserves took up rich and fecund prairie lands. In an astonishingly short time Mennonite expertise made that fecundity bear fruit.

Though they lacked wood for log houses or fencing, they knew how to build mud huts until they could afford lumber for frame buildings. They planted trees extensively (to serve as windbreaks, beautification and future lumber supplies), including the fast-growing cottonwood. As for farming methods, they introduced crop rotation and summer fallowing (to retain moisture in the soil). And they prospered – in spite of some drought and frost in the early years.

Their prosperity was enhanced by their solidly communal way of life: not collective, for individuals held property, but co-operative. A number of families would group themselves in a village, with elected officials in charge (and a general assembly of heads of families to resolve major questions). Within the village a farmer owned the land on which his house and other buildings stood, and a patch of garden. The farmland, however, was divided into allotments – strips of land on different quarter-sections, allowing an equitable distribution of fertile soil. The crop rotations and summer fallowing were arranged by communal consent, again to ensure equity. And the fields remained open – unfenced – because pasture land was common land where everyone's stock grazed together, and herdsmen kept them off the crops.

The west may not have realized it, but the Mennonites had established two vital aspects of the settlement and immigration pattern that was to come. First they had proved that the open prairie was cultivable; second, they had shown that Canada would welcome the immigration of ethnic groups, and would make the way easy for them. From then on many such colonies of hard-working and knowledgeable Europeans would be moving in, to inhabit the country and make it habitable.

The next ethnic group in Manitoba, the Icelanders, left their rugged island to escape a land shortage – and perhaps (as romantics would have it) to satisfy the old Viking wanderlust. For them, sadly, Canada proved, at first, to be a land of hardship and suffering.

Several Icelandic colonies had existed in Wisconsin before 1872, when Sigtryggur Jonasson became the first of his countrymen to visit Canada. His praises of the Dominion drew others, mostly to Ontario, in the next two years; and in 1875 Jonasson and others ventured westward to Manitoba. Again the government became interested in the prospect of more new Canadians, especially when the Earl of Dufferin, Canada's Governor-General, who had visited Iceland, recommended their desirability. With some federal help, a colony was established – northwards in the wilderness beyond the boundaries (as they then were) of Manitoba. The Northmen were looking for a second home, and found it on the chilly, well-timbered, grasshopper-free banks of Lake Winnipeg. They called their settlement Gimli, which means Elysium or Paradise.

In late 1875 about 250 Icelanders arrived, including seventy young children, with barely enough time to prepare for winter. The men threw up thirty log houses in three weeks – but nevertheless they suffered a long and violent winter, perhaps more like one at home than they had bargained for. In spring a new contingent of about 1,000 arrived. Their usual occupations – farming and fishing – began well in 1876, though money was scarce for seed, supplies and tools. As always, though, the Icelanders made more than they bought: they built their own boats, as well as nets, harness, furniture and many farm implements.

Then, that winter, Gimli failed to live up to its name. Smallpox struck, ravaging the community as fearfully as ever it did in Indian camps. One-seventh of the settlers died – most of them children.

During the height of the epidemic the province of Manitoba offered not help but callous selfishness. The authorities posted an armed guard on the trail from Lake Winnipeg to the provincial border, to keep the infected Icelanders out, at gunpoint. The quarantine lasted well into the spring. By that time, as a side-effect, it had prevented the Icelanders from buying (in Winnipeg) the seed they needed for that year's crop. When the quarantine was lifted the season was too far advanced, too late for sowing. Many of their number had left in despair for Wisconsin; those who remained planted what they could and through autumn and winter eked out their survival on potatoes and fish. When spring came again, they turned to the task of restoring their colony's viability.

The Dominion Government helped with $8,000 worth of make-work road-building, which brought some money into the settlement. Also, many of the young people went to Manitoba to work – on farms, or logging, and the girls as domestic servants. They sent money back to Gimli, helping to pay debts and bring in the supplies and articles which they could not grow or make. Slowly they regained their feet. As circumstances improved, more Icelanders came to settle, some starting small daughter colonies nearby. By 1881, when Manitoba expanded her boundaries a few degrees of latitude northwards, and encompassed the Icelandic settlements, she was delighted to find that, along with several thousand excellent pioneers, she had acquired a large and successful fishing industry. But one wonders if the Icelanders of Gimli remembered, at the time, that gunpoint quarantine.

These new arrivals, Mennonite and Icelandic, altered the blood lines in Manitoba. No longer could the province, or the west, be neatly and inclusively divided into French and (or versus) British. And more ethnic group settlements were about to follow the lead of these forerunners, as upheavals in Europe, or simple overcrowding, drove the 'huddled masses yearning to breathe free' into the spaces of North America. For example: individual Jews and Jewish families had already appeared in the west (as fur traders, gold miners, farmers, merchants and so on); then a *group* immigration of Russian–Jewish refugees arrived in the early 1880s in Manitoba. They were escaping the first of a terrible series of pogroms begun by the Czar: with the help of leading Britons (including the Archbishop of Canterbury and Sir Alexander Galt, Canada's High Commissioner in London) many hundreds of Russian Jews escaped to Canada. Some 300 came to Winnipeg, where the poor and tiny Jewish community (fewer than thirty traders and merchants) did all they could to make homes for the newcomers.

In the second western province, immigration and settlement in the 1870s remained limited and sparse. The floodtide of gold miners had swept in and out again, leaving behind its debris of camps and shack towns. With economic depression and lack of transportation British Columbia offered little attraction to would-be settlers: the few immigrants, largely British and American, who did find their way to the province usually made their homes in the towns. With this thin trickle of newcomers, the towns' populations slowly swelled – principally Victoria, Nanaimo and New Westminster.[1] Some of the mining centres were reclaimed from ghost towns: but even Yale, which was the second largest mainland centre in the 1870s, held only 500 inhabitants. (Later, of course, the railway would bring an immense stimulus to urban growth in British Columbia, which would not alter the tendency of immigrants to gravitate to the towns.)

Non-urban settlements in this period remained few, minute and isolated. They were populated, as was seen, by former miners, fur traders or others who visited the province to make their fortunes and decided to stay. The late 1860s had seen a few embryonic ranches begin in the grassy valleys of the southern Cariboo area, and in the perfect pastureland of the Okanagan and Kamloops regions. A few small farms had sprung up, in the early days, in the Fraser valley: the rich fertility of the delta region assured its prominence (which would be magnified by the C.P.R.'s terminus at Burrard Inlet); farming communities also found good land in the Chilliwack and Langley areas of the lower Fraser.

At Burrard Inlet itself, a few pockets of civilization had appeared, anticipating the railway. A man named Sewell ('Sue') Moody began a sawmill on the Inlet in the 1860s, and shortly the spot had become a village called Moodyville.[2] Elsewhere on the Inlet, Jeremiah Rogers operated a spar-making industry: his location became Jerry's Cove, later Jericho. Further, New Westminsterites who came down to the sea to swim at Burrard Inlet nostalgically named their bathing spot Brighton – but shortly changed it to Hastings. An hotel was built at another location by a colourful Yorkshireman named Captain

[1] By 1886 Victoria would have reached the population figure of 12,000. But New Westminster, even then, would contain only 4,000 people – and Nanaimo, incorporated as a city in 1874, only 4,500.

[2] Not to be confused with Port Moody, at the head of the Inlet, named after Colonel Moody of the Royal Engineers.

John Deighton, who for his garrulousness was nicknamed 'Gassy Jack'. The hamlet that grew up around his hotel was therefore called Gastown, though it later acquired the more dignified name of Granville. As an indication of size, in 1869 Moodyville contained 200 people; in 1873 Gastown had only 65. Within a few years, of course, the Inlet would be the site of the C.P.R.'s terminus, where a new city would rise in an incredible population explosion.

The doldrums of the 1870s had not, however, reduced the flow of Chinese to the province. In 1871 there had been about 1,500 Chinese in British Columbia; ten years later there were 4,000. The anti-Chinese racial hatred (which was discussed in Chapter 5) increased as their numbers grew, and as the depression of the 1870s, when jobs and money were scarce, strengthened white fears of Asian competition and the 'yellow peril'. Various provincial attempts to legislate against Chinese immigration were disallowed[1] by the federal government, which was seeking to avoid disturbing Sino–British trade relations. The disallowances, however, could not affect the hatred. A provincial Select Committee considered the problem in the 1870s, and in 1879 reported its opinion that Asian immigration should be restricted.

Evidence heard by the Committee stank of racist irrationality: one witness, asserting that the Chinese could never be good citizens because they took no interest in politics, admitted in the next breath – with no awareness of the contradiction – that of course the Chinese had no vote in the province, nor should they have. (Other immigrants could easily become naturalized and gain the vote. Chinese could not.) The Committee was chaired by Amor De Cosmos, who was prominent in the anti-Chinese political agitation: one may well wonder at the investigators' objectivity.

Then, in the early 1880s, the C.P.R. began construction along the Fraser. Andrew Onderdonk, fighting his heroic battle against the mountainous mainland, hired almost all the available white labour on the Pacific coast and still needed more. So he began to import Chinese workers in their thousands. British Columbia remonstrated, but Onderdonk pointed out that men had to be found: if the province wanted a railway it

[1] Immigration was, according to the British North America Act, to be entirely the concern of the federal government.

would have to have Chinese. To some extent the racist furore was overcome by the heady joys of railway building, which brought a flush of prosperity into the province. The furore would return, however, and mount to a crisis, when the completion of the C.P.R. threw that immense Chinese labour force into unemployment, along with many thousands of whites. But that crisis must be left until a later chapter.

In the Northwest Territories through the 1870s, a few hardy pioneers would venture now and then into the loneliness – mostly Ontarians pushing past Red River in search of *lebensraum*. Generally they were drawn into the ambit of the older centres, such as Fort Macleod, or Prince Albert. But some, in a fine spirit of optimism and business, created new centres – at locations where they expected the C.P.R. line to come through, raise land values, and make them all rich.

The town of Battleford had such ambitions. It had first appeared in 1874 as a camp of telegraph linemen, who were putting a line along the proposed northern C.P.R. route. They set up a temporary headquarters at the junction of the Battle and North Saskatchewan rivers, calling it Telegraph Flats. Two years later the N.W.M.P. built a fort there, and around the fort – as always occurred around such nuclei – a small cluster of houses gathered.

In 1877 Telegraph Flats achieved the high honour of being chosen as the capital of the Northwest Territories, and was then renamed Battleford. Its fortunes seemed assured. It acquired government buildings to house the Lieutenant-Governor (though logs of sufficient size for the buildings had to be floated 300 miles downriver from Edmonton). Shortly the first newspaper in the Northwest, the *Saskatchewan Herald*, began operations under P. G. Laurie – who had been a Schultzite in 1869 at Winnipeg, and who brought a printing press on a Red River cart across 600 miles of prairie from Winnipeg.

The first shipment of wheat, according to Battleford's historian C. Wetton, went out from the settlement in 1881; a log church was built, which summoned the faithful by raising a flag, for bells were scarce in the west; and with these amenities and achievements Battleford comfortably awaited the C.P.R. and real-estate wealth. Then came a succession of shocks and catastrophes.

The river rose in 1882 and inundated the flatlands, wrecking fields and homes, and forcing the settlement to rebuild on higher ground – on the plateau between the Battle and the North Saskatchewan. The same year the C.P.R. decided, in its last-minute change of route, to move its line south – leaving Battleford stranded, and spelling the end of its role as capital. As if these blows were not enough, in 1885 the town was attacked and plundered by Indians during the Riel Rebellion – as described in the following chapter. (The final injury occurred years later, when the Canadian Northern railway unkindly laid its track *north* of the Saskatchewan river – spawning a railway town, North Battleford, which grew into a city and left the old town to wither among its memories.)

Among other tiny pre-railway settlements which formed themselves in the park belt, the farmers of the Carrot River valley deserve special mention. A group of eighteen settlers, led by a Canadian named Sanderson, took up land in that beautiful location in 1878 entirely on account of the excellence of the soil – not to profit by a railway. And, justly, when the Canadian Northern came through the valley in 1904 they benefited in spite of themselves. Less lucky was one J. F. Clark, who established himself on land at Clark's Crossing – the spot where the C.P.R. was originally to cross the South Saskatchewan. When the route was changed, he stubbornly stayed on: but he had to wait years before a Canadian Northern branch line brought him the railway station he had hoped for.

As has been seen, once Van Horne had chosen the new route across the prairies, construction went ahead without pause. In 1881 trains were running north to Winnipeg on the Pembina branch line and work had begun in both directions from that city. Van Horne's five-hundred-mile summer, in 1882, left a chain of tiny western towns in its wake, towns composed (it seemed) largely of land speculators, real-estate agents, profit-seeking merchants, and a sprinkling of actual homesteaders. The same was true of Winnipeg. Those years brought the frenzy of a land rush, and artificially inflated boom times: as town lots and near-by lands were bought and sold, and fortunes were being amassed by amateur and professional alike, the whole speculative balloon got out of hand. Top eastern auctioneers, imported by realtors and desperate for more and more land to feed the insatiable buyers, eventually were offering lots in

Edmonton and beyond to the Winnipeggers. At its peak the boom raised prices on town lots – in a small and fairly primitive frontier town, remember – until they were higher than prices of lots in downtown Chicago.

West of Portage la Prairie, on the Assiniboine, the town of Brandon experienced a similar rush. Two years before the C.P.R. arrived, a few premature landholders had settled and were squabbling over town lots in the wake of the surveyors. By 1882, according to Martin Kavanagh, the population was fluctuating around 3,000 as homesteaders and speculators flocked in on trains: nearly twenty new hotels went up in Brandon that year.

The land booms in and across the prairies tended to peter out rapidly, leaving unwise or careless speculators with an armful of worthless paper. In the Territories, speculation around a shack town graphically called 'Pile of Bones' left some political embarrassment behind as well.

The site itself lay near a small and muddy creek where buffalo hunters had liked to camp, and where they littered the surrounding countryside with buffalo bones. When the C.P.R. surveyors came through, after the change in route, they were surprised to find that some squatters had preceded them: one of the squatters, named Gore, himself a surveyor, had predicted the path that the survey would choose. The land speculators then descended as usual, and a group of them formed a syndicate which, as E. G. Drake tells it, bought up many sections of H.B.C. reserve land in the vicinity of the creek because they knew a town was projected for the site. The syndicate, reportedly, included Edgar Dewdney, Lieutenant-Governor of the Northwest.[1]

As the town began to appear, in 1882, the land was worth a paper fortune – for plans were laid (and urged forward by Dewdney) to make this spot the new capital of the Territories. But the C.P.R. was anxious to sell *its* lands, and so located its station – always the focal point of a new railway town – well away from the syndicate property. Both sides accused each other of double-dealing – and when the dispute dragged on, the government was forced to mediate. It laid out a town site that took in lots from both syndicate and C.P.R. land. And, Drake says, the new arrivals themselves provided a just denouement

[1] See p. 270.

when they bought very few lots from the syndicate side of town.

It was an odd choice for a capital city, for the site possessed little water, less wood, and not much of anything except dust and wind. But the railway was the deciding point along with, presumably, Dewdney's desire for a profit. So Battleford lost the capital, and Fort Qu'Appelle (where, in one of the most beautiful districts in Saskatchewan, a small settlement had sprung up around the H.B.C. post and N.W.M.P. fort) failed to gain it, though many residents of the Territories might have preferred Qu'Appelle had they been asked. Pile of Bones was given the name of Regina.[1] By the following year it had also gained a well, a newspaper (the *Leader*), eight hotels, about 1,000 people, and a reputation for unpleasant environmental conditions – not only driving snow in the winter, wind driving dust in the summer, but (after a rare rainfall) thick sticky 'gumbo' mud. The *Leader*'s editor, the enthusiastic and poetic N. F. Davin, wrote that persons walking through Regina's streets after rain 'picked up a homestead on one foot and a pre-emption on the other'.

But then such conditions prevailed in all the unprepossessing prairie towns cast up by the C.P.R. Moose Jaw, west of Regina, made of a few shacks and tents; Swift Current, which became a central freight terminus from which carts and wagons supplied the Saskatchewan valley; Medicine Hat, where the C.P.R. crossed the South Saskatchewan, and where the brawling, saloon-filled town apparently resembled U.S. western towns more than most; and finally Calgary, where an N.W.M.P. fort had preceded the railway and had gathered to itself (as one pioneer described it) 'a long line of frame stores, tarred-paper slab shacks, and tents'. It also acquired a strong 'wild

[1] Place name origins are always diverting – too much so to be included extensively in these chapters. But Regina's name deserves comment. Pile of Bones Creek was actually called Wascana (a mutation of the Cree word for 'bone'), which, sadly, was considered too aboriginal for a capital. So stuffy, unimaginative British loyalty triumphed – as it had with the deadly names of Prince Albert, New Westminster, Victoria, and indeed British Columbia and Alberta – in spite of the availability of indigenously beautiful Indian names or unique and traditional fur-trade names (mostly French). For this writer, years of repetition never overcame the incongruity of finding places named Prince Albert and Regina in a place named Saskatchewan.

west' reputation from the early growth of cattle ranching in the area (see Chapter 11).[1]

So the C.P.R. spanned the prairies, and the incoming settler could travel by train considerably nearer to his chosen home than before. But, even then, in the early 1880s, no vast surge of immigration came about. Growing anxious to put *some* settlers on the land, the C.P.R. and the Dominion Government encouraged various schemes – among them co-operative farms, philanthropic enterprises, and commercial colonization companies.

One co-operative experiment produced Cannington Manor, begun by Captain E. M. Pierce in 1882 as an attempt to bring 'gracious living' to the empty frontier. Pierce took up land near Moose Mountain, in southeast Saskatchewan, and peopled it with well-to-do English families or young men with capital. The Cannington people brought their finery of leisure – dinner jackets and ball gowns, cricket bats and tennis rackets – and occupied themselves with fox hunts, dances, shoots and sports while hired labourers attended to the farming. A farm instructor reportedly remarked that he was glad 'when the young gentlemen took to tennis, so I could get on with the work'.

When three brothers at the Manor began raising thoroughbreds in 1889 they had immense success, even internationally. Horses heightened Cannington's reputation, and brought even more horsy young people from England. But gradually the experiment flagged. Some families moved away to less oppressive climates (for instance, British Columbia); young bachelors were drawn off to the Boer War, or to gold-hunting in the north. A few remained to farm, but the golden days of Cannington – as an oasis of leisured-class civilization in the raw west – ended in the 1890s. A N.W.M.P. sergeant pronounced its epitaph and described its heyday: 'We had a very good class of people in and around Cannington. . . . Most of them had a remittance,

[1] Some of these place names, too, are irresistible. Moose Jaw Creek, from which the town was named, is said to have been the spot where a traveller repaired his Red River cart with the jawbone of a moose. Others say that the creek flows in the shape of a moose's jaw. Medicine Hat may come from an Indian legend in which an apprentice sorcerer obtained, after various tests, a magical hat from a great demon. Alternatively, the name came from an incident during an Indian battle when a Cree medicine man lost his hat. Calgary's name is both certain and prosaic: it is borrowed from a Scottish castle.

a jolly good time, a pack of hounds – and to hang with the farm.'

Another co-operative venture created the equally famous Bell Farm at Indian Head on the C.P.R. line. The idea had been devised by an ambitious Ontarian, Major W. R. Bell, who formed the Qu'Appelle Valley Farming Company in 1882 and approached the government for land. Ottawa sold him the even-numbered sections within a tract some nine miles square, requiring him in return to place settlers on the land, to cultivate 20,000 acres and to spend $60,000 on improvements, all within six years. At the same time the C.P.R. sold him 29,000 acres from the odd-numbered sections. Then Bell put his farm company into action.

In 1882 Bell had nearly 3,000 acres ploughed, while builders erected a 16-room house and a giant circular barn (64 feet in diameter) – both of stone – along with a few cottages, stables, and so on. Before the workers came $91,000 had been spent. By the end of 1883 7,000 acres had been cropped, and the farm held over 100 buildings. Yet many westerners feared a disaster, doubting that farming in Saskatchewan could be treated like an industry, with gangs of labourers mass-producing grain. They felt that Bell had bitten off too much.

Trouble eventually arrived. A few squatters had, as usual, followed the C.P.R. on to the land before Bell bought it, and they refused to move. The court fight that resulted harmed the farm's public image. Also, Bell had spent nearly $250,000 by 1884, but typically vicious weather had damaged crops and reduced income. An early frost in 1884 destroyed more hopes. In 1885 the Farm might have recouped, but much of the labour force left the Farm during the Riel Rebellion, and only a small part of the land was cropped. Facing debt and continuing expenses, Bell obtained a mortgage with which to pay the government its annual instalment and to continue farming. But it was not enough. Creditors swooped on to Bell, taking farm machinery and other necessaries. In 1889 the Bell Farm Co. was formally liquidated. Bell himself retained a kingly portion of the land – reported to be 13,000 acres – and managed to farm it during the next years with the help of a loan from private finance. But in 1893 a fire destroyed buildings and flour and grain; in 1894 the weather destroyed his crops. The financiers sued, seized his property and auctioned it off.

Yet Bell's doomed enterprise had done the Territories a service. It left behind a number of farm workers, who became settlers, and its mills, grain elevators and other useful amenities. It had also proved the fertility of the Indian Head area to a wide audience, for the progress of the farm had been reported internationally – which helped the Dominion's plans to encourage colonization companies.

Some charitable, non-profit-making organizations also gathered immigrants for new settlements. A group of Scots crofters were sent in 1883 by Lady Gordon Cathcart from her estates, to settle in the Moosomin area of what is now southeast Saskatchewan. (The park belt of the southeast, reasonably close to settled Manitoba, gained the bulk of settlement in this period.) Near-by, a settlement was created called the 'East London Artisans' Colony', sponsored by Baroness Burdett-Coutts. It brought in 1884 twenty families out of London working-class poverty and settled them on homesteads. None had ever farmed before; all were city dwellers who may never have been out of London. But an experienced farmer was hired to teach them, and within a few years the Londoners – who are among the most resilient people in the world – were almost all thriving, though some had moved to the town to revert to artisanhood.

Commercial colonization companies generally did less well. Often they were encouraged by Ottawa to take up land farther away from the C.P.R. than most homesteaders were willing (then) to go. A Saskatchewan Royal Commission on immigration, in 1930, looked back on these ill-fated speculations:

. . . on the whole they were poorly conceived, developed without reference to underlying economic realities, and . . . caused, consequently, heavy loss of capital as well as waste of human material.

In fact, many of the companies failed to place even one settler on the land. But at least the founders had control of land that could only grow more valuable. And of course exceptions existed. The York Farmers' Colonization Company, begun in Ontario in 1882, settled its eight townships (in the area of the present town of Yorkton) with little apparent trouble. But, usually, the successful companies offered some special inducement. Some of them were sponsored by religious groups; one of the most enterprising companies was formed by people with only a principle in common. They became the Temperance Colonization Company, seeking an island of abstention[1] in the (appropriately) dry farming area.

Within a few months of its formation the company had received 3,000 applications. (Applicants were required to sign the pledge.) They found their island in central Saskatchewan, as it now is – 200,000 acres straddling the South Saskatchewan river. The members who chose the land had lunched on a berry (proliferating on the riverbank) which the Crees called 'saskatoons': thus the present city of Saskatoon gained its name and its temperate beginnings. Unfortunately, the company was able to buy only odd-numbered sections, and had no legal way of keeping non-abstainers off the free-homestead land. So the ideal of a drink-free stronghold was eventually thwarted.

Before the C.P.R. crossed the prairies, travellers westward relied upon a limited variety of transport, all of them primitive. Some, for instance, walked, like an Ontarian in Manitoba:

> We walked ninety miles in search of homestead sites, but returned unsatisfied. [In spring] I bought a team of oxen, two carts and some equipment, and my brother and I set out walking one hundred and twenty miles north-west from Winnipeg. . . .

Others, if they could afford it, bought some form of conveyance. How they travelled, and the routes they took, reveal much about the nature of pioneer life. First, the routes.

The old trails which crisscrossed the emptiness ranged from a pair of ruts that linked two homesteaders' shacks to great prairie thoroughfares many wagon-widths across. Of the latter, none took prominence over the Carlton Trail (sometimes called the Saskatchewan Trail). Winnipeg was the starting point for westward-bound travellers, and the Carlton Trail was their chief artery into the interior. Like all arteries, it had its subsidiaries: the entire complex can be briefly outlined in terms of points on a line.

From Winnipeg, aside from the deeply grooved trail to Pembina, the main trail ran west to Portage la Prairie, and there split into three. All three converged again at Fort Ellice,

[1] Temperance organizations, with the full *apparat* of pledges and propaganda, had considerable power, as political pressure groups, in the east.

near the border; but one, the lower of the three, had crossed the Assiniboine near the present site of Brandon and had wound south of the river. At Fort Ellice more tributaries branched off. One went north to Fort Pelly; another went southwest, past Moose Mountain to Wood Mountain near the Montana border. Two trails, on either side of the Qu'Appelle river, led to Fort Qu'Appelle.

From that point an important trail cut across the open plain to the Cypress Hills, while a minor trail went north from Qu'Appelle to link again with the main trunk of the Carlton Trail. The Carlton then stretched northwest through the parkland, up to Batoche,[1] where a ferry carried travellers over the South Saskatchewan. A part of the trail then remained south of the North Saskatchewan, passing through Battleford, staying south of the Battle river, finally reaching Edmonton – the end of the line. But the main trail out of Batoche went on to cross the North Saskatchewan at Fort Carlton, and followed the north bank of the river to Edmonton.

In what is now Alberta, a main artery lay through the centre of the territory to link Edmonton with Calgary, and was called the Old North Trail. It left the N.W.M.P. fort at Calgary, and passed through Morley (the home of the Rev. John McDougall) on its way to the northern clearing-house.

Probably the trails, or parts of them, were originally laid down by Indian bands following the buffalo. But their final forms were carved out by the traffic that flowed regularly from civilized Winnipeg to the settled centres of Carlton and Edmonton. Métis, who left Red River for the North Saskatchewan valley in 1870, moved out along the Carlton Trail; missionaries covered their vast parishes along these trails; surveyors used them, and visitors such as Captain Butler or the tourists Milton and Cheadle. Above all, the trails supplemented the rivers in the early days as the supply routes for the northwest outposts: they were highways for freighting. And therefore they were simply *cart* trails, laid down by the ubiquitous Red River carts that still remain the most familiar symbol of Canada's Old West frontier.

The Red River cart resembled in some ways the peasant carts of Europe. It was designed to be drawn by one animal (usually an ox), and to be light and easily repaired. But Canada's cart,

[1] The central métis settlement in the northwest. See Chapter 9.

in other ways, stands unique. It was made entirely of wood, with its parts joined by wooden pegs or buffalo rawhide (*shaganappi*) fastenings. Its two wheels were from five to six feet high, deeply dished, with eight to twelve spokes jammed into hubs of elm (a wood unlikely to split). The axle, of maple or oak, held a balanced plank platform with a railing around it. The shafts were attached to the axle. Also, carters often wrapped the wheel rims with rawhide 'tires', which could be replaced easily.

The Red River cart's special features, ensuring its value and its fame, included extreme lightness and considerable strength: it could carry up to a ton over the by no means smooth wilderness trails. Rivers presented no problems: the wheels were strapped underneath the cart, for added buoyancy, and the whole thing floated like a raft. Above all, it was easily repaired: one needed only an axe and a drawknife (a saw and an auger helped, though, if repairs had to be especially neat and quick) and a handy clump of trees. (If legend is to be credited, jaws of moose could fill in where trees were absent.) Finally, it displayed a special feature found in no other conveyance: the cart dispensed with any form of lubrication – because dust would have mingled with grease at the hubs and soon would have abraded the wood. The price paid for this greaselessness was hellish noise, wood rubbing agonizingly on wood, squealing and screeching, to be heard for miles. A historian of pioneer Saskatchewan, George Shepherd, mentions an Indian story explaining the disappearance of the buffalo: the animals had hidden to escape the noise of the Red River carts.

Without doubt the opening of the west owes much to the existence of these all-round conveyances. Winnipeg grew through its links with St Paul, and those links were forged by the carts. Edmonton, Carlton, and other oases in the emptiness depended for their survival on the cart's freight. The métis drew most of their livelihood from the carts: they were the chief cart-makers, and the freighters; they also used the carts in their mass buffalo hunts. From Captain Palliser to the Dominion surveyors, all the mid-century travellers needed the carts to achieve their prairie crossings.

But by the time the C.P.R. main line reached Calgary, the heyday of the Red River cart had nearly passed. Freight now travelled shorter distances over the open prairie, and (to supply

Sir John A. Macdonald

Sir William Van Horne

The Canadian Pacific Railway, laying track on the prairies. On the right, an N.W.M.P. constable stands guard

A trestle bridge (on log pilings) in construction for the Canadian Pacific
Railway, in the 1880s

Chinese laborers working on a C.P.R. cutting in the Rocky Mountains

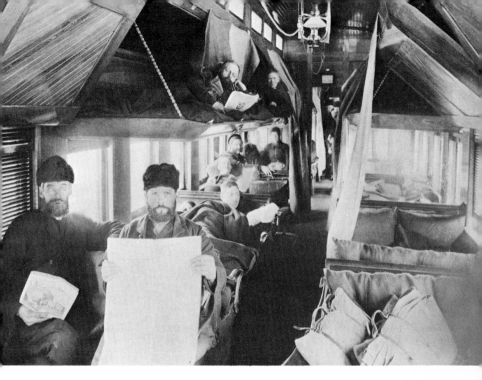

A special C.P.R. "colonist car" carrying immigrants to the west

The great circular stone stable on the
Bell Farm, southeast Saskatchewan

Louis Riel

Clifford Sifton

One homesteader's first home — a "dugout," cut into the side of a rise, with a sod roof. Note the buffalo skull over the doorway

An early homesteader and his family, outside their sod

The Klondike stampede: in 1898 gold seekers gathered at the base of Chilkoot Pass, and waited their turn to join the single-file line of men struggling up over the pass

Another view of the Klondikers climbing through the snow at Chilkoot Pass. Miners followed this trail, in a nearly continuous line, for two full years

Klondike gold miners working on Eldorado, the richest creek for placer mining

Dawson City, Yukon, 1899 — as the gold rush began to die away

Camp of the Barr Colonists at Saskatoon, 1903

Part of the Barr Colony camp at Saskatoon; the Rev. G. E. Lloyd
is third from the left

The log shack of a Barr Colony family. Note the fireguard ploughed in the foreground

Ukrainian (or Galician) immigrants arriving at Quebec City in the 1890s, en route to the west

homesteaders) tended to be heavier and more extensive. So the 'bull trains' – huge freight wagons, drawn by six to eight yoke of oxen – replaced the brigades of carts that had first gouged out the old trails. Again, a homesteader moving out from some point on the C.P.R. with all his goods, farm equipment, and so on needed a wagon that carried more than a ton. So the larger, stronger, wood-and-steel covered wagons ('prairie schooners') were imported from America. And the Red River carts, mere prairie dinghies, were pushed into the background.

Some of the smaller trails vanished as well: the brigades of Red River carts, not following in one another's tracks but spread out across the prairie to avoid making impassably deep ruts, could follow paths on which the heavier and as it were steel-shod wagons became mired to the axles. By the mid-1880s stagecoaches were running on some of the trails, and their speed demanded even smoother surfaces. Where the bull trains took two weeks on the Old North Trail (Calgary to Edmonton), the stagecoach took one – in favourable circumstances. Naturally sudden shifts in weather could hold up progress. Also – true to southern Alberta's 'wild west' reputation – stages were often held up otherwise, by gun-toting bandits. But at least, as one laconic lady westerner remarked, 'there was no traffic jam at any time'.

The wagon ride along a rutted, treacherous, muddy trail may have been the worst part of a new arrival's journey to the land of promise. But earlier stages often produced their own terrors. Comparatively well-to-do immigrants could cross the ocean in comfort, according to their means, but for others there were varying degrees of overcrowding and connected hardships. At worst, the ship might be a converted cattle-boat, thinly partitioned into corridors of cubicles, with passengers left to shift for themselves as regards food, sanitation, privacy. On arrival, most newcomers made their way to 'immigration halls' – barn-like buildings set up by the government (and sometimes by the railway) where they could stay in more cubicles, eat in a communal kitchen (doing their own cooking), store baggage, and acquire information and propaganda about the west. Many of the halls, of course, were reasonably well-run, pleasant places; all were free or extremely cheap.

From these special immigrant quarters in the east, the

newcomers embarked westward on special C.P.R. trains. From the colonist coaches, the newcomers took their first looks at their new homeland – with eyes somewhat jaundiced, no doubt, by the trains' overcrowded discomfort. Pairs of seats, facing one another, pulled out into hard wooden beds that would sleep two; above the seats, another hard wooden bed, the 'upper berth', swung down from the wall like a shelf. Every car had a kitchen range, with fuel supplied, as well as wash-basins and drinking water. But fuel often ran out during the trip, and the immigrants would have to forage during stops. Toilet facilities were non-existent and the immigrants again had to utilize the train's regular stops – which sometimes could be embarrassingly short. Also, utensils were not provided: if any optimistic newcomer had put off buying pots and kettles, and had not laid up a store of transportable food for the ride, they would be very hungry by the time (a matter of days) the train had run from Quebec to Winnipeg – unless some more thought-ful immigrants acted hospitably, as so many did.

At the mainline station nearest their prospective homestead, the immigrants disembarked and prepared for the last lap. In most cases their farm machinery and other heavy belongings, and often horses and oxen, had come out by train as well, the man of the family riding in a freight car with these possessions while his family rode in the colonist coach. The trip could be hazardous for the men, especially if they were unfamiliar with the fine points of freight loading. A favourite pioneer joke contains the suggestion that convicted criminals should ride to prison in these trains: they would all be overjoyed to reach their destination after travelling in a freight car loaded by an amateur. Upon arrival, after the difficult task of unloading had been over-come, the family set up a tent for the night or stayed in some shack. Next morning they moved out across the prairie towards the quarter-section they had not yet learned to call home.

Gerald Willoughby, in his pamphlet *Retracing the Old Trail*, describes a harrowing cross-country journey which must stand as the best account available of newcomers' tribulations. Several families of homesteaders unloaded their possessions from the train at Moose Jaw, in 1883, on a bitterly cold April day. (Like all wise homesteaders, they had gone west early, so as to be able to plough and sow some land in their first summer, which meant that they were travelling in the last vicious days of winter.) The following day they arose at dawn to load wagons, pack tents, and hitch horses; then they took the trail northwards. The horses were driven slowly, because they were eastern stock, unused to western trails, or winters, or water and hay. Many settlers preferred oxen, which were less demanding. Of course they were slower – requiring a man to walk beside them much of the time – and tended to react to the hordes of mosquitoes by bolting off the trail into mudholes, but they also had the strength necessary to break, initially, the incredibly tough prairie sod. And they could thrive on grass alone, needing no grain. Finally, in the last resort, if all else failed, they could be eaten. Nevertheless, this group of homesteaders had chosen horses, and however well they were tended, the horses suffered. Willoughby writes, 'Even if there had been no trail a stranger could have found his way into the north country by the bones of the horses that had died by the way.' Some of this group's animals added their bones – especially after a howling blizzard had trapped the travellers in their camp (on the bald, unsheltered prairie) for three days.

When the snow had stopped and the wind subsided, some of the group found that the pioneer urge had been blown out of them, and they turned back. The others, jettisoning some belongings to lighten the loads for the surviving horses, moved on. Reaching a clump of woods in rolling land that provided shelter, fuel and game for food, they rested there for some days to collect themselves. So far, exhausted themselves and with weakened horses, they had been making only a few miles a day. The terrain flaunted all its worst features in their path: there was the open prairie with its razor winds; there were creeks and streams, unbridged, often without fords, where the wagons had to be floated over and the animals had to swim; and there was the thick mud, which as the weather cleared buried wagon wheels to the axles, forcing the men to unload each wagon and sometimes even to dismantle the wagons to get them out.

The crippling, dispiriting work went on for days, and the end of each day required the added effort of setting up camp, gathering fuel and cooking meals. But finally the journey ended, and then the homesteaders, guided by a rough map, began to search among brush and prairie grass for the corner stakes that marked their quarter-sections. The search might take days, if the terrain had changed; a stake driven into a low spot in summer, by the surveyor, might be covered with water in spring. With some luck, though, the correct sections were eventually more or less determined. Then the wagons were unloaded for the final time; the homesteaders were home.

But home, of course, was a patch of nothingness in a flat immensity of the same – an artificial island of wild prairie, in no way different from the vast sweeping ocean of grass around it. And as far as they could see standing alone on their land – and they could see for many miles – the homesteaders were unable to perceive a sign of any other pocket of humanity, any sign that they were not alone from horizon to horizon. They had moved for days over the endless swells of grass, and then had stopped – and where they had stopped was home.

The arrival of those settlers in the 1870s and early 1880s came as the last and probably most important event in that period of momentous development. Those fifteen years form a crucial watershed in the history of the west's transformation. They began (to recapitulate) with two new provinces carved out of the wilderness, and they contained the formation of the N.W.M.P., the beginnings of the C.P.R. and the first growth, however thinly spread, of prairie settlement. Many more new arrivals would be needed before the west could be said to be truly opened. And, tragically, before that could happen the inhabitants of the *old* west – the Indians and the métis, 'true children of the prairies' – would try with their lives to halt the inevitable processes that were turning them into anachronisms.

9

Northwest Rebellion

Federal ignorance and indifference provoked the métis into a rebellion of sorts (properly a resistance) in 1869, when Canada had taken over the west without reassuring or even informing its inhabitants. And, predictably, the métis found that Canada's dealings with them after 1870 continued to be typified by ignorance, indifference, and administrative bungling. It will be remembered from Chapter 4 how the métis suffered persecution from the anti-French, anti-Catholic Ontario settlers; how governmental delays in the distribution of their land grant brought forth an issue of scrip, which meant little to the more naïve métis but much to the speculators and confidence men who bought it up at ridiculous prices. Worse, the old buffalo-hunting, wide-roaming days had definitely ended in Manitoba, as Winnipeg thrust towards cityhood and swarms of settlers carved the province into quarter-sections. So the métis' wounds, social and political, festered. A minority chose assimilation, took up land, and became Manitoba farmers. The majority, once they had sold off what they had won by armed resistance, loaded their carts and moved west – to the great lone land where the buffalo herds too had found sanctuary.

There they squatted on land, practised some desultory farming, and went out on to the plains in the great community hunts.[1] There, too, they formed their settlements – or swelled the numbers of earlier communities that had filtered into the Territories before 1869. The Catholic mission of St Albert, near Edmonton, came to contain 700 people in 1870; similar missions in that area, Lac Ste Anne and Lac la Biche, held around 500. The Qu'Appelle valley sheltered some smaller

[1] Marcel Giraud estimates that about 300 families of Red River métis reverted to full-time nomadism on the Saskatchewan plains.

encampments, as did the Cypress Hills. And through the 1870s the incoming métis also created new homes, many of them in a cluster south of Prince Albert: settlements such as Duck Lake, St Louis, or Batoche (where a ferry crossed the South Saskatchewan). The first segment of this cluster, and eventually its premier settlement and the leading métis community in the Territories, was the hamlet of St Laurent.

The Church came to St Laurent in 1871, giving it solidity and permanence. And government came soon after – but a government of the métis by the métis. At the time, of course, the N.W.M.P. had not yet been formed: the métis saw the need for law and order in the west, and so created their own. In 1873 all the métis of the district gathered at St Laurent and – imposing the social organization and discipline of the buffalo hunt on to their daily lives – elected their rulers. (The Church approved this orderly evolution of responsible government, and provided advice and guidance.) A leading citizen of St Laurent, Gabriel Dumont – who will shortly reappear in a less peaceful role – was chosen president, with eight councillors. A code of law was adopted, setting out various rules by which peace would be kept in the community, and various penalties for breaches of the peace. At *no* time did the métis consider their government at odds with Canada: they protested their loyalty to the Dominion, and made it clear that they would abandon their provisional government as soon as the Territories acquired a true government, able to impose the rule of law.

So the métis found peace and freedom in the valley of the Saskatchewan. But it was, inevitably, a temporary lull. The 1870s, as the last chapter showed, brought the advance guard of prairie settlers; the early 1880s brought the railway, and slowly the frontier began to roll back. The métis now knew from experience how even the thinnest stream of white immigration could erode and undermine their way of life. So, before the stream could become a flood, they sought to protect themselves. They were squatters in Saskatchewan, without legal title to their lands; now they needed assurance of their right to keep the land before incoming whites began encroaching on them, using the homestead laws to shoulder the métis aside. Petitions, resolutions and complaints flew to Ottawa – for the métis were never inarticulate when it came to defending their rights, and local priests and other friendly parties added their voices. Ottawa replied that the situation was being considered.

It went on being considered for years, and no action was taken – not even an empty gesture. Meanwhile, the encroachments continued. In Red River the métis had balked at the arrival on their lands of government surveyors – who seemed to pose a threat to their ownership of the land. Now in the 1880s the situation recurred. The métis had always preferred the traditional, picturesque, Québecois method of laying out a farm in river lots. The new surveys, however, imposed the neat and efficient squares of the section-and-township system that Canada had borrowed from the U.S.A.

The métis simply refused to accept the imposition. Under the avalanche of letters and petitions, dwarfing previous submissions, the government gave way. But it did so in a strange, grudging, quibbling manner. It permitted the river-lot method in the already *established* métis areas – especially St Laurent – but insisted on the township form in the near-by unsettled areas. Therefore, as the communities expanded and the métis took up new lands they would be forced to accept the new surveys. Later, when this situation arose, the métis requested a resurvey of the land their way. The government refused. When they pointed out the unfairness – that some métis areas should have river lots, and some not – the government, as it were, shrugged. More petitions and complaints had no effect.

(A localized effect was achieved by a delegation from St Albert – a priest and a métis, who travelled to Ottawa and saw Macdonald. Their demands, covering the sore points regarding land titles and surveys, were more or less met – but *only* for St Albert: the relaxation of the rule was not extended to other métis areas. So the rankling continued.)

For the métis, the villains of the piece were the various Dominion Lands Acts, setting out the areas where settlers could homestead lands, and the means by which they could gain title.[1] The law made no exceptions: if the métis wanted to claim legal title to their lands, they would have to follow the Act's procedure, which meant waiting three years before filing a claim. The métis, who had been on their land before the Act was thought of, naturally resented being made to act like newly arrived homesteaders. Others, settled on land for which the Act

[1] See p. 162.

demanded payment (H.B.C. reserves, C.P.R. reserves, or Crown lands – odd-numbered sections), refused to pay.

It is important to remember that each of the specific grievances mentioned, concerning the land, not only seemed unfair in itself to the métis, but flouted a great principle of the métis nation. They believed that they, as well as the Indians, were the original children of the west. The interloping whites sought, by the Indian treaties signed in the 1870s, to 'extinguish' the Indian title to the western lands. But part of those lands, the métis believed, was *theirs* (by right of inheritance from their Indian parentage) – and *their* title too should be acknowledged, by a treaty that would guarantee the métis and their descendants reserved lands for ever. This principle, it seemed, had been tacitly accepted in 1870 when the Canadian Government – on its own initiative – had given the Manitoba métis a 'reserve' of thousands of acres. The métis communities of the Territories were merely asking for similar consideration of their birthright. They grew embittered when that consideration was refused.

The established white settlers of the Territories did not remain passive while métis discontent grew and petitions flew. Indeed, the agitation that developed in the early 1880s found its leaders among the whites. Among them the land regulations were even more unpopular; also, being wholly dependent on farming for survival, they suffered gravely from economic recession, crop failure, the bursting of land speculation bubbles, and other growing pains of an agricultural frontier. The white farmers felt, as they were to feel for many years thereafter, and as many still feel today, that their troubles might have been avoided or alleviated if government and big business in the east had shown proper concern for western problems. Their resentment led to the formation of the Manitoba and North-West Farmers' Union – the first agricultural organization in the west. From that forum they complained to Ottawa. Astonishingly, Ottawa noted their complaints and did precisely nothing.

So the two most powerful groups in the west found themselves confronting a common enemy – complacent and apathetic federal government – and seeking more or less similar ends. It did not take long for the English-speaking agitators to form a solid front with the French métis, and to begin making decidedly threatening noises.

In the face of this turbulence, only two governmental moves stand out as even vague gestures towards pacification. In 1881 a Land Office was finally established in Prince Albert. (The métis and other old settlers had not only been forced to abide by the Lands Act with regard to registering claims, but had been unable to complete the registration due to the absence of an Office.) And in 1884 an official – the Inspector of Dominion Lands – investigated the western situation on behalf of the Ministry of the Interior. But the blind federal indifference persisted even here. The inspector was not bilingual, and therefore restricted his observations to the English-speaking areas in and around Prince Albert. The French métis were entirely ignored. Later that year the local land agent sent in a report concerning grievances in the métis areas, but it was side-tracked apparently in a welter of bureaucracy.

Yet, even in 1884, when the agitation was rapidly approaching a peak, no one honestly believed that it would really ever be 'too late' – that the agitation would produce violence and organized resistance. The English-speaking farmers were taking political steps to improve their lot; their organizations were political pressure groups, not revolutionary cells. And it was with the same political purposes in mind that some of the whites decided, in conjunction with the métis, that a leader – and rallying point – was needed: the very man who had already made the federal government listen to the west, whose efforts in 1869–70 had wrung concessions and assurances out of Ottawa. So out of a resolution passed in 1884 at a general meeting of the white and métis agitators came a delegation empowered to visit Louis Riel in his exile, and bring him back as leader of their movement.

The intervening years had not been kind to Riel. After being expelled from Parliament, where he had never been able to take his seat, he had left the country under the terms of the amnesty and had tried to pick up the pieces of his life in the U.S.A. He wandered through the northern New England states, visiting friends and fellow French-Canadians, never staying in one place for long. Occasionally he visited Montreal and other Quebec centres, but always furtively and briefly. More and more he occupied his time and his mind with religious observances, which seemed to be turning his interests away from politics. And slowly, as it seems from his own writings and the statements of people in contact with him, the idea grew in him that his political role as a métis leader was in fact a religious role. A grandiose letter written to him by a bishop apparently strengthened this feeling: the Bishop had spoken of Riel's 'divine mission', and seemed to imply that Riel was a favourite of God's who was destined for great things.

So it appears that loneliness and strain and the introversion of exile, deepened by the religious mysticism that had grown in him and by his brooding on past glories and future possibilities, damaged the balance of his mind. He began to be overcome by hysterical seizures, and in 1876 was taken by friends to a mental hospital in Montreal.

Later, fearing his discovery, the friends moved him to another hospital in the city of Quebec. There he alternated between violent, manic periods, and lucid (though morose and brooding) periods when he fulfilled religious duties, wrote poetry and rested. And gradually he began to heal.

Eventually Riel was able to leave the hospital for brief periods, and meet people – including Wilfrid Laurier, a Quebec member of Parliament and later prime minister, who was impressed with his lucidity. But on religious or political questions he remained subject to hysteria, or so his doctors warned when they discharged him in late 1877. He planned to go west, perhaps to farm, in order to find the tranquillity the doctors advised; but, lacking the capital to begin farming, he instead went to find work in New York. Before he left, however, he met, courted and became engaged to a French-Canadian girl in the American town where he had gone from the hospital.

City and fiancée both failed to keep Riel. His health suffered, and he deserted New York in 1878 to return to his first love, the prairie west. There (in Minnesota) he regained his health; he reawakened his old interest in politics and the métis' welfare; and he revived old friendships, as Manitobans came down to see him. Abruptly he broke off all contact with his fiancée – perhaps in a gesture of renunciation, of the lonely years and breakdown, of the east where he had not felt at home. To everyone in Minnesota he seemed to be the old Riel – as energetic and extroverted, as eloquent and forceful as ever. Only a few noticed – or thought they noticed – an occasional tinge of the frenzies that, Riel freely admitted, had landed him in an asylum. (Some associates later reported that Riel claimed to have been *feigning* madness.)

For the next few years Riel joined a wandering band of buffalo-hunting métis and drifted with them across the prairies of Montana and Saskatchewan. He married a métis girl; in 1882 she bore him a son, and the next year a daughter. That year, too, Riel's five-year exile ended; but he asserted his new allegiances by taking up American citizenship. Only then did he return to Manitoba, publicly, to be sought out by the newspapers and generally made a fuss of. While there, he learned more about the position of the métis, and their discontent, in the Territories. What he learned apparently revivified the old obsession with his divine mission, in terms of the métis nation.

So he was ripe for the persuasion of the delegates from Saskatchewan when they asked him to lead the agitation for the métis' rights. The distinction is crucial: when Riel arrived in the North Saskatchewan valley it was as a leader of an *agitation*, a political movement – not as the leader of an incipient revolt. He found the métis unanimous in their unrest, and in their confidence that he would be able to help them. Moreover, he found the whites firmly on his side (gratifyingly, for the English-speaking settlers had been at best neutral in Manitoba). He encouraged them with a rousing speech in Prince Albert, urging the propriety of organized agitation, demanding responsible government in the Territories. It was what the Prince Albertans wanted to hear: Riel, always a spellbinding speaker, impressed them most of all with his concern for legality, for constitutional means of redressing wrongs. Armed rebellion had not even been hinted at.

When he gained the faith of the English-speaking areas Riel had in fact gathered the entire Territories behind him – whites, métis and Indians. The Plains Indians of course had always been readily and extensively influenced by métis leaders; naturally they were most influenced by the greatest métis leader. When Riel returned, therefore, the Saskatchewan Indians visited him to seek his help and advice regarding *their* grievances.

Next to the Indian troubles the métis problems of land titles and surveys seem trivial. The Indians were simply facing *death* as a direct result of federal policy. Not that Ottawa had adopted the unofficial American tendency to wage wars of extermination, but in the fullness of its ignorance the government of Canada had initiated policies that would, if continued, have had that effect.

The sufferings of the Indians had begun much earlier. It has been seen in Chapter 6 how the tribal treaties were drawn up through the patient persuasion of the N.W.M.P. But agreement was one thing, obedience another. The treaties allowed the Indians to roam over unsettled areas off the reserves; and since most of the land remained unsettled during the 1870s, the Indians' nomadic lives were not in the least curtailed. It was as if there had been no treaty, no decisions about Indian reserves. But then – for some Indians – there *had* been none. Some lesser chiefs, notably the Cree Big Bear, had refused to sign a treaty. They, too, roamed freely in search of the buffalo.

Then a day came when the roaming had to stop. The buffalo had vanished from the plains.

Knowledgeable westerners had been predicting its extinction for years. The vast slaughter during the days of the whisky trade – when buffalo hides and tongues drew top prices – had begun the process. Another cause had been the effect of America's great transcontinental railway, the Union Pacific, which (because the herds would not cross the tracks) divided the over-all buffalo population into two sections, north and south. In the U.S.A., buffalo hunting had become massacre. Settlers slaughtered the animals to keep them off the fields; professional hunters (like Buffalo Bill Cody) vied with each other for record killings; Indians continued killing them for their trading; and the prairies were carpeted with corpses, usually intact save for skins and tongues. North of the railway, the U.S. Army pitched in as well – because someone had realized that buffalo slaughter was a way to control (or exterminate) the hostile Plains Indians, who depended on the animals for almost all their needs.

The northern herd migrated regularly to Canada, and there, too, the slaughter had reached incredible proportions. Ottawa finally awoke to some of the warnings, but passed the buck to the Northwest Territories Council. In 1877 the Council created a clumsy ordinance forbidding various forms of buffalo hunting, setting up a hunting season, and so on. It was so complicated that Indians and métis ignored it; complaints arose, and it was shortly repealed (not amended or replaced).

Then the Sioux crossed into Canada, and the U.S. Army had to find a long-range means of getting at them. The buffalo provided the means. Reports at the time, quoted by G. F. G. Stanley, note that a series of prairie fires began – coincidentally – along the border at about the same time that the U.S. Army had stationed itself there ostensibly to keep the Canadian Indians on their own side of the line. (The Blackfoot, it was said, had been hunting too often on U.S. territory.) The move worked, of course, both ways. Soldiers and fires kept the buffalo in the U.S., away from the Sioux and Canada's Indians, where the efficient mass-slaughter arrangements continued and eventually concluded the depletion of the herds.

So by about 1880 the buffalo had gone except for a few scattered handfuls. And the Indians had begun to starve.

They reacted in two ways. They demanded assistance and provisions from the government; and what they were not given, they took. They raided cattle herds, they ran up unpayable debts at kindly trading posts, they even broke into Fort Qu'Appelle in 1879 and stole provisions. Like the métis, the Indians also ran into government inaction and delay. They had hoped for ready assistance: disillusioned, increasingly desperate, they sank into bewildered bitterness. The white man had proved untrustworthy. As their resentment increased, the danger signals became more obvious. Even the N.W.M.P., whose reputation had been assured among the Indians, became guilty by association. No longer could the special magic of the Mounties command respect and obedience. Instead, the police found a threatening sullenness when they went among the tribes. And, in late 1879, the danger became more real when – for the first time – a N.W.M.P. constable was killed by an Indian whom he had gone to arrest.

Under pressure from the police and the Indian agents, the government finally acted. Stop-gap provisions were sent to the west (100,000 pounds of beef, 500 head of cattle, and more). At the same time Ottawa took the administration of Indian matters away from the Ministry of the Interior and set up a separate Department of Indian Affairs. The department devoted itself to reinforcing the Mounties' and missionaries' heart-breaking exertions to calm the Indians, to settle them on the reserves, to start them cultivating the land – where they could learn to support themselves not by hunting but by agriculture.

Some Indians resigned themselves to learning to be farmers. Others – more than half of the Plains Indians – refused to try farming, or gave up too soon in the face of farming failures. Many of these left the reserves, gravitating to the Cypress Hills and the independent groups gathered around Big Bear and the other hold-outs from the treaties.

These free bands raided across the border, stole cattle, and lived on the edge of starvation. The N.W.M.P., however, displayed enormous patience, and eventually managed to coax and bribe many of them to return to the reserves, where the government had now established farm instructors to help the Indians adjust to their new life.

Flaws soon appeared in that idea. The instructors were rarely devoted to their charges: the reserve schools were often badly run: and the government built up more resentment by trying to suppress other traditional tribal ways – including the religious dances and ceremonies. In fairness, the reserve system was not wholly vicious. At least most tribes were allotted reserves in regions that had traditionally been their territory, not hustled off to useless land out of the way of settlers (which, for a long time, was U.S. policy). Yet, however tactfully handled, the treaties were at best a mess of pottage offered in exchange for the Indian's ancestral lands, undermining in the process his ancient way of life, restricting his freedom, and permanently destroying his self-possession and self-respect. He became what he is today: a ward of the state, barely tolerated if he adapts to white ways and persecuted if he does not. Because he is totally dependent, and mostly inarticulate politically, his viewpoint is rarely taken into account by government policy-makers – even when the government takes steps that affect his welfare directly.

Some very serious measures concerning the Indians were taken in the early 1880s. The strength of the economy, restored when Macdonald returned to power in 1878, had dwindled again and the new recession required a reduction in spending, including the government's. 'Non-essential' expenditure was cut back: and the Department of Indian Affairs fell under this heading. More money was not available to keep provisions flowing west. The Indians' rations were suddenly cut. An official of the Department paid a flying visit to the west, and returned convinced that no hardship would result – for he believed that most of the Indian agents had been lining their pockets, on the side, by means of the provisions. New regulations, he felt, would stop the graft and rechannel the supplies to the Indians, so they would get as much as they always had. He was wrong.

The Indians suffered the depths of famine. Dry weather damaged their small and generally poor crops, and the famine worsened. As they grew weaker, disease spread on the reserves. Children and old people especially fell victims to the combination of starvation and sickness. Deaths became more and more frequent. The agents, who were mostly as fair-minded and honest as could be expected, remonstrated, complained, resigned in protest. The Mounties issued stern warnings: Superintendent Crozier called the cutback a 'false economy', insisted that supplies be increased, and made it clear that the hardship could easily lead to an Indian uprising. Other agencies – missionaries, the western newspapers – added to the clamour. Ottawa paid no heed: the reductions continued in force.

Famine due to the disappearance of the buffalo could be accepted, if not understood, by the Indians. Famine due to the inaction of the whites – who themselves were *not* starving – was unacceptable. The Indians' resentment soon showed signs of reaching that pitch of hatred which had existed between the races in the U.S.A. And, to add to the danger, as in the U.S.A. many of the new settlers in the Territories proved to be prejudiced, ignorant people, contemptuous of the Indian, unable or unwilling to give an inch, or to understand the Indian's problems. For instance, the Indian had difficulty in adjusting to the notion of private ownership of land. For generations the land had been open to anyone; now if he walked or rode across a field he was liable (as frequently happened) to be sworn at, struck, or even shot at by a white man who claimed to 'own' it.

Soon, as was to be expected, the Indians turned defiant; their resentment boiled over. They deserted their farms, and many took to theft and raiding. And all the time, ominously, the old charisma of the Mounties diminished in power. Since the murder of the constable, the N.W.M.P. had felt their authority receding. In 1882 four Mounties tried to arrest a Blackfoot who had shot at a white; but his tribesmen refused to permit the arrest, and threatened the police, who were forced to retreat to their fort. Several hundred frenzied and armed Blackfoot surrounded them. The arrival of Crowfoot, the head chief, lifted the siege, for he did not want to unleash a war, but he had visibly lost much of his respect for the Mounties. No more peaceful, single-handed restorations of the peace would be possible for the police now: the constables rode in groups, watchfully.

Throughout the build-up of the crisis, Big Bear remained at large, bound to no reserve, yet receiving provisions now and again from agents who would not see his band starve. The Indians on the reserves grumbled about this. Also, they could not hide their admiration for Big Bear's successful defiance of the order to settle on reserves. Other chiefs – especially the influential Cree, Poundmaker – emulated Big Bear, leaving their reserves from time to time, their restlessness increasing daily. In late 1883 Big Bear received an ultimatum: get on to a reserve or no more supplies. The proud Cree ignored the order and kept his freedom.

The frightened Territories knew that any incident, however slight, might set off the explosion. And incidents began to occur. In early 1884 a band of armed Indians at Crooked Lake (near Qu'Appelle) demanded food from the farm instructor. That unlucky man, under orders, had to refuse. But these Indians had come to the end of their patience. They stormed the storehouse, severely injuring the instructor in the process. When police arrived, the Indians barricaded themselves inside the house and threatened them with rifles. The usual N.W.M.P. techniques – overawing and bluffing the opposition – failed to work. But even so the police saved the situation, and contained it: they negotiated their way out of trouble by tactfully dropping charges, and giving only suspended sentences to the main culprits.

Later that year a similar incident occurred, and again the west held its breath. An Indian on a reserve demanded food from another farm instructor, and attacked the man when refused. The violence began a wild riot among the Indians.

Police mustered, fortified buildings on the reserve in case they needed to fight, and proceeded to do their duty. Superintendent Crozier, in charge of the detachment, stepped into the raging mob and seized the wanted Indian. Immediately the rioters circled around in a roiling, hysterical mass, waving weapons, screeching threats. A single shot would undoubtedly have set off the uprising. Yet, in the face of the utmost provocation – Chief Poundmaker nearly killed an inspector – the N.W.M.P. remained calm, and pulled no triggers. With their prisoner they retreated slowly to the fortified buildings. Safe inside, they threw food supplies to the Indians to divert them. The trick worked, thanks largely to Big Bear's presence, for he had been struggling to calm the rioters. (Big Bear, like a few other chiefs, had no desire to start a futile and bloody war, which his people could not win. He still hoped that protest and agitation would rescue the Indians from their misery.)

Incident followed incident, crisis piled on crisis. The whole west knew that any day might bring massacre and racial war – unless there was a major policy change. Yet the blind and deaf policy-makers of Ottawa ignored the agents' and Mounties' reports, and made no changes. Then the news went out that Louis Riel had returned to the Canadian west – and the Indians, who respected and admired the métis leader as much as did the métis, sought his advice and leadership.

So Riel had returned to fill an already prepared role, to lead and focus the justifiable ferment of bitterness and unrest among métis, Indians, and the long-established whites. At first, his leadership was entirely devoted to launching a political movement. Riel visited the key settlements of the North Saskatchewan, organizing a campaign whose declared goal would be self-government for the Territories (which was the end he had achieved in Manitoba). He met with the Indian chiefs, especially Big Bear, and yet managed to avoid alienating his white following who were afraid of an Indian rising. Finally, in the autumn of 1884, he cemented the national feeling of the métis by uniting them into *L'Union Métisse de Saint Joseph*, including almost all the métis from St Laurent, Batoche, and the surrounding districts.

Farther afield, Riel's influence indirectly stimulated other protest movements: in Qu'Appelle, grievances were voiced through a Settlers' Association; meetings and rallies mush-roomed in many settlements. The Manitoba Farmers' Union continued to breathe fire over land injustices. And the clamour-ing of these groups grew in volume as 1884 saw a general crop failure throughout the west.

Hardly any knowledgeable people doubted the reality of the protest movement, or rejected the fear of its culmination – from the métis and Indians at least – in violence. Regrettably, Ottawa and the east held few people who could be called knowledgeable on western matters. The protests still went ignored, the fears discounted. (The government's reluctance to believe in the extent of the danger probably grew from suspi-cions that the Liberal opposition was exaggerating the western discontent to embarrass Macdonald's administration.)

So Riel had to accept the fact that constitutional methods of protest had failed to break down the supreme indifference of Ottawa. And it seems that he decided then, before any new developments forced the decision on him, to turn to more direct methods. Drastic steps had worked in Manitoba (so his thinking ran) and would work again. But Riel did not consider that the situation was changed. What in 1869 had been a *resistance* – when H.B.C. had given up the west before Canada had claimed it – would in 1885 be *rebellion*, high treason against the constituted authority of the federal government, and the Crown behind it.

Presumably Riel did not ponder long on questions of legality. In early 1885 he began appearing ominously among the settlements accompanied by a phalanx of armed men, and made statements about taking up arms and forming (as in Manitoba) a provisional government. The clergy disapproved of such threats, and tried to sway the métis to reject Riel. At mass one Sunday, Riel accused a priest, who had been preach-ing against the movement, of being a traitor; in the ensuing conflict the métis confirmed their willingness to follow Riel, whatever the Church's view.

Then in March Riel, believing in the value of *faits accomplis*, declared the formation of a provisional government. The step took the métis community by surprise, but they were rallied by a ruse: Riel claimed that the Mounties were about to march against them, and the government was formed to organize the resistance. The declaration unnerved the English-speaking settlers, however unwilling to commit themselves, they reverted to the safer stance of neutrality, approved by the N.W.M.P. As for the Indians, though they had had, as yet, no direct invitation from Riel to take part in active resistance, they grew wild with excitement as the rebellion was launched.

For, of course, it was now rebellion: the declaration of a provisional government was tantamount to revolt. Riel then added the final touch by issuing an ultimatum to Superintendent Crozier and the Mounties at Fort Carlton. They were ordered to surrender, or the métis would attack the fort.

Crozier, who was something of a hothead for a Mountie, refused. Worse, though reinforcements were on their way to the fort he declined even to wait for them. With a mere fifty-three men, along with about forty Prince Albert volunteers who had gathered for just such an emergency, Crozier sallied forth. To fight at all, without the reinforcements, was a fateful error. To fight the métis on their own ground – in the vicinity of Duck Lake – was a disaster. Gabriel Dumont, the powerful métis leader who directed the military side of the rebellion, led a few men out to meet the Mounties in a gully where brush beside the road afforded good cover. (At first the métis were outnumbered, but more men came to join them during the battle.) The police advanced – more heroically than strategically – straight down the road.

When the two forces met, words were exchanged, but neither side was likely to back down. The words became threats, and someone fired a shot. Wholesale firing broke out. The police set up a barricade across the road, while the métis scattered. Some moved into the brush to outflank the police. Others, from the cover of a near-by hut, fired on the Prince Albertans, who were exposed. Soon, the flanking movement shattered the N.W.M.P.'s defence, and forced them to retreat – with ten dead and thirteen wounded. By this time Riel had appeared on the scene and, reportedly, held the métis back from following the police and continuing the slaughter. They had won their victory. The N.W.M.P. had been defeated in combat for the first time and Colonel Irvine, who had arrived too late either to reinforce or to restrain the hasty Crozier, organized the evacuation of Fort Carlton – to Prince Albert, where the settlers feared an imminent métis attack.

So ended the Battle of Duck Lake – a battle that had never

been necessary. Crozier might have waited for Irvine, and the combined forces of police, more wisely deployed, might have quashed the revolt at the start. On the other hand, Riel had never intended a battle. He had (perhaps naïvely) expected the N.W.M.P. to surrender and provide hostages – which would have been a bargaining point as before in Manitoba. Now Riel was committed to war – which, being well aware of the limited resources of men and weapons he had, he would have preferred to avoid.

But then those limited resources were dangerously augmented. The Indians took the Duck Lake victory as their cue. The last vestige of their respect for the N.W.M.P. had been wiped out. Cree war parties mustered for action – and Riel, now anxious for allies, roused them further and pointed them in the right direction: the town of Battleford. Poundmaker's reserve was near the settlement: other bands came to join him, ready to take their revenge for a winter of incalculable suffering. The combined Indian forces swooped on Battleford, killing six whites. The survivors fled to the safety of the town's fortified N.W.M.P. barracks, and Poundmaker's warriors occupied and plundered the deserted settlement.

Elsewhere, farther to the northwest, the tiny settlement of Frog Lake (near Fort Pitt) faced the same terror. The fighting men of Big Bear's following, who had finally cast off the chief's attempts to keep the peace, surrounded the settlement and demanded supplies from the H.B.C. man. The Indian agent stood up to them – as much as he could, for the Indians had overrun the village – and one maddened warrior turned on him and shot him dead. The shot unleashed a holocaust. In a few minutes nine of the village men, including two priests, lay dead.

A survivor fled to Fort Pitt, which was hastily fortified for a siege. Soon Big Bear (retaining his position as chief by going along with the wild ones) and about 250 of his men had moved in on the fort. Their fury had died down, however, and they were willing to let the whites pass out safely if they abandoned the fort and its contents. Finally this arrangement was made, and Big Bear took command of Fort Pitt.

Big Bear's success drew more and more Indians to his leadership. It also sparked further outbreaks of raiding and plundering across the prairie. Rumours and wild exaggerations increased the terror among the settlers. But in spite of the massacre at Frog Lake, the later Indian raids had been mainly in search of loot, not blood. This restraint was especially true of the Woods Crees, brought into the fight by Big Bear's men. The Plains Crees, however, were more anxious to strike blows at white dominance: they wanted to drive the whites from the land. For this purpose the chiefs sent messengers to rally the tribes – for so far only a comparative handful of Crees and Assiniboines had entered the fight. Many hundreds remained uncommitted. So did the Blackfoot, who might have been induced to join the rising, and would have then reproduced the terrible days of America's Indian wars. Also, there were the American Indians themselves – the Sioux especially, with their racial hatred still at the boiling point. To the white westerners in that year of armed rebellion, it seemed possible that before the summer's end every Plains Indian in Canada might be inflamed with the urge to war. And Canada's western settlers were few, mostly unskilled with guns, with no army near by to protect them.

But the fear of a general Plains Indian rising gradually filtered through to eastern Canada. The authorities – who had previously sneered at the idea that Riel, or starving Indians, or disaffected métis, might offer a threat to the peace – now clamoured for speedy action to quell the outbreak. Action came. Wisely, the government's first step was an order to send extra provisions to the tribes who were not yet committed. With their sufferings alleviated, many Indians – including the warlike Blackfoot – stayed on their reserves. But credit for restraining the Blackfoot must also go to those two influential missionaries of the Territories, Père Lacombe and Rev. John McDougall, who lost no time in visiting Crowfoot and his chiefs and advising peace. Similarly, a hastily-formed government commission met and examined métis grievances. Soon scrip was being issued to assure their land claims, a move which might have prevented the whole rising, but which at this late date merely underlined the government's irresponsibility and served as a tacit admission of its guilt. Meanwhile, in the east, regular troops awaited orders, and in the settlements of the Territories volunteers took up arms.

The force that was being mobilized against Riel, Big Bear and Poundmaker eventually numbered nearly 8,000 men, not including the 500 N.W.M.P. Over 3,000 of these soldiers came from eastern Canada, in early April, when snow and ice still made travel difficult. But this was no slow march of many weeks, as it had been when Colonel Wolseley brought his men out to pacify Red River in 1870. Within *ten days* of the battle at Duck Lake, the eastern forces were mustered at Winnipeg. And in that statement lies the fact that the C.P.R. – not yet finished, full of gaps – had come into its own.

Macdonald urged Van Horne to transport the soldiers with all haste, for he was anxious to show that Canada could now quickly and efficiently handle her own crises and control her own Territories. But Van Horne needed no urging. The C.P.R. had to prove itself, too, to restore public confidence. So he organized the military's progress into a miracle of precise timing at top speed.

The detachments from the east boarded their trains on March 30, and rushed west towards the half-completed trackage north of the Lakes, where a series of gaps in the line – over the worst terrain – barred the way. As their train reached the first gap a brigade of horse-drawn sleighs was waiting for them: the men were bundled off the train, and the sleighs hurtled over the snow, on a rough service road, to a point where the tracks began again. There another train – only flat cars with hastily improvised protection against the wind and snow – stood ready, with a good head of steam, to carry them to the next gap. And so it went, the full distance of the bleak lakeshore, from gap to gap. Van Horne had even seen personally to the men's food: ample hot meals would be waiting for them in tents when they disembarked, hot coffee would be ready when they boarded the train at the next point. On April 4 the first detachments from the east arrived at Winnipeg.

By that time the companies of volunteer militia had moved west from Winnipeg and from other prairie centres. Less than a week after the soldiers had come from the east, almost the whole military force was mustered on the still frozen prairie, and was moving north to crush the rebellion. But – unlike the process of transportation – the process of crushing suffered some delay. It seems clear that the delay was largely due to the inept and hesitant deployment of the troops by Major-General Middleton. The General, apparently not at his ease with cavalry, relied on ponderous infantry tactics in that land of horsemen. He moved slowly, giving the métis ample time to prepare for him. (According to Stanley, Riel had to restrain Gabriel Dumont from sending out a force of mounted métis sharpshooters to make mincemeat of the foot soldiers.)

The General and his troops advanced slowly north from Fort Qu'Appelle towards the métis stronghold at Batoche. At the same time other forces moved out of other bases: Colonel Otter marched from Swift Current (on the C.P.R. line west of Moose Jaw) to rescue the citizens of Battleford, still surrounded by Poundmaker's warriors; and General Strange departed from Calgary, to search for Big Bear in the North Saskatchewan valley near Fort Pitt.

As the soldiers moved nearer Batoche, Dumont overcame Riel's pacific hopes and led his men out to fight. Riel went with them until an alarm from Batoche sent him back with some of the men to defend the town against a possible N.W.M.P. attack. With only 150 men against Middleton's 800, Dumont used all the tricks of the plainsmen; he stationed his force in a ravine called Fish Creek and lured the inexperienced enemy into sitting-duck positions, depending on the métis' marksmanship and skill at using scanty cover to maximum advantage. But the odds were too heavy and Middleton had artillery. The métis lost nearly 100 men: though they had temporarily halted the soldiers' advance, they had not won a victory. As Middleton regrouped, Riel, growing desperate, sent calls for help to Big Bear and Poundmaker.

But by then the Cree leaders themselves needed help. Strange's force had reached Edmonton – having by its presence quelled any remaining thoughts of war among the Indians of that region – and was moving downriver towards Big Bear, who was slowly making his way in the general direction of Battleford. Big Bear was growing dubious about continuing the battle: his allies and cousins, the Woods Crees, were refusing to fight any longer; only the warmongering of a strong faction among his own Plains Crees kept him on the warpath. These bloodthirsty Crees, in common with the Crees and Assiniboines of Poundmaker's force, were anxious to join Riel. Big Bear vacillated and his camp moved slowly in fits and starts.

Meanwhile, in Battleford, Poundmaker was waiting for Big Bear – though his wild-eyed warriors wanted to assault the N.W.M.P. barracks without reinforcements. So as Riel was asking the Indians to come and fight Middleton, Poundmaker simultaneously sent to Riel for help in besieging the Mounties.

Shortly, however, the Cree chief was himself besieged. Colonel Otter had arrived in the area. The Colonel did not delay his attack, but planned it poorly. He tried to surprise the Indians, in their camp on Cut Knife Hill. He might have known that regular soldiers could not creep up on Indians. Suddenly Otter found himself surrounded by the Crees, who had slipped silently through the brush on the hill and were directing a withering fire on to the exposed soldiers. Sensibly, he retreated; and Poundmaker – as Riel had done at Duck Lake and elsewhere – held his men back from the pursuit and slaughter.

Big Bear, barely able to hold his followers together, learned at the same time of the battle of Cut Knife Hill and the advance of Strange's troops. He prepared for battle on a piece of high ground called Frenchman's Butte. There Strange attacked him, but he had little success against the Crees' well-fortified position, and withdrew. Big Bear promptly withdrew in the other direction – while Strange remained unaware of his retreat – and escaped through the tangled brush north of the river. Some days later a detachment from Strange's force came upon the fugitives, but had insufficient men to fight an effective battle and again withdrew. Big Bear's flight – or forced march – continued.

For the métis at Batoche, flight was impossible. They had their backs against the wall. After the Fish Creek setback, Middleton's forces licked their wounds for a few days, then fell on Batoche – where the métis had dug trenches and well-protected foxholes along the riverbank. Middleton arrived on May 9, attacked, and was repulsed. But the métis position was hopeless: Middleton's artillery poured death on to their fortifications, and their ammunition and supplies were running out. After several days of attacks and withdrawals, the army wore the métis down. On May 12 a quick flanking movement and a powerful charge emptied the métis fortifications, and the defence of Batoche was broken. Surviving métis fled into the forest. Gabriel Dumont and a handful of men slipped away from the mopping-up action, and headed south for the border. But Louis Riel gave himself up.

Poundmaker, moving away from Battleford after the battle of Cut Knife Hill, heard of the métis defeat, and shortly gave himself up as well – to Middleton, who had marched to Prince Albert after his victory and then towards Battleford. Only Big Bear remained. Middleton, still clinging to his rigid British ideas of foot soldiers and thin red lines, decided against pursuing Big Bear with mounted police and cavalry – and so lost the use of his only experienced plainsmen. Instead, he marched heavy infantry into the dense, muskeg-and-mosquito under-brush around Loon Lake. Big Bear eluded him easily, and Middleton marched out again. But then Big Bear's forces split permanently, as the Woods Crees absconded to seek a separate peace with the authorities. The chief now had no choice: salvaging some pride, he continued to elude the soldiers that were searching for him and travelled to Fort Carlton to sur-render to the N.W.M.P.

So the last rebel had been taken, and the revolt ended. The principal leaders were taken to Regina for trial: there métis and Indians received sentences ranging from one year for felony to hanging for murder. There Big Bear and Poundmaker were each sentenced to two years' imprisonment for 'treason-felony'. And Louis Riel, found guilty of high treason, was sentenced to death. After lengthy investigations and several stays of execution, he was hanged in November 1885.

The uproar that accompanied the sentence and that followed the execution moved like an earthquake across the Dominion. It tore at the new and flimsy bonds forged between Ontario and Quebec: Quebec's French Catholics insisted that the sentence was a plot instituted by maniacal Ontario Orangemen; Ontario's British Protestants countered with accusations that the Catholics were trying to protect a treasonous murderer. The Press, at all levels, had a field day with the controversy. Details of the turbulence in eastern Canada do not belong here: but it might be noted that the widened gulf between the nationalities did considerable harm to Macdonald's Con-servative party, in the old master's declining years, and probably helped to bring about a resurgence of the Liberals – and especially a strengthening of Liberal power in Quebec under Wilfrid Laurier, the French Canadian who was an impassioned defender of Riel. In the end the question remained and remains controversial: how should we, and history, view Riel and the rebellion?

Answers cover every extreme. To some, Riel was merely a

mystical maniac who had a brief moment of power, thanks largely to some unfortunately misled Indians. To others, Riel was an important working-class revolutionary seeking to lead the downtrodden in their fight against imperialism. In this writer's personal view, the latter conception (though a wild exaggeration) holds rather more water than the former – simply because the question of Riel's sanity seems to obscure more issues than its importance warrants.

Remember that the métis sought Riel out. He did not organize them from the beginning of their unrest. He served mainly as a rallying-point, even a figurehead – a source of inspiration more than of decision or planning. Of course, Riel had a share in creating the violence, but it seems likely that, once arms were taken up, he sought merely a show of force, with hostages to be used as bargaining counters. Events – and Gabriel Dumont – got away from him, and the resistance became armed revolt. But it did *not* become so because its leader was insane. The métis' organized, pre-Riel agitation might well have developed into armed revolt even *without* Riel – and certainly it developed regardless of the leader's state of mind.

So the insanity question – and this is still a personal and freely speculative view – becomes pertinent only with regard to the execution, in terms of whether Riel should have lived (aside from considerations of the pointless brutality of capital punishment). In terms of the revolt itself, it was mostly irrelevant. Some distinctions must be made, when examining the rebellion, between the end, the means, and the justification.

At its simplest, the *end* in view for Riel and the métis was an assurance from the authorities that their rights, their lands, and their old free way of life would be secured in a changing world. Such a goal, in the light of one's knowledge of frontiers and settlers, may seem naïve, but it does not smack of insanity. Riel was not mad to seek this end.

The *means* to the end began as a protest movement and grew into armed rebellion. The escalation was undeniably due partly to Riel's decision; but certainly that decision was bolstered by the urgings of some of the métis fighting men. Undeniably, the majority of the métis rejected the idea of violence, or went along with it only grudgingly; and it has already been stressed that Riel himself tried to hold back, tried to wield only the *threat* of arms (to make Crozier surrender, for example), and launched no major offensives. With regard to the means, then, Riel made errors; perhaps the errors sprang from the stress of the situation, perhaps even from his growing panic and loss of control over it, but this, if anything, is weakness, not madness.

If the thin edge of something resembling insanity creeps in anywhere, it is in Riel's own *justification* for the agitation and the revolt. Here his heightened religious sense played him false. During his breakdown and after, he believed firmly that he had a mission in life, and that he had been chosen by God for that mission. He believed himself to be delegated to lead, protect and save the métis nation from ruin – and to save the west from tribulation. He also believed, as a sidelight, that his connections with God occurred in terms other than his role: that he was a descendant of the prophet David (he signed himself 'Louis "David" Riel') and was himself a prophet. In these beliefs, and their variations and exaggerations in his statements and actions, can be found what we may call madness: paranoia – megalomania – delusions of grandeur.[1]

But it seems certain – as the doctors who examined him agreed – that at no time did Riel's paranoia affect his ability to distinguish between illusion and reality. Certainly not between right and wrong. His *insanity* (which had been accompanied by hallucinations and ravings) had been cured in an asylum. It left him with a mild paranoia, which may have strengthened under stress. But he had been restored to normality in terms of perception, understanding, awareness. And therefore, while he may have been wrong in what he was doing, he was mentally unbalanced only in the realm of *why* he was doing it. In every other respect he can be seen as an honest man (if weak and wrong-headed) fighting for his people. And fighting a last, lonely, futile, impossible battle.

The Northwest Rebellion of 1885 became the last stand of the old Canadian west. The métis had made a stand before, in Manitoba, the free prairie hunters against the builders of towns

---

[1] Riel himself, during his trial, denied his insanity – when to plead it would have saved his life. Paradoxically, this act might itself seem mad: but Riel was then showing more concern for his name, his honour, his memory among the métis, than for his life.

and fences and farmhouses. They had lost, and had retreated to the great lone land of the Territories to take up their own way of life again. There the tide of settlers had caught them up again, and they had again resisted. Now they retreated once more, in disarray, never to stand or fight again. The Indians accepted the irrevocable and went to their reserves and stayed there, facing the alternatives of making the best of it or dying away in resignation and apathy. The métis scattered to what pockets of emptiness remained: the forests of northern Saskatchewan, the far plains of the Peace River. Civilization would find them there, too, eventually. Their day was as undeniably past as the buffalo's. The future, and the west, belonged to the settlers.

10

O Pioneers!

The Riel Rebellion had publicized the west around the world, but not entirely favourably. Now its rapid conclusion publicized the fact that the west was under control – that law and order, as well as freedom and fertility, prevailed. Immigration, from abroad, from new European sources, began to swell. But before these new westerners could be readily admitted, the railway had to be completed.

Before the Rebellion, as one financial crisis (staved off by a government loan) gave way to another, George Stephen had had every reason to fear that his C.P.R. would never be finished. Its enemies, the Grand Trunk and others, were busily plotting; a new recession had badly shaken the Canadian treasury, and rocked the stock market; and the costs of construction had mounted. In early 1885 creditors stormed the offices of Stephen and Donald Smith, who were using every manœuvre in their enormous repertoire to raise funds – a few thousand here, a few there – for day-to-day operating expenses. Even so, vital outlays – for necessities like the men's pay – were delayed. That spring a rash of strikes added a further impediment to progress. In one, the strikers rioted, downing tools and taking up makeshift weapons to march on the local C.P.R. headquarters and demand their money. Eight N.W.M.P. men held off 300 workers in that incident, without bloodshed; and some cash rushed out from the east eased the tension. But such payments were only temporary stop-gaps.

As Van Horne pressed for more money, Stephen and Smith turned to what was nearly the last resort, and something which Stephen called 'absurd on any kind of business grounds':

pledging their own resources. (They were both several times millionaires.) Using their personal credit, they endorsed a million-dollar note for funds to hold off creditors and build a few more miles. Both men were ready to commit themselves further, for Stephen is reported to have told Smith, regarding creditors: 'When they come they must not find us with a dollar.'

As the threat of the C.P.R.'s collapse grew stronger daily, John A. Macdonald offered no hope in answer to Stephen's desperate requests for help. The government had helped once; now, with the stock market in its current state, and with the railway's reputation becoming increasingly tarnished as its costs rocketed, the government was unwilling to throw good money after bad. Macdonald – old, tired, facing political strife on many fronts – was unwilling to try again to pressure Parliament into aiding the C.P.R. So he hedged, delayed, avoided Stephen, and generally justified his nickname: 'Old Tomorrow.'

But then the métis and the Indians broke out in armed rebellion – and Van Horne's superbly organized movement of the troops over the incomplete railway crushed their dreams before they had been fully launched. The C.P.R. had proved itself worth saving, and Macdonald, taking advantage of the propitious moment, at last swung into action. Like his old self, he introduced resolutions in Parliament proposing financial aid for the railway, waited while the storm of political fury spent itself, and then bulldozed the proposals through. The new arrangements included an immediate loan to pay creditors and provide operating funds, and a guaranteed issue of bonds. As if to underline the fact that the C.P.R. was saved, financiers from Britain – who had previously been indifferent to the railway – leaped on the bandwagon as agents for the bond issue. Soon the C.P.R.'s finances swung into the black.

Van Horne then whipped his men into a frenzy of work to finish the line that year. Inch by inch, the British Columbian track advanced towards the Selkirk mountains. Above Lake Superior, Van Horne ordered the construction of more temporary trestlework, which could be replaced later, at the engineers' leisure. By autumn the line was whole from Ontario to the mountains. And there, on November 7, the British Columbia line met the westward line, in Eagle Pass in the Selkirks, at a spot named Craigellachie.[1]

True to his individualistic temper, Van Horne created a unique ceremony around the Last Spike. He rejected gold or silver spikes (claiming to have seen too many bankrupt railways begin in a flush of golden spikes) and chose a plain iron one. He also restricted the area to persons who were connected with the railway: no governors-general or other ceremonial functionaries were present at Craigellachie; only C.P.R. men such as Sir Sandford Fleming, Major Rogers the surveyor, a group of the chief engineers, and a scattering of general employees. John A. Macdonald, whose vision had transformed a railway dream into a reality, and whose political skill had saved reality from ruin, was absent. So was George Stephen, the financial wizard who had kept the C.P.R. company alive in the dark days when even its friends were ready to mourn it. Van Horne, the supreme railway builder, was there, but refused the privilege of driving the last spike. It was driven, in the end, by the person who, among all the men involved with the railway, probably least deserved the honour – Donald A. Smith. Nevertheless, the spike was driven, the continent spanned. And in June 1886 the first trainload of passengers crossed the continent from Montreal to the edge of the Pacific.

The C.P.R. directors had every intention of exploiting the railway's front-door view of the Orient by means of trans-oceanic trade: and for this they needed a deep-sea port. Port Moody, the official terminus at Burrard Inlet, proved unsuitable, so Van Horne extended the line a few miles around the north side of the Inlet to Coal Harbour (near Granville). He named the spot Vancouver, overriding protests from the Island of that name, and there, in 1886, a small town was incorporated as a city. But its status as the end-of-the-line soon gave its incorporate name a reality: two years later (in spite of a fire in its first year that destroyed nearly every building) Vancouver was an industrial and commercial miracle, with a population of more than 8,000, riding high on a wave of construction, immigration and trade.

[1] The name of the Highland gathering place of the clan Grant, from which the clan derived its battle-cry: 'Stand fast, Craigellachie!' which was the content of an encouraging telegram, from Stephen to Smith, in the darkest hours of the C.P.R.'s financial desperation.

And here the pattern of immigration into British Columbia continued. It was not a province where a fairly well-designated frontier was being slowly pushed back: no one could push very successfully against that mountainous wilderness. Instead, settlement took the form of separated pockets (as Chapter 8 showed); and the majority of new British Columbians settled in or near the main urban centres.

So the boom times of the Terminal City drew newcomers, for the smell of money carries a long way, and only fools failed to make money in that roiling, bustling young commercial capital. With the new arrivals came still more Chinese, adding their numbers to the thousands who had been thrown suddenly out of work when Onderdonk finished his part of the C.P.R. Thousands of whites had been in a similar position, and now all the unemployed competed for jobs – not a situation designed to promote racial tolerance. Few British Columbians in the 1880s and 1890s could manage the clear-eyed view of the Port Moody *Gazette* (quoted by J. M. Gibbon) describing events at Yale when the ex-railway employees arrived:

> A thousand white men . . . rushed out of the cars and into the saloons. In two hours the streets were full of lunatics; they roared and raved and attempted to force their way into private houses. Twelve hundred Chinese arrived by the same train, and went into the woods and cooked their rice.

By these tokens, they were model citizens. But to the whites, the Chinese faults were legion.[1] Mainly, of course, the Chinese kept to themselves, retained their own ways and language, and were another colour. So the hatred fed on itself, and grew.

The Dominion had previously disallowed the province's legislation against the Chinese influx: Macdonald was worried about possible effects on Anglo-Chinese treaties and on Sino-Canadian trade by means of the C.P.R. He had also seen that without the Chinese there would be no C.P.R. But at last – with the railroad approaching completion – the province's demands could no longer be put off. In 1885, a few months before the last spike was driven, a bill imposing a 'head tax' on Chinese immigrants, $50 each, payable upon entry, was passed in Ottawa. (British Columbia grumbled that the tax should have

[1] As indicated on page 111.

been $100.) Clearly the Chinese were no longer needed, and so were definitely no longer wanted. The tax and the completion of the C.P.R. caused the immigration of Chinese to drop considerably: from 4,000 in the first half of 1885 to fewer than 1,000 a year throughout the late 1880s. Yet even those few proved too many for the British Columbians – who also remained fretful concerning the thousands of Chinese still in the province. Small and usually isolated clashes between the races occurred often (in 1887 the workers of Vancouver rioted in an anti-Chinese demonstration). Later in the century, as will be seen, other Asian arrivals would stimulate new excesses of discriminating legislation and violent racial hatred.

Beyond the mountains, the year of the Riel Rebellion and the completion of the C.P.R. marked a decisive turning point, in many ways, for the west – but not in terms of settlement. Prospective homesteaders were still flocking westwards: but it was not yet time for the great floodtide that would inundate the prairies. That would have to wait for (among other things) the remaining free-homestead lands of the U.S.A. to fill up. Nevertheless the vanguard of prairie settlement continued to grow steadily throughout the late 1880s and 1890s, and in that time the nature of pioneer life emerges most clearly. The life had little to recommend it: none of the heroic glamour imputed to it by Whitman's poem,[1] little of the simple satisfaction of honest toil and rugged individualism with which modern urban nostalgia colours it. Pioneer life was an exercise in survival – an endless round of immense labour to scrape up a bare subsistence. Even if the result surpassed mere subsistence, the overall flavour of homestead life seems to have been as flat as the land where it was lived, dismal and depressed – from the inevitability of hardship, the primitive living and working conditions, the knowledge that natural catastrophe could destroy in minutes the result of several months' labour.

The pioneers grubbed in the earth, and lived in it as well:

---

[1] Which reads, in part:
   We primeval forests felling,
   We the rivers stemming, vexing we and piercing deep the mines within,
   We the surface broad surveying, we the virgin soil upheaving,
   Pioneers! O pioneers!

their first houses were usually made of sod. The pioneer needed a home that was reasonably solid but also quick to build, for he had little time – after arriving in the spring – and had to get on with breaking the land and seeding his first small crop. The sod house answered his needs. He ploughed a few furrows of virgin prairie, choosing the low land, which collected water ('sloughs') for part of the year, and which when dry held grass with long and tenacious roots. He then cut the sod into manageable lengths, usually three feet long and a foot or more wide, and simply laid them like bricks to make his walls. He left the bare earth as his floor, and stretched poles across the walls, covered with hay and more sod, to make the roof. Some homesteaders brought window-frames and glass with them; others did without windows. Openings for doors might merely be floor-to-ceiling spaces left in a wall (ceilings were low) and doors, too, were usually bought elsewhere and brought along. 'Soddies', as the shacks were called, could be built any size, but the smaller ones went up faster, and their roofs were more secure. Most were single rooms: sixteen feet by twelve was a common area, but larger families required more space as well as makeshift partitions.

A sod house deserves some praise: it was warm in winter and cool in summer. (Some builders made their walls a double thickness, for added strength and insulation.) Also, it was fireproof and extremely cheap to build. On the other hand it required some skill in the building, especially in the selection of sods: if the grass did not bind them well, a prairie wind could simply blow the shack over, or it could collapse with its own weight. Oxen might break down the walls; rain might dissolve them. Rain invariably had one effect on the best-built soddy: a three-day rain outside, as a pioneer saying put it, meant a five-day rain inside.[1]

On an even more primitive scale, some early pioneers imitated the prairies' own burrowing rodent, the gopher, and lived in holes in the ground. More precisely, they bored their

[1] An old western song, both more realistic and less sickly than Whitman's treatment, concerns this subject:

> Oh for the days of the old-time shack
> When the rain begins to fall:
> Drip, drip through the mud on the roof
> And the wind blows through the wall.

way into the side of a low rise (if one was available) and roofed and fronted their cave with poles and sod. Frequently the roof sods regained their grassy aspect, which – unless the poles supporting them were unusually strong – could lead grazing oxen or horses to disaster.

In the park belt, some pioneers took the time to build small log shacks, often hauling logs many miles from the nearest 'bluff' of trees. If the builder was skilled, the logs would fit well, and would be tightly chinked with clay or other materials; otherwise the logs served only as a framework, and were sodded on the outside. The inside walls might be plastered with clay, or (where limestone existed) with crude sand-and-lime plaster.

The interior of the house was the place where individuality – and the pioneer wife – took over. Every home had a few special furnishings which the homesteaders had brought with them as mementoes of civilization: perhaps a favourite chair, but more likely something impractical like a picture or a carpet. Otherwise furnishings usually remained sparse, until the pioneers could afford better homes. Prairie winters demanded that stoves and heaters dominate the décor, but beds, chairs and tables could be makeshift affairs. One family slept for months on the packing-cases in which they had transported their belongings; most homesteaders, though, built rude tables and benches from cheap slab lumber.

Food as well as furniture taxed the pioneer's ingenuity and hardihood. The land offered some sustenance: wild fruit, berries and, of course, game: deer, moose, bear and wild fowl for those who owned guns and could shoot, snared rabbits for the rest. The settlers had a wry rhyme on this subject: 'Rabbit hot and rabbit cold, rabbit young and rabbit old; rabbit tender and rabbit tough; thank you, but I've had enough.' In a bad season gopher stew might dominate the menu. Domestic stock was prohibitively expensive for most early settlers, so all their meat was wild: anyone who could afford a cow kept her for milk. Pioneer wives grew and tended gardens, which – drought, frost and fire permitting – contributed to the larder. Those essentials that could not be shot or grown necessitated trips to the nearest village which, for many, meant a journey of fifty or more miles. Sugar and flour, oatmeal and syrup, salt, baking soda and tea predominated on shopping lists.[1] To pay for these staples, the settler might sell a wagon-load of fresh vegetables, if his garden had been productive. Or buffalo bones might be gathered from the prairie and sold for $7.00 a ton – at a time when, for instance, brown sugar sold for $2.00 per ten-pound sack. As will be seen later, the heads of the household often left the homestead for months, working elsewhere – on the railway, or for more established farmers – to raise the money that would pay for the essentials of prairie life.

Essentials were all that the early pioneers could hope for, and they pared their definition of 'essential' to the barest minimum. Clothes were patched and repatched and handed down; many prairie people tortured their feet by wearing shoes that had long passed their usefulness. In the earliest days, medical help was usually too far away to be considered an essential – though smallpox and typhoid were well known among the settlements. Diseases were fought at home, with home remedies, as well as they could be. A birth might be attended by a neighbour's wife (if neighbours lived within reach); otherwise the man of the house learned midwifery in a hurry. As for dentistry, aching teeth were simply and unceremoniously pulled – at home.

Needless to say, pioneer life meant work – months and years of tedious, crushing, endless work. The houses had to be built, and frequently rebuilt or repaired. The tough, unyielding prairie had to be broken, which put a strain even on a yoke of oxen, and caused crooked furrows at best, wrecked ploughs at worst. (Many 'greenhorn' homesteaders set out to plough too deeply; the secret was to cut in only a few inches for the first breaking.) Then seeding followed. Usually some part of a pioneer's 160 acres contained brush that demanded clearing, or stones that had to be picked off. Stables had to be built (of sod) for the oxen or horses, hay gathered for their winter feed, fences built to keep them off the crops. Gardens had to be planted and tended; enormous quantities of fuel had to be gathered – which might require lengthy trips to bluffs of trees on empty land, miles distant, in both summer and winter. Wagons, farm implements and harness needed looking after; other minor and monotonous chores were interspersed. The

[1] In the early years of homesteading coffee was an impossible luxury. Some settlers improvised a substitute by roasting barley, or even wheat.

216

women and children took on much of the latter work, as well as
the grinding routine of household tasks – with special attention
given to baking bread and preserving food for winter – and
preparing, all the while, regular meals from scanty supplies.

The early pioneers undertook this work – much of which was
simply typical nineteenth-century farm labour – in the face of
hardships and calamities peculiar to the prairie. They faced
their first real western trial almost before the wagons had
stopped, for only a few homesteads boasted anything like a
regular supply of water. Some had sloughs that appeared in
spring, grew increasingly stagnant, then dried up in the hot
winds of summer; the majority merely had hopes of a well.
So arduous digging and re-digging, in search of water, must be
added to the foregoing list of pioneer labours. In the end, if no
water was found, a settler would have to abandon his land,
after first trying to live by transporting water from the nearest
source. One inventive Scot constructed a giant water tank on
his wagon and hauled many gallons in a dry season, but most
drove their stock for miles to reach water, and carried their
own drinking water back. The search for water occupied a
vast amount of the homesteaders' time and energy; if he hired
someone to search for him, the cost could be crippling. Lloyd
Rodwell, the Saskatchewan archival assistant, in an article on
early homesteads, quotes an account of one man's pathetic
experience:

> I have persevered in trying to get water and thought I was
> successful after digging 124 feet and boring 50 feet but it has been
> an endless expense for the last two years. . . . I paid in the first
> place for digging and kerbing a well 97 feet and boring 50 feet
> $195. As there was no water a man witched the land so I dug
> where he indicated and had to move my house, dairy and stable.
> The present well cost $291 the first outlay and as it was impossible
> to pump by hand I had a geared Windmill erected which with
> the pump cost me $400. And now it is useless. . . .

That man, understandably, abandoned his homestead. Others
reported better luck with water 'witching' or dowsing, which
became largely the monopoly of local Indians. Still others, as
Mr Rodwell adds, owned a surfeit of water, having unwittingly
selected a quarter-section on low, marshy ground that might
well be flooded in spring.

Throughout the prairies, when the spring run-off had

subsided and the windy summer had evaporated the moisture, all those miles of dry grass became a fearsome fire hazard. To the pioneers, prairie fires were an annual event, occurring regularly in autumn. So every pioneer, as one of his first tasks, placed a fireguard around his home and possessions: he ploughed up a few furrows, then left a space and ploughed more, then burned off the grass between the ploughed areas. Naturally, a number of newcomers, misjudging the wind, started prairie fires in the process of burning off their fireguard.

The pioneers fought the fires as best they could, not only with fireguards but with sacking and blankets soaked in their precious water, with which they kept the flames away from their homes. In the dry autumn, men might be firefighting many nights in a row, riding to help neighbouring homesteaders whose danger was advertised by the glow of fire in the distance. Hardly an autumn night passed without the red flickering light appearing in the sky. Yet their firefighting could only dabble at the edges of some gigantic blazes, which rushed across the grass at the speed of a galloping horse, advancing on a front many miles wide. In the case of the largest fires the homesteader could hope only to use his wet sacking against the possibility of the flames jumping his fireguard. And even then he might be overwhelmed. In one account, a fire sweeping the prairie on a thirty-mile arc was said to have jumped a broad fireguard *against* the wind. In another, a man in southern Alberta reportedly lit his pipe carelessly, and the resulting fire burned off fifty square miles of prairie, taking scores of cattle, horses and homesteads with it. In the face of such terrors a pioneer could only gather a few possessions and run – returning later, perhaps, to the blackened acres, where neither house, crop, stock nor hay remained, to start over again.

Another prairie speciality wreaked its share of homestead destruction: the wild life. Gophers, rabbits, mice and birds plagued the gardens and crops; coyotes and other predators fed well if a settler dared to bring in young livestock or poultry. For the humans, there were the insects – especially that Canadian scourge, the mosquito. These repulsive little bloodsuckers – along with various breeds of biting flies – were (and are) both innumerable and persistent. They drove animals wild, interrupting ploughing when the berserk oxen sought relief in slough mud. They drove humans wild as well, and even the most rugged of pioneers wore veils when working outdoors. Burning green wood and leaves for smoky smudges sometimes helped, but the wind was unpredictable and the insects were not. A favourite pioneer joke tells of a man who wanted to know the time, and who therefore cut a hole in the cloud of mosquitoes around him to have a look at the sun. But it was literally true that, often, one could not tell the colour of a horse from even a short distance; it would merely be a grey cloud of insects.

Throughout the long winters, the homesteaders exchanged one set of hardships – gruelling labour, insects, fire – for another. It is probably unnecessary to detail the problems of survival in the winter months, when deadly blizzards reduced visibility to inches, and heaped snow so high that a man might be cut off from his own stables only yards away; or when deceptively still, sunny days lured settlers outside into eighty or more degrees of frost, to face the threat of bronchial damage and snow-blindness. Then the whole world would seem frozen – but at least meat would keep, and snow could be melted for water. The danger of fuel shortage, however, became an obsession: and the winter was treacherous. The cold could insidiously freeze hands and feet and face before one was aware of it; the wind could summon up a blizzard, suddenly, to trap a man miles from home.

Above all, winter added to the homesteader's most familiar and most cruel hardship: isolation. Even if he lived only a day away (as the ox plods) from some neighbours, winter made the effort and the risk of a visit too great except in emergencies – and not many early settlers were even that close to companionship. So they stayed huddled around the stove in their shacks, venturing out (when they could) only for fuel or to tend stock, all through the long winter months. The tribulations of the rest of the year dwindled in the face of the impenetrable winter loneliness. Loneliness, too, breeds fear – fear of accident or disease or shortage of food – and this haunted the snow-bound shacks from October to April, and never quite departed even in high summer. For this reason bachelor homesteaders often shared a house, though farming widely separated quarter-sections; for this reason many settlers abandoned good but isolated land for poorer land that was near others. Yet even then the clot of neighbours remained isolated, cut off from the world, an island in the emptiness.

Contact with the outside world was re-established infrequently, when the homesteader drove for days to get supplies at the nearest store. There, too, he might find mail waiting for him, and months-old newspapers; but mail travelled slowly and erratically. A letter would come west by train, then move nearer its destination by stagecoach (these travelled only a few trails, and mostly the Calgary–Edmonton) or in one of the goods wagons that supplied the scattered stores. Then it might wait for months before its recipient came out of the prairie and picked it up, or before a neighbour passed it on. A story is told of a man who, living far from town, received supplies and mail through a chain relay of neighbours. The neighbours (many miles apart) never made special journeys to pass on letters, however, and his wife and children, arriving from the east to join him, had to wait six weeks at the local immigration hall before he received the letter telling him to meet them.

The cruellest isolation, of course, beset a homesteader who chose to venture alone into an unsettled area, ahead of a mass movement, but even farmers in more populous regions knew the prairie loneliness during the depths of winter when the snow made travel impossible. For them, however, summer brought relief. After the heavy work of spring seeding had been done they could indulge in their only real form of relaxation, casual visiting: where knots of neighbours existed, in the more settled areas, a man knew that he could always drop in unannounced and he would be made welcome, fed and put up for the night if necessary. So arose the tradition – now a cliché, but very real nevertheless – of western hospitality.

But then in a land where everyone was scratching for survival, neighbourliness became less of a virtue than a necessity. However poor you were, however unable to offer more than unsweetened oaten porridge or rabbit stew, you offered it – because some time you might be in need of a similar offer. Not that this attitude was ever any more than semi-conscious: the giving was rarely grudging, and often unasked for. A homesteader named Edward West, in his reminiscences, tells of the surprises he received in his first days on the prairie: how some neighbours arrived with fresh vegetables, and others came unbidden in the autumn to help gather his hay and build a hayrack.

And in this is revealed the true nature of pioneer social life: it revolved around *work*. Newcomers might begin awkwardly building their first sod house only to find their more experienced neighbours riding up from all directions and erecting the house in a day, while the women produced and cooked food for the entire group. Neighbours banded together, pooling their animals and their limited machinery, to bring in one another's crops, or hay, or winter fuel. If one man's crop was destroyed – say, by fire – his next year's seed might come from a more successful neighbour, as a gift. If another homesteader ran short of food, his neighbours would dip into their own slim resources. In this way the pioneers achieved a truly communal existence – not the poor battening on the rich, but the poor banding together with other poor for mutual aid. In the laconic words of one early homesteader, 'nobody had nothing and we all used it'.

Co-operation, therefore, rather than individualism, stands out among the characteristics of pioneer life. Of course as the frontier melted away and population grew and spread, this spirit diminished and independence became more possible. The narrowing of the actual spaces between people served to separate them, in this other sense, breaking down the co-operative commonalty. (Outside the urban centres this familiar spirit of agrarian hospitality can undoubtedly still be found; but because circumstances no longer demand it, it grows more rare.) The breakdown was furthered by the growing immigration into the west of homesteaders whom the Anglo-Saxons – the majority of settlers in the early 1880s – were pleased to call 'foreigners'.

From 1885 onwards the nature of immigration to the west altered: the balance swung away from total domination by the Britons and eastern Canadians. These, of course, continued to come in search of opportunity in the raw, unformed Territories, but the Europeans, too, arrived in force, seeing the prairies not as a colony to be tamed but as a haven to provide a fresh start, away from poverty, oppression, or other tribulations. More and more, western settlement became characterized by ethnic group immigrations. In the great rush of settlement after the turn of the century, 'foreign' immigrants and Anglo-Saxons arrived in nearly equal numbers. New languages and new ways formed the beginnings of the western Canadian ethnic *mélange*, of which the following is only a sampling, taken from the last two decades of the nineteenth century.

Swedish settlers – suffering a depression, fleeing compulsory military service, or simply feeling restless – arrived in Saskatchewan in the path of one Nils Johanson, who had been led west by an enthusiastic immigration agent. Johanson saw the green and wooded hills of the Qu'Appelle Valley and felt at home; a Swedish settlement soon materialized north of the Qu'Appelle River. The newcomers, calling their Canadian home New Stockholm, proved to be ideal pioneer material. They knew forests and fields, axes and ploughs: they put up sturdy log houses at record speed, broke quantities of land and progressed steadily towards prosperity – thanks largely to their ability, in the early days, to wield their axes in the woods and sell the timber for fuel or for building.

The woodcraft of the men of the north almost always led them into the forested regions. So it was with the few Finns who made their way west before the turn of the century. Some Finns had been employed in Alaska by the Russians and had moved south to British Columbia after the U.S.A. Purchase. There they found jobs with the C.P.R., and then in the late 1880s they settled – a few taking up farming, the majority turning to the growing logging or mining industries in the north of the province. Other Finns had come to the prairies from Minnesota during the C.P.R.'s advance, and after its completion settled in the park belt on the fringe of the north woods. As for other Northmen, the 1880s saw Icelandic settlements grow up in the Territories. First of these was Thingvalla, near Yorkton, which later linked up with a community called Lögberg to the north. Still later, in 1891, some venturesome Icelanders trekked westward to the Foam Lake area, some 100 miles from the nearest civilized establishment, and made themselves a home on the bald prairie.

Unlike the Manitoba forerunners of Icelandic settlement, these new arrivals devoted all their time to agriculture: their situation offered little opportunity for fishing and other familiar occupations. But the Icelanders had little experience of grain farming, since it was seldom practised in their homeland's short growing season. Instead, they turned to extensive mixed farming, and were soon able to show older residents how to raise stock in the west. Other farmers might turn their herds loose during the winter; not the Icelanders. They cut and stored vast quantities of hay, and when others lost a predictable number of young or weak cattle in the hard winter, the Icelandic settlements lost none. Hay had attracted the Foam Lake group to the area, for in the early 1890s the lake was dry and formed an ideal hay meadow – though the handful of homesteaders (less than twenty, including children) were even more vulnerable to prairie fires than others.

Religious minorities continued to look for a haven in the open spaces of western Canada. The Mennonites of Manitoba, flourishing in that area, met the danger of overcrowding by setting up 'daughter' colonies farther west: so the adventurous young, as well as new Mennonite immigrants, were directed to a settlement north of Saskatoon after a railway[1] had connected that town with both Prince Albert and Regina.

Jewish immigrants, mainly from southern and eastern Europe, had been pouring into Canada in numbers that swamped the few philanthropic organizations set up in the east to look after their welfare. The bulk of this influx had come through Britain, where London organizations soon passed them on to the roomier colony. Many remained in eastern centres, especially Montreal; but when the Russian pogroms broke out the immigration swelled even more, and the overflow was caught by the west. The first Jew in the Territories settled in Qu'Appelle in 1877; but western Jews in the 1870s and 1880s preferred Winnipeg to the homesteading west. They suffered in that city – they were all poor, yet wages were low, jobs scarce and prices high – and many among them were educated professional men, unused to the harsh labour that the west demanded of most new citizens (especially of 'foreigners').

Various plans emerged for Jewish agricultural colonies in the west – in spite of the fact that most of these immigrants' experience of European ghettoes would hardly have trained them for farming. This lack of experience – and of encouragement – wrecked the hopes of the first Jews who settled in the southeast of what is now Saskatchewan in the 1880s. New

[1] See p. 234.

223

Jerusalem, as their colony was called, did not live up to its name: the usual hardships of western homesteading drove these willing but inept farmers back to Winnipeg, or to the U.S.A.

As eastern Europe's pogroms mounted in ferocity – for Poland and Rumania and other countries followed Russia's example – later organizations tried again to place Jews on land in the Territories. One ambitious plan set out calmly to establish a colony for 10,000 Jews. In fact the first Jewish settlement in the Territories held forty-seven people. Western conditions soon weeded out those who were ill-suited for homesteading, and the settlement, called Hirsch (also in the southeast region), dwindled to a population of nine. But at least it was a beachhead. Other Jews arrived in the early 1890s: a few made homes at Oxbow, near Hirsch, others at near-by Wapella. Gradually they began to overcome the difficulties that all pioneers had had to learn to live with, and a few special problems of their own – among which, for most of the Jewish immigrants, was the problem of maintaining their dietary rules and still finding enough to eat under frontier conditions.

The poverty-ridden religious groups from Europe contrasted strongly with the prosperous American Mormons, who also moved into western Canada in this period. But they, too, were fleeing from persecution – specifically, from the anti-bigamy laws imposed by the Territory of Utah in the 1880s. Certain leaders of the Church of the Latter-Day Saints became fugitives, sought by the authorities. And, while their Utah brethren were escaping punishment by accepting monogamy, they found a suitable home in the grasslands of what is now southern Alberta. There Charles O. Card, son-in-law of Brigham Young, founded a settlement (partly financed by the Church in Utah) whose centre was given the name of Cardston. The first Albertan Mormons worked on local ranches, especially the giant Cochrane ranch,[1] to amass capital – though some (including Card) brought small fortunes with them, or were assisted by the Utah brethren. Within a few years flourishing shops appeared in Cardston, and industry – a cheese factory, sawmills and gristmills – had grown up to add to the settlement's success.

The Mormons were among the first to see that the ranch

[1] See p. 245.

lands of southern Alberta could be rich farmland if the problem
of water were solved. To them, with their Utah background,
irrigation was the natural answer. By the mid-1890s the settlement was able to rent, and later buy, half a million acres (at
$1.00 an acre), and launch an irrigation scheme to reclaim it
for agriculture. Later still the Mormons bought out the
Cochrane lands, and extended the bounds of 'Mormon country'
by another 500,000 acres. The settlements continued to swell
as more Latter-Day Saints came up from the U.S.A. – no longer
impelled by repressive laws, but drawn by economic potential.

Of all the religious sects whose members helped to populate
the west, the Doukhobors of Russia have taken the honours as
the most noteworthy (or newsworthy) and, to say the least,
colourful. But let it be stressed now: the acts that brought the
Doukhobors into international notoriety – the demonstrations
and nude marches, the arson and dynamiting – were perpetrated by a sect within the sect, a splinter group of fanatics
calling themselves the Sons of Freedom. With the average
journalist's tendency to get his facts only half right, the Sons
have been allowed by association to muddy the overall name
of the Doukhobors.

Their name, Doukhobor, 'spirit-wrestler', is a nickname
bestowed contemptuously by the orthodox church-goers in the
Russian Caucasus, but readily adopted[1] by the sect as an
indication of their willingness to battle against evil with (and
only with) the weapons of the spirit. Their battle had begun –
no one knows exactly when, or where – during a great crisis
and eruption in the Russian Orthodox Church in the late
seventeenth century, when many Russian 'protestant' movements were thrown up. The seeds of Doukhoborism germinated
under influences both mystical and social, to produce a dogma
that includes belief in the equality of all men, in pacifism, in
common ownership of property, in individual interpretation of
the Bible, and in rejection of the high church ritual. Yet in
spite of the first two tenets, the Doukhobors in Russia had
traditionally been organized under one autocratic leader, and
had never hesitated to defend themselves fiercely if the law of
the land pushed them too far.

[1] Just as the Society of Friends took on their originally pejorative
nickname.

225

Eventually they were pushed out of Russia entirely, and Canada inherited them. The same compulsory military service that sent Mennonites around the world drove the Doukhobors from their home. Count Leo Tolstoy heard of their sufferings – and of the fact that their peasant communalism and pacifism reflected in many ways his own thinking and teaching. He lent his weight to a movement designed to help the sect out of the country by raising funds[1] and by finding them a new home. In 1898 a British Tolstoyan, Aylmer Maude, led the first Doukhobors to Canada – a small group on a tour of inspection. Canada, hungry for new Canadians, welcomed them, and huge blocks of land were set aside for them in what is now Saskatchewan.

By 1899 about 7,500 Doukhobors had settled on the prairies. The majority lived in a colony north of Yorkton, others in a colony near Rosthern (Saskatchewan) and more in a colony between these points. Though they had been poor, they had not suffered unduly: Tolstoy and the Quakers, and the few well-off members, had seen to their immediate needs. And they were self-sufficient colonists, saving capital by making most of their communal possessions (including farm implements), farming fairly expertly, and hiring out their labour to build up their funds. Being illiterate peasants who had stepped out of a still-feudal society into the whirl of North American free enterprise, they were shamelessly exploited when they went to work for others, but they were used to working hard for little, and never objected to the pitiful wages paid for woodcutting, farm labour or other jobs. (The Anglo-Saxon working men, priced out of the market, objected strenuously and even petitioned Ottawa.) The Doukhobors were happy: they had land, rich and productive, more than they had ever owned, and – most important – they had a guarantee from Canada of military exemption, which indicated they would be left alone.

Indeed, they were left alone, for even then the west was roomy enough to permit their self-possession. Of course some of their more primitive ways occasioned comment: a story flew across the west that the Doukhobor women actually pulled the ploughs. (In fact a few women had done so, in one village, before the community could afford horses and while the men

[1] Quakers contributed enormously, not only funds but organizational work, as they had done and continued to do with Russian Jews and other refugees from oppression.

were away wage earning. But it was definitely an exception.)
Eventually their unity, thrift and ceaseless labour produced a
degree of comfort, if not actual prosperity. And as they grew
comfortable they gained time to consider fine points of dogma
and, inevitably, to disagree. Their titular leader, Peter Verigin
(who had been imprisoned in Russia, as the instigator of the
Doukhobors' seditious refusal to bear arms, and remained
there until 1902), believed himself, and was believed to be,
divinely inspired. His inspirations fanned the flames of fanaticism among this naïve and harmless sect.

Verigin's vague concepts of a 'promised land' apparently led
to the first major split: a quarter of the population of the settlements set out on an early winter march to nowhere, in sub-zero
weather, hoping that the promised land would manifest itself
along their route. Before long, however, the Mounties halted
the procession and herded the frozen visionaries back to their
homes. It was the first important clash – though non-violent –
between the sect and the Canadian authorities. Even the more
or less soothing arrival of Verigin himself, in 1902, could not
halt the new fanaticism. That year the first nude demonstration
occurred – their way of protesting against governmental 'inter-
ference' – and again the Mounties stepped in. A number of the
marchers were briefly imprisoned; from that number grew the
Sons of Freedom, with their devotion to opposing all authority
on all grounds.

So began the story that continued, almost without pause,
up to the 1950s – by which time the centre of the Sons' activity
had shifted to British Columbia. In the process, not only the
peaceful segments of the Doukhobor population but to some
extent all eastern Europeans found themselves condemned as
second-class citizens. Not that the Sons' excesses were wholly to
blame. They did, however, reinforce the Anglo-Saxons' inevitable xenophobia. Also, in a land where all have been at one time
foreigners, the last to come can be sure to meet the full blast of
snobbery from their entrenched predecessors. So it was all the
more unfortunate that, at the turn of the century, the latest
arrivals should be poor and generally illiterate peasant farmers
from the Slavic countries.

The advance guard of this new immigration came from
oppressed nationalities subsumed in the Austro–Hungarian
empire. At first they moved to the U.S.A. – where in the 1870s

coal-mining enterprises brought in thousands of Hungarians as 'contract labour', a pernicious form of near-slavery that was banned by Congress in 1882. Slavic immigration to Canada got its start after 1885, when the C.P.R. acquired a colonizing agent in the person of Count Paul Esterhazy (or d'Esterhazy), a Hungarian nobleman. The Count first aimed his colonizing persuasiveness at Hungarian settlements in Pennsylvania, and skimmed off a few potential settlers. He would have attracted more, but mine-owners who wanted to keep their miners apparently launched a campaign to discredit him, accusing him among other things of being an impostor, a commoner whose real name was John Papp. So only thirty-five Hungarians moved north, in the first wave to be settled on land in Manitoba.

Later, helped by a government loan, Esterhazy brought more Hungarians out of the U.S.A. and settled them in the Territories (near the town of Whitewood in south-east Saskatchewan). Then organizational difficulties, as well as the effects of the American mud-slinging, forced the Count out of the picture. Hungarian immigration, however, continued – and began to come from Europe as well throughout the 1890s. A good many immigrants found their way to the prairie colony near Whitewood, where the nucleus of the thriving town had acquired the name of Esterhazy.

At that time, of course, Austro–Hungary contained a good many mingled ethnic groups, and later writers have a problem with their names. Not all the Slavs of the Esterhazy district, or of the later influxes which worked in Lethbridge coal mines or farmed in Alberta, could properly be called Hungarians – though they were listed as such by the indifferent Canadian authorities. Among the immigrants were crowds of Slovaks, Croats and Serbs as well as the Magyars who are the true Hungarians. There were also sprinklings of Czechs, Ruthenes and even Germans. In the same way, the later arrivals from eastern Europe whom we now term 'Ukrainians' almost never went under that name. The Ukraine, as we know it, was partly Austrian and partly Russian, so confusion reigned in the minds of the Canadian immigration agents. Were the newcomers Galicians, Ruthenians or Bukowinians – were they to be called Austrians, or were they Russians? Any of these names might have been put on the documents. Some agents included Ukrainians as Hungarians, or Poles – or simply avoided the difficulty by calling them all 'Slavs'. Just as the public, in general, avoided the difficulty by calling them all by that ugliest of racial nicknames, 'bohunks'. Nor did the term 'Ukrainian' come into general use until the time of the First World War, when the people of the Ukraine proclaimed their national identity.

Like their brothers in flight from eastern Europe, the Ukrainians exchanged their European debts, poverty and small patches of overworked land (often five acres or less) for 160 acres of western soil and freedom from the heavy hand of government or aristocracy. They first learned about this land of opportunity from a venturesome farmer, Ivan Pillipiw, who with his friend Wasyly Eleniak[1] had paid his way to Canada in 1891. Impressed by the wealth of the empty land, Pillipiw returned (Eleniak stayed, near a Manitoba Mennonite settlement) to propagandize the New World to his countrymen. The authorities threw him in prison for daring to suggest emigration – but by doing so only underlined the Ukrainians' need to escape, and publicized Pillipiw's journey. In the end several families (including Pillipiw's when he was released) sold their meagre possessions for the fare to western Canada. Some of them took up land some forty miles west of Edmonton, for they preferred the park belt: and according to Paul Yuzyk, a Ukrainian–Canadian historian, this was the first Ukrainian settlement in Canada. Others remained in or near Winnipeg, where they could be sure to find people who spoke a language they knew: Russian or German.

In 1895 the reputed Ukrainian scientist and author, Dr Osyp Oleskiw (translated as Josef Oleskow), toured Canada and wrote about it. His book, praising the west's fertility and providing useful advice to would-be emigrants, was widely read in the Ukrainian provinces, and led to a mass immigration – assisted to some extent by the C.P.R., and by the new, dynamic Minister of the Interior, Clifford Sifton[2] – who provided the settlement movement with a slogan:

I think that a stalwart peasant in a sheepskin coat, born on the soil, whose forefathers have been farmers for ten generations, with a stout wife and half a dozen children, is good quality.

[1] Ukrainian names, transliterated into the English alphabet, receive a variety of spellings.
[2] Whose work will be discussed more extensively in Chapter 11.

'Sifton's Sheepskins', the east Europeans were sneeringly called (among other names). But the Minister was proved right.

To put it simply, the Ukrainians desperately needed what Canada had to offer – the land and the opportunity – and so they responded to it. As they poured in, in their thousands, in the late 1890s and early 1900s, they brought with them the willingness and ability to build up the emptiness from scratch. As tough and skilful farmers who knew, from long experience, how to survive on very little, they were the ideal homesteaders. When they were allowed to be.

But at first not all of them were allowed. For they were also illiterate and comparatively unworldly peasants, too used to bowing before the directives and whims of authority. They were ripe for the plucking. And the migration schemes invariably attracted professional exploiters, sharks who set their teeth into the Ukrainians before they left home and more who were there to meet the boat.

In Austria the confidence men developed their techniques. They would hear on their grapevine of someone in a village who was planning to leave. They would call on the would-be emigrant, claiming to be immigration agents – or actually *being* official agents, lining their own pockets – hinting that free land was no longer available in Canada, and trying to sell the emigrants poor or even non-existent lots. Or perhaps they would arrive with money to lend, at heavy interest; or to take money on a promise of obtaining good land, whereupon they would never be seen again. En route to their departure point (usually Hamburg), Ukrainians were deluged with more agents and 'officials', all of whom seemed able to smooth the progress if a little money changed hands. Yet the progress became no smoother. V. J. Kaye, another Ukrainian–Canadian historian, tells of two clever agents who posed as doctors to give expensive 'check-ups', who cheated the travellers in exchanging currency, who overcharged for tickets or even sold non-existent tickets on ships. And they acted with impunity, having neatly bribed the police and local officials.

Their counterparts in Canada had the same success, though Dr Oleskiw tried to set up proper reception committees that could bypass the swindlers. Again worthless land was sold to the newcomers, or money was taken on promises of a 'good thing'. Exorbitant over-charging and profiteering, on any kind of commodity, but especially food and shelter, was the simplest and most common form of swindle. And, when Ukrainians sought work – for a great many turned to manual labour to gather enough money for homesteading, and to send money home – wages invariably seemed to be far lower for them. So they not only remained poor (in the face of Canada's prices), but earned the rancour of the non-Slavic workers, who saw these new hordes as a threat to their pockets and their jobs.

Only the exceptional Ukrainian managed to avoid poverty and suffering in his first year in Canada. Those who home-steaded generally lived at first in dugouts, and broke the land with spades – being unable to afford ploughs or other implements. Nor could they afford draft animals: they walked for supplies, or when they went looking for work as farm labourers or railway workers. Some, it is said, walked barefoot to save on shoes, tying their footwear around their necks. One of the first Manitoban Ukrainians, looking for work at his trade of carpentry, walked 240 miles along the C.P.R. line from the Regina area to Brandon – in four days.

But they were hardy – none hardier – and they survived confidence men, exploitation and plain western hardship. (They even made extra work for themselves, often choosing homesteads – in the park belt – covered with brush and woods that needed clearing, in spite of the millions of acres of open prairie that was available. But then they added to their finances by cutting the trees and selling cordwood to other farmers in winter.) The men worked on the railways, the women grubbed out stumps and cultivated small patches of land. And gradually the patches grew bigger. Less gradually the railways were built: with the frenzy of railway-building in the 1890s (to be described in Chapter 11), it cannot be denied that the Ukrainians, providing the bulk of the railway force, had come in time to finish the job of opening the west.

In the face of the Ukrainians' submissive, backbreaking contribution, the Anglo-Saxon Canadians continued to speak of the 'scum of Europe', and to propagandize against the immigration policy that had turned to backwaters of the old continent to people the backwoods of the new. Xenophobes offered a weak rationalization: the Slavic immigrants would drag down the 'standards' or 'quality' of the western population; they might become a majority and take over the west.

But the Territories' population remained too scattered, and its Anglo–Saxon character still too pronounced, in the 1890s, for these complaints to have any meaning or to be taken seriously by Ottawa. Sifton stuck to his policy: the more 'stalwart peasants' there were breaking ground in the west, the better. Eventually, the Ukrainians' blood and sweat transformed their poverty into reasonable comfort, mellowed by their national customs and songs and foods – and broadened by the Canadian ways which they took up, as well and as quickly as they were able.

So the 'nineties – which displayed very little gaiety on western homesteads of whatever nationality – moved to a close. Clifford Sifton remained in his ministry, and by the close of the century his policy began to bear fruit – assisted by turns of fortune. The smothering depression that had lingered like a fog over North America for the decade, or longer, lifted: the free lands of the U.S.A. reached saturation. And at the same time – to complete the job of opening Canada's doors to the multiplying swarms of immigrants – the western lands were made both more accessible and more agriculturally profitable.

11

Finishing Touches

The completion of the C.P.R.'s transcontinental main line undoubtedly seemed a glorious culminating achievement – in terms of railway building. In terms of settling the west, it was a bare beginning. The scattered homesteaders became very much aware that the C.P.R. provided a narrow band of steel through an extremely wide void. Though strips of settlement grew up along the main line, or fanned out from it in especially fertile areas, vast stretches of good land remained inaccessible except for very hardy, or foolhardy, homesteaders. Then a number of businessmen and politicians saw the point: sow railways and reap settlements. Suddenly Canada went railway-mad.

Of course the C.P.R. had built branch lines – or, in some cases, had allowed small local companies to build the branches and had then bought them out. The notorious monopoly clause, when in force, shackled would-be competitors, except, perhaps, in Manitoba during the 1880s, when the provincial government challenged the monopoly in a series of pointless clashes with Ottawa. Manitoba issued charters for railways south of the C.P.R. main line; Parliament promptly disallowed them; Manitoba just as promptly issued more. The province was trying to make the point that a monopolistic railway harmed the province: it did not expand its branch lines rapidly enough, and without competitors there was a danger from arbitrary freight rates. Ottawa's view was that the C.P.R. needed some time free of competition to establish itself. Of course the prohibitions were Ottawa's prerogative, under the British North America Act; but they inflamed a growing feeling in the west that eastern interest lay in draining off and profiting from western resources, and stopped short of an interest in the west's welfare. It is a feeling that persists, not without justification.

During the same period, Manitoba began construction on a valuable line running north of the C.P.R. and so outside the monopoly clause's precincts. The new line began at Portage la Prairie, and moved northwest, past Lake Manitoba, towards some well-settled areas. Later, under the name of the Manitoba and North-Western, this line will have a part to play in another flare-up of the railway craze.

The C.P.R. first spread its tentacles in the east, to combat its old enemy the Grand Trunk, before concerning itself with too many additional lines in its monopolized western region. Though the eastern branches do not belong in this story, it might be noted that the C.P.R. built at this time the famous 'Short Line', cutting across Maine to the Maritimes, and the 'Soo Line', dipping south of the Great Lakes (the Grand Trunk's stamping-ground) from Sault Ste Marie to Minneapolis St Paul.

Railway activity began in the west, in earnest, about 1890, when an important branch was extended north from Regina, to pass through Saskatoon and end at Prince Albert, opening a new strip of railway lands for farms and town sites. The C.P.R. did not build the line directly, but acquired a lease for it after its completion. In the same way the C.P.R. leased another vital north-south artery, built shortly after, linking Calgary and Edmonton, as well as a line built privately from the C.P.R. main line to the newly opened coal fields of Lethbridge (Alberta) – which presented a valuable opportunity. American railways had been extending feelers towards the interior of British Columbia: to block them, the C.P.R. extended the Lethbridge line westward and pushed it through the Crow's Nest Pass (far to the south of Kicking Horse), where it also provided a useful route to the rich Kootenay region.

While these and lesser branches were progressing, trouble had boiled over regarding the monopoly clause. Manitoba had long wanted a line of its own along the Red River to the border – a line which would be controlled by the province, in opposition to the C.P.R.'s Pembina line. In 1886 Manitoba chartered such a line, and Ottawa passed the ball back with the usual prohibition. But the province responded with a new approach: it would ignore its federal masters and build anyway.

So the Red River Valley line began construction. Soon, however, it foundered financially – at which point (in the C.P.R. view) Manitoba contracted with the devil. It brought in the American railway, the Northern Pacific, another old nemesis of the C.P.R.: the Red River Valley line was to be built by a new joint venture called the Northern Pacific and Manitoba Company. The C.P.R. and Macdonald's Tories pulled out all the legal stops to block the line's progress, but Manitoba stubbornly pushed it ahead. Then the province and the American intruders decided to extend yet another line out of Winnipeg, this time running south of the Assiniboine towards Portage. To reach that town, however, this second anti-monopoly line would need to cross C.P.R. tracks – which would add insult to injury. The C.P.R. set out to stop it.

Van Horne brushed aside suggestions of legal action, injunctions, restraints and so on. Manitoba and the Northern Pacific had ignored court orders before; so the chief of the C.P.R. gave them something they could not ignore. He sent a crowd of men to wait at the planned crossing point, and he had a locomotive derailed at the spot. The rivals came up to the line with a good-sized force of their own, including some special marshals hastily sworn in by the Manitoba government. For several days and nights the two groups prowled on either side of the C.P.R. line, watchful and threatening. One night, the Northern Pacific men found the other side less vigilant and hurriedly set in place the 'diamond' which allows tracks to cross. The next morning the C.P.R. men tore it up again. Yet, astonishingly, the rising tempers never exploded (perhaps the presence of the marshals contributed to the peace). Soon the rival companies agreed to refer the quarrel to the Supreme Court, and the men were called off. The only casualty of the entire drama was a C.P.R. employee who had been punched in the eye.

The litigation that followed, and the publicity that accompanied it, put Ottawa and the C.P.R. in an embarrassing position. Neither wanted to be stigmatized as an iron-heeled monopolist. And besides, there was some justice in the province's anger at being told, as the Manitoba *Free Press* put it, 'that we are not to build a railway with our own money on our own soil'. After all, the monopoly clause had been intended primarily to keep out American railway encroachment. So – without too much reluctance – the C.P.R. gave up its monopoly in 1888, even though the contract had meant it to remain in force for twenty years.

Rails, not monopolies, now had to do the job of blocking American threats to C.P.R. power in the southern areas of the Territories. So in the early 1890s a C.P.R. branch extended out of Moose Jaw, through the embryonic towns of Weyburn and Estevan (Saskatchewan), to a point in North Dakota – from which, along U.S. lines where the C.P.R. obtained running rights, it linked up with Chicago, Duluth, and the Soo Line.

But in this period the focus of railway building shifted northwards. A new crop of railway builders had their eye on the park belt – on the well-off settlements that already existed, and on the immense stretches of fertile land waiting to be filled. It was two young unknowns from Ontario who grasped the opportunity, and who were to weave a railway web throughout the northern prairies. They were William Mackenzie and Donald Mann.

Mann knew railways: he had held sub-contracts for small sections of the C.P.R. Through those connections, he also knew the west's potential for a railway-minded company feeding lines into sparsely settled areas. Mackenzie knew finance: he had been showing, in the east, a rare skill at promoting business enterprises and squeezing money out of other people to back them. The two came together because Manitoba had run into financial trouble over a new line – a sub-branch, as it were, running from the Manitoba and North-Western line towards Lake Winnipegosis. The province gratefully accepted Mann's offer of help; Mann, remembering Mackenzie from a brief association earlier, called the other in. The partnership was formed, in 1895, with a springboard to railway success waiting for them. They took over the flagging Winnipegosis line, raised money, got a guarantee from the province, and proceeded to build. Apparently the settlers in the locality (the Dauphin area), delighted at the prospect of being on a railway, came and pitched in as labourers, for no pay, as if it were one of the community barn-raising or harvesting efforts. And when the line was operational in 1897, the partners reciprocated, giving out free seed grain to the settlers. So the western spirit of communality could even supersede business.

Mackenzie and Mann were gifted with youth, confidence and flair: in the modern jargon, they thought positively and they thought big. But they had subtlety as well. No one suspected their ultimate ambitions when, with Manitoba's blessing, they took over another small line – a valuable branch running from St Boniface southeast to the U.S. border at Lake of the Woods. This line, too, they built in a hurry. And though the construction may have been below main-line standards, it carried trains – in spite of the heavy muskeg that barred the way, and that gained the trains the title of 'Muskeg Special'. Costs were covered by another provincial guarantee, a rich land grant, and the partners' clever innovation of cutting and selling timber from along the right-of-way. Both lines belonging to Mackenzie and Mann began to show profits almost before they first carried trains.

The partners' plans aimed at providing railways not only where they were then needed – as with the Dauphin line – but where they *would be* needed later as the park belt became settled. They were gambling on the agricultural potential of the more northern farmlands. So it followed naturally that in 1898, they should build westwards, from their Dauphin line, towards Prince Albert. (Mann had for some time held a charter for a near-impossibility: a line from Winnipeg to Hudson Bay, through all the Pre-Cambrian horrors of scrub brush, rock, bog and barrens. With some finagling, he switched the charter and the land grants to richer prairie lands, to sponsor the Prince Albert line.)

At this point the partnership acquired its new name, the Canadian Northern. The name implied the objective: as Mann stated, in 1899 they had 300 miles of rail north of Winnipeg, and hoped to push their lines as far as Edmonton. But he added, soothing flutters in C.P.R. or Ottawa bosoms, that 'we have no plans at present for a transcontinental line'.

What plans they did have proved disturbing enough for the existing transcontinental. Mackenzie and Mann extended their 'Muskeg Special' from Lake of the Woods to Port Arthur at the head of Lake Superior – gaining access to the lake steamers which carried freight to Ontario. Almost overnight the Canadian Northern had thus become a major grain-carrying railway for Manitoba farmers. Simultaneously the partners used their preferred position with the provincial government to snatch a cluster of small, new lines in the south of the province before the C.P.R. or the Northern Pacific could engulf them. Manitoba was delighted to see that the C.P.R. had competition – and grew more delighted when in 1901 the Canadian Northern lowered freight rates. It had become the farmers' friend, and Manitoba assured the partners of its continuing support. To the C.P.R., a small thorn had become a major threat.

Talk began that the Canadian Northern would grow into a second transcontinental, but the partners continued noncommittal. Yet their bites now became bigger. They sniffed out charters that had been issued to fly-by-night companies that had failed before a spike was driven, bought up the charters (which often included land and cash grants) and scattered spur lines through the northern park belt. With healthy profits from this expanding web, they thrust out trunk lines east and west. The western line advanced in a frenzied season of track-laying that equalled Van Horne's mighty achievement on the prairies. A Canadian Northern tentacle had already been extended from the Dauphin line to Kamsack (Saskatchewan): suddenly this line became a main line, and stretched north-westwards. From April to December, in 1905 track was laid through Humboldt, through *North* Battleford, all the way to Edmonton – nearly 550 miles, including five major bridges. And in the same year the Canadian Northern proved its strength by wresting a valuable property from the C.P.R.: the north–south line from Regina to Prince Albert, which the C.P.R. had leased, casually, on a year-to-year basis.

With these trophies still freshly gleaming, Mackenzie and Mann seemed destined to be the second transcontinental. Then their headlong progress was arrested. In the east, the Grand Trunk – still smarting from the C.P.R.'s clever penetration of Ontario, Quebec and the Maritimes – put up a stiff fight against the newest interloper, balking, at every turn, the Canadian Northern's attempt to buy or lease lines into the eastern urban centres. And in British Columbia, a furore of political juggling arose over the partners' proposed entry, mainly concerned with the province's financial participation. Mackenzie and Mann were as capable of moving slowly, or waiting patiently, as they were of spectacular speed. But while their patience was being tried, the Grand Trunk moved into the west with *its* transcontinental ambitions.

It will be remembered that in the 1870s the G.T.R. had been a likely contender for the right to build the first Pacific railway, but its desire for a route south of Lake Superior had clashed with Macdonald's all-Canada idea. With extensive contacts in New York and London, and close association with the Liberal party, it had harassed the C.P.R. and Macdonald throughout the railway's construction. Now the Liberals were in power in Ottawa: and it was inevitable that, when Prime Minister Laurier began thinking in terms of another Pacific railway, he should think of the Grand Trunk.

The new scheme's origins can be traced to a desire in the east, especially in Quebec (Laurier's province), to have an all-Canadian route that would be rather more under Ottawa's thumb than the C.P.R. For in Canada railways were (and are) literally arteries, carrying the life-blood: they are indispensable, simply because the population is thinly spread out in a relatively narrow but immensely long east–west band. So railway strikes, even today, can cripple Canada more rapidly and thoroughly than such strikes can in most other countries. So, too, in Laurier's time, it was seen that such power and responsibility could not be left indefinitely in the hands of one private company. Commerce and colonization demanded more railways; Canada needed to retain some authority over them. So the decision was made to approach the G.T.R. It jumped at the chance, for – watching the C.P.R.'s success in the east – it had realized that it would have to go west or go under.

In the negotiations Ottawa and the G.T.R. chose to ignore the fact that the Canadian Northern had already built a sizeable portion of a transcontinental. Mackenzie and Mann had indicated their unwillingness to sell out, and the G.T.R. had no intentions of undertaking a joint operation. So Laurier pushed his plan through Parliament, just as old John A. had done for the C.P.R. years before, steamrollering the opposition down. (Some growlings, however, were heard in his own ranks as well: Clifford Sifton, for one, thought the plan premature.) Nevertheless, Laurier obtained Parliamentary approval and the Grank Trunk Pacific (G.T.P.R.) was born – a strange hybrid creature.

The proposal divided the new railway into two sections. The eastern section would be constructed *by* and *for* the nation. The western section would be built by the G.T.P.R. and owned by it. Upon completion, the eastern trackage would be leased to the G.T.P.R., which would give Canada a continuing hold over it. Also, the G.T.P.R.'s own construction would be over-seen by government inspectors, to ensure that it measured up to specifications. (In practice the G.T.P.R. also oversaw the government construction, for the same reason.)

Construction began at a frenetic rate in 1906–7, which takes it beyond the extent of this narrative. Yet the progress of the second transcontinental is worth following briefly, for a few years. First, then, the engineers took advantage of part of the route laid down by Sandford Fleming for the C.P.R. The prairie line moved northwest from Winnipeg across the central region of the Territories, through Saskatoon (justifying the Temperance Colony's choice of locale), then to Edmonton, aiming at the Yellowhead Pass. Above the Lakes, the original route was again more or less adopted, and the rails ran through the swampy forests below Lake Nipigon but well above Superior. In British Columbia, instead of joining the C.P.R. down the Fraser valley, the G.T.P.R. chose to take its Pacific outlet well to the north, near where the Skeena river empties into the Pacific – and where, by means of a public competition, the terminus received the unappealing name of Prince Rupert.

Actual construction brought all the usual hardships that Van Horne had faced, and a few more. Manitoba, angry that Mackenzie and Mann had been passed over, sulked and proved unco-operative; British Columbia struggled mightily to protect its self-interest in the negotiations over land, the terminus, and other questions. But the provincial attitudes were to some extent provoked, as G. R. Stevens makes plain in his brilliant history of these railways: for it seems that the G.T.P.R. rode roughshod over some provincial sensitivities, especially regarding formal requests for permission to alter routes or town sites, cross highways, and the like.

As for Mackenzie and Mann, they, too, were hurtling to-wards the Pacific by this time, haunted by fears of losing business to the approaching national transcontinental. They also forced their way – finally – into the east, tapping the mineral wealth of the Shield in northern Ontario, constructing a line between Toronto and Ottawa, and reaching Montreal. In British Columbia, a deal with the province was eventually completed, and the Canadian Northern entered the Yellow-head Pass, proceeded along the ankles of the mountains to the valley of the North Thompson river, then to the lower Fraser and finally reached a terminus, called Port Mann, four miles from New Westminster.

As the two new transcontinentals advanced, competition became murderous. One line would alter its route, constructing a loop to dip into some choice part of its rival's path; a furious race for the best route through Yellowhead was barely won by the G.T.P.R., leaving the Canadian Northern the more expensive path. And in the end the two lines were within a stone's throw of each other for more than forty miles.

By 1915 the Canadian Northern had found a way to the sea, and its first through train from Toronto steamed into Vancouver to announce the fact. But the rival had reached the coast first, with a through train into Prince Rupert in 1914. As each consolidated, the lines threw branches across the prairies – the Canadian Northern especially, swollen by land booms and tempted by wholesale immigration. The G.T.P.R. was a trifle more restrained, largely because a new Conservative government had launched an investigation into the finances of its construction, and claimed to have discovered immense (and, by implication, slightly shady) wastage. The uproar contributed in great part to a sudden disenchantment with railways throughout the country. And none too soon: by then, according to Stevens, Canada had some 30,000 miles of track – which meant about one mile for every 250 inhabitants. The U.S.A. could claim only a ratio of one mile for every 400; Britain had a mile for every 2,000.

Clearly the young and impecunious country had dashed off in all directions without counting costs. Now, with the outbreak of war, the earnings of both the new transcontinentals were drastically reduced: wartime inflation sent costs sky-high, and the government had cut freight rates. Both companies had needed a post-construction breathing space to establish themselves firmly, and it had been denied. They both began to totter. Fragments of government aid shored them up, but only postponed ruin.

Yet, as a Royal Commission pointed out, the railways could not be left to collapse – not when Canada needed them, in her war effort, more than ever. So the government considered, and finally accepted, the only solution: nationalization. To shorten the story, the Dominion acquired control of Canadian Northern stock in 1917 and, after a squalid wrangle, took over the Grand Trunk and the G.T.P.R. in 1919. Out of the complex, cluttered mass of trackage and subsidiary possessions, a new and theoretically non-political board of directors created the Canadian National Railways.

Now to jump back into chronological propriety. In the 1890s the railway boom provided the homesteader with more extensive means of getting to his land. Even before then, agricultural progress had begun to provide him with slightly more security once he had reached the land. Most important of all, in those years, was the new strain of wheat that had been produced by a young Scots amateur experimenter in Ontario, David Fife.

Fife had been breeding wheat in search of a high-grade, hard wheat that would mature early enough to overcome the west's short growing season. Finally he achieved a few heads of wheat that fulfilled the qualifications: though a wandering cow almost destroyed his success by eating most of the heads. From the wheat he salvaged, the new strain – named Red Fife – spread itself across the prairies, furthered by government and C.P.R. encouragement, and by the fact that new milling processes had replaced the older methods for which hard wheat had been generally unsuitable. The more rapidly maturing wheat reduced the threat of early frosts on the settled prairie, and allowed settlement to edge farther north.

In the 1890s another experimenter went a step further, producing a new strain (a cross between Red Fife and a similar hard red wheat) which, after some years of tests, went out to farmers under the name of Marquis. All things being equal, Marquis had a still shorter growing season and slightly greater productivity than Red Fife. And the agricultural frontier moved even farther north.[1]

As new wheat opened up more land to more people, new farm machinery came along to make the work easier. Machines were produced to hurl the seed 'broadcast', or to drill it into the soil (to take advantage of subsoil moisture). Machines came along that could reap the wheat, though men still had to

[1] Research continued and continues. Later new breeds, such as Reward or Garnet, grew even faster and yielded more. Then disease, especially rust, became a problem: more modern research has had to concern itself with wheat possessing rapid maturation, high yield *and* built-in resistances.

bind the sheaves – until 1877 when, from an American inventor's nightmares, a machine appeared that could tie knots in twine. Mechanical threshers evolved in a series of monstrous creations, leading to the self-feeding, steam-powered separator, which took in wheat at one end and blew out straw at the other, like some giant herbivorous dinosaur.

With mechanical aids promoting bigger farms and larger crops, the harvest season exploded into an annual pandemonium as hired crews and 'harvest excursions' of transient labour (brought in on special trains) gathered to help bring in the wheat. The work was fearsomely hard and almost without respite, for each day that the ripened crop remained on the fields lowered the odds against its being ruined by frost, rain or snow. The gangs laboured in every second of daylight, laboured on by the light of lanterns, and perhaps went without sleep for days in order to do the work and keep the Rube-Goldberg machinery in repair. Farmers' wives laboured too, serving up an incessant round of enormous meals for the gangs (which normally numbered from about 10 to 25 men). One Saskatchewan lady remembers cooking daily, at dawn, at least six dozen eggs for breakfast for fewer than twenty men; in planning provisions she estimated a loaf of bread a day per man.

The culmination of farm machinery – and the end of the rowdy, myth-making days of harvest gangs – came later in the twentieth century with the invention of the combine, a machine which both reaps and threshes while moving like an immense metal grasshopper around the field. The resemblance is heightened by the fact that, today, most combines are self-propelled. Earlier versions, like all farm machines when they first appeared, had been pulled by tractors. And tractors too went through an evolutionary series, from vast steam-powered behemoths to the neat and powerful motorized vehicles of today.

Along with the labour-saving devices, agricultural progress brought soil-saving techniques, to offset the situation described by a disillusioned homesteader named E. W. Elkington:

> When a farmer has taken every ounce of good out of his land, and for three years has found his crop decreasing, he begins to look about for a purchaser, advertising his property as an improved farm and accordingly raising the price. . . . Not one farmer in fifty ever manures his land . . . not one in ten ever changes his crop. . . .

But of course the new techniques were intended to make more land productive, not merely to protect the land that was in use. And new techniques were necessary if settlers were ever to move, in force, on to the dry open prairie and prosper there. In spite of the fact that the Manitoba Mennonites in the 1870s, and the Bell Farm in the 1880s, had proved the value of letting land lie fallow for a season (to gather moisture and nutrients), summer-fallowing required heavy propagandizing before it was widely adopted. Finally extensive tests run in the 1890s at a government experimental farm at Indian Head (Saskatchewan) allowed the chief experimenter, Angus Mac-Kay, to prove that dirt farmers in the semi-arid southwest could not do without summer fallowing. The message got across one dry year when crops in southern Saskatchewan had come to nothing while MacKay, on fields summer-fallowed the previous year, harvested twenty-three bushels to the acre.

With summer-fallowing came other techniques to defeat the droughts: deep seeding, autumn ploughing, and more. Also, where water supplies permitted it, many farmers took up mixed farming – in which livestock, poultry and their products give the farmer something to fall back on if his crop fails. But even these advances did not always mean that the west's great dangers had been bypassed. Advanced machinery is still useless if, the day before harvesting is to begin, a hailstorm flattens every head, leaf and stem. Summer-fallow and the rest has little effect against several successive years of heavy drought; and a long, hard winter can play havoc with a farmer's stock.

Farming entered very slowly into the southwest region of the Territories: before the new techniques had been established, and before heavy immigration had begun, farmers were content to find land as near as possible to the park belt. The southwest – which had been the greatest of buffalo grazing lands – was taken over instead by ranching.

Cattle came into what is now southern Alberta as early as the 1870s, when Rev. John McDougall imported a few head, and the N.W.M.P. brought a nucleus of a herd to their posts. When the buffalo had finally vanished, and when the Indians – who could never see why they could kill buffalo but not cows – were safely on reserves, the ranching industry expanded mightily. Majestic cattle drives brought herds up from Montana and (using the railway) from the east: one small herd rode a train to Winnipeg and then were driven 800 miles to a ranch west of Calgary, a drive that took from April to autumn. Still others came from the Kamloops area of British Columbia, often called the birthplace of Canadian cattle raising, where ranching had sprung up from a few head of cattle left over from herds that fed the gold rush.

One of the Territories' biggest ranches began in 1881, when M. H. Cochrane bought some 12,000 cattle in Montana and brought them up to land west of Calgary. Unfortunately, in the series of drives that brought the cattle to the ranch, the cowboys seemed bent on breaking a record: they pushed the herds so fast and so carelessly that many hundreds died en route. The remainder had been sufficiently weakened that a harsh winter killed many hundreds more. An even crueller winter, in 1882–3, made huge inroads into Cochrane's fortunes: by the following spring he was left with only 4,000 head.

Winters in the southwest did not always kill cattle, however: the 'Chinook' wind[1] blew fairly reliably, and when it blew the snow melted visibly and exposed the grass. The grass itself was the principal reason why the land was so valuable as ranch property: it was the kind of grass that cured as it stood, without losing any nutritiousness. So if the Chinook exposed it, the cattle could grow fat on it all winter. (One winter, when the Chinook failed, a desperate rancher hired a horse-breeder to drive 500 stout mustangs through the chest-deep snow, breaking the hard crust and scattering the snowdrifts. It is said that the horses themselves were nearly trampled to death by hungry cattle rushing to the grass.) The winter of 1886 is still remembered as the fiercest of all, when the Chinook failed completely, and cattle died in their tens of thousands. Only then, apparently, did the complacent ranchers learn their lesson, and begin cutting that rich grass to make emergency stores of hay.

[1] A velvet-warm westerly wind, which produces startlingly sudden thaws in the depths of winter, and which is one of the few mitigating aspects of the prairie climate. The Indians, understandably, believed it was a magical gift of kindly spirits; the whites, too, developed semi-mythic legends and 'tall tales' about it. One such concerns a farmer who set out one January day driving westwards in a horse-drawn sleigh. He looked up to see the awesome cloud formation called the 'Chinook arch', heralding the approach of the wind. Turning for home, so as not to be stranded, he raced the Chinook for miles over the prairie – with, as the legend says, the sleigh's front runners on hard snow and its back runners on dry grass.

The 1880s were the great days of ranching, when the industry reached its peak, and hundreds of thousands of acres were sold or leased to the cattlemen, or the horse-breeders, or the few scattered sheepmen. They were also the days of the cowboy in the Canadian west. But the Canadian cowboy was even further removed than his American counterpart from the glamorous, violent legends perpetrated by novels and films today. The N.W.M.P. frowned on cowboys (or anyone) even *wearing* guns, let alone shooting them. Many tales are told of a wild group of cowhands, on a cattle drive from Montana to Alberta, being met by a lone red-coated policeman at the border and being ordered to place their guns in their saddle bags and keep them there. In Canada's well-policed west, the cowboy was a working man, quite unmythical. They used to say that if you saw a man wearing a huge hat, heavy spurs, a coloured shirt, and perhaps a holstered gun, you could bet he just got off the train from the east.

Ranching continues to be a prominent feature of Alberta life today, but its extent has considerably diminished from its nineteenth-century heyday. Then the new methods of farming led settlers to look greedily at the empty ranchland, and led squatters to encroach. When immigration took on a new momentum in the 1890s, the government came down on the farmers' side: ranch leases were not renewed, pressure was exerted on cattlemen to sell their lands. So the farmers crowded in, planting their crops and fencing the open range: and the ranchers dwindled. Cochrane himself gave it up in 1904, selling 500,000 acres to the Mormons – at $6.25 an acre, when he had paid $1.00. Canada had decided that the few cattlemen who used the land must be replaced by the many farmers who would fill it.

That decision formed part of the new general policy formulated in Ottawa towards the close of the century, designed to people the west at great speed and at all costs. The policy originated in the resourceful mind of Clifford Sifton, Laurier's Minister of the Interior.

Sifton, a Manitoba lawyer and newspaper proprietor, came to power (when he was thirty-five) as one of the brightest new brooms in the Liberal government, which had won the election of 1896 on the general platform of 'getting Canada going' after years of Tory stagnation. The west had suffered perhaps more than any region from that stagnation. Settlement, especially, had been a disappointment. New arrivals had generally huddled near the railways; while thousands of homesteads had been claimed, thousands more had been cancelled or abandoned. In the economic doldrums of the 1880s and early 1890s it was being said that a Canadian homestead was just a way-station en route to the U.S.A. In 1896, according to Robert England, only about 900 immigrants filed for homesteads, and in the same year 400 homesteaders cancelled their applications and left the country.

Laurier's victory, however, coincided with an upswing in the North American economy, and with the first signs of a shortage of good homestead land in the American west. Clifford Sifton grasped the opportunity. With his typical crisp energy he reorganized immigration policy, to turn the west into a magnet for settlers. He cleaned up the Ministry of the Interior (which he called a department 'of delay . . . of circumlocution'), and set out to improve the situation of settlers already in the west. For example: the railway companies had never hurried to choose the land that they acquired in their grants – for once they had chosen, they would have had to pay taxes on the acreage. So huge blocks of reserved land, in the best areas, stood idle: the railways could not sell it, settlers could not homestead it. Sifton freed these lands in an instant, by abolishing (from then on) the policy of land grants – substituting cash subsidies or guarantees of loans – and forcing the railways to make their selections. Again, Sifton gladdened the farmers' hearts by tidying and centralizing the bureaucratic machinery set up to deal with grievances, complaints and conflicts regarding homesteads. Red tape decreased, official flexibility increased, and a two years' backlog of unsettled problems was cleared up.

With these and other improvements securing his footing, Sifton turned to overhauling or creating machinery for attracting immigration. He increased the number of agents in Britain and Europe; he made arrangements with steamship companies whereby the companies would bring in immigrants (gathering them through advertising campaigns and special offers) and would receive governmental bonuses. Then he turned to the fine art of public relations, of which he was a master. As well as the usual glowing advertisements and pamphlets extolling Canada's virtues, Sifton expanded the use of publicity brochures – much more believable – consisting of descriptions of the country written by actual farmers, addressed to their countrymen. The following sample comes from an Englishman in the Alberta park belt:

> The land is all that can be desired, mostly a rich loam capable of growing anything. . . . Grain can be raised with very little trouble. The average yield for wheat is forty bushels to the acre . . . and, as the expenses are very low, it means a good living. . . . I think that if the farmers of England only knew of the advantages here they would bring their capital and families to this country, and not grind year after year, and have nothing to show for their years of work but debts and semi-poverty.

Sifton's department kept track of visitors and tourists, and made sure that they were well treated and that they took note of Canada's prospects. At the nation's expense he brought groups from various countries to tour the west and report back on its potential for immigrants. He even invaded the U.S.A. with a flood of agents and high-powered publicity – with what results the next chapter will show.

These new methods, and the new air generally in the sunny early days of Laurier's administration, spelled success. The Ukrainian influx, sponsored by the Sifton policy, has already been described: within a few years immigration generally began to keep pace. It was not an overnight transformation of a stream of settlement into a flood, but it was quite rapid enough. In the late 1890s, with railways, agriculture and government all at last improved and eager for new Canadians, the west waited like a bride for the multitudes of immigrants that the new century would bring. It would also bring the final steps in the opening of the west.

12

The New Century

As the world turned into the twentieth century, the Canadian west turned with it, to enter a new era of growth – rapid, bountiful, intoxicating growth which made real all the plans and hopes and expansive visions of its past leaders. Trainloads and wagonloads of immigrants, in their tens of thousands, rolled in to fill the lands which had been waiting so many years. In less than a decade (from 1896 to 1905) the interior was transformed: from a frontier society into a semi-civilized agricultural society. Another generation or more would be needed to dislodge the qualifying prefix 'semi-' (though there are expatriate westerners who will say it has never been dislodged). Nevertheless, the frontier – which had lingered on, in spite of all the high-sounding phrases of 1870 concerning immigration and settlement – finally retreated, into the backwoods of the northwest.

A word about this vague and over-used concept of a frontier. In practice, and in connection with the west, the term refers not to a clear line that is being pushed back steadily and evenly by the advance of settlement, but to an ill-defined *area* – an intermediate or transitional stage between outright untamed wilderness and outright civilization. Within this area the wild ways and the settled ways mingle and jostle uneasily. And always the settled ways multiply and gain full control of more ground, forcing the whole frontier area back, shrinking the wilderness beyond it.

Paul F. Sharp, the American historian, speaks of the 1890s as a time when the American western frontier 'moved north': when western Canada offered a new frontier just at the time that the U.S.A.'s frontier had vanished. The view is misleading. Canada's central prairies did not offer the Americans or anyone else a *frontier* in the 1890s and 1900s – simply because the old wild ways were long gone. They had vanished when Riel died, when the métis scattered, when the Indians resigned themselves to the reservations, when the C.P.R. and its rivals built a network of rails over the land. Instead, the prairies offered the Americans and the others abundant *lebensraum,* expanses of free, fertile and unclaimed farmland, within the bounds of a fully tamed area. The frontier, that region neither wild nor settled, had moved on.

About the turn of the century a true frontier could be found among the lovely northwest landscapes of the Peace River region – a rich enclave of rivers and forests and open parkland, taking in northern portions of both Alberta and British Columbia. The river that gives the region its name is the largest tributary of the Mackenzie, and flows both east and west of the mountains. Its valley contains munificent farmland; and the region also holds a wide plateau, of at least 30,000 square miles, with forests and wide stretches of prairie (of which the widest explains the name of a leading settlement, Grande Prairie). For all its northerliness, the Peace River receives the Chinook winds in winter and – as residents boast – is rarely any colder than Winnipeg, 1,000 miles to the southeast. (But then Winnipeg can be very cold.)

With its woods, plains, parklands and mountains, the Peace River region displays in a small area all the features of the western terrain. It also displays much of the west's history in microcosm. Consider the parallels. Like the entire west, Peace River remained inaccessible for a long time, cut off from Edmonton and other southern parts by 200 or more miles of muskeg and forest, which barred all travel except by water. So the fur traders were the first, and for a long time the only, Peace Riverites. As in British Columbia, gold miners came next, pushing north after Cariboo had petered out. And, as on the prairies, missionaries then struggled in: the frontiersman-priest Father Grouard, who ministered to the north from the 1860s until his death, in 1931, at the age of ninety-one. Or the Anglican Rev. Bompas, who also arrived in the 1860s and used Peace River as a spring-board for his work in the north.

A few of the gold miners who penetrated the area exchanged their pickaxes for other ways of earning a living. They became free traders – wandering the north with packs of trade goods, dealing with Indians, other miners, and anyone else available, and acting as gadflies to the H.B.C. monopoly. Along the way, they bequeathed some remarkable tales to the west: such as that of 'Nigger Dan' Williams, a Negro and an ex-miner, who carried on a feud with H.B.C. for years. Williams claimed 'squatters' rights' on a piece of land which H.B.C. had wanted as a site for a trading post. The feud climaxed when an H.B.C. factor claimed that Williams had shot at him. Williams was arrested, but received only a light sentence, thanks largely to his defence by a crony named Banjo Mike. The H.B.C. man, said Mike, claimed that he and Williams had been within speaking distance when the shot was fired. Therefore the shot could not have been fired by Williams, or the H.B.C. man would not be alive to tell about it, for (as Mike put it) 'Dan Williams at a distance of one hundred yards can take the eye out of a jack-rabbit at every pop'.

Another free trader became perhaps the most famous character in the region: an American from Vermont named 'Twelve-Foot' Davis. His nickname came from an achievement during the Cariboo gold rush. Davis had noted that two extremely rich claims, lying side by side, seemed over-large: upon measuring, he found that a twelve-foot strip between the two was actually unclaimed, for the two claims had extended over their legal limit. He promptly filed on the strip, took thousands out of it, and earned his name.

Davis was one of the vanguard of miners in the north of British Columbia, then turned to trading, bringing in his goods and setting up a string of posts from British Columbia or from Edmonton overland. His trade flourished, because of his fame but also because of his unaffected western generosity. As he put it, in his own epitaph for himself:

I never killed nobody, I never stole from nobody, I never wilfully harmed nobody and I always kept open house for all travellers all my life.

The traders and the missionaries raised a few fields of crops, and several gardens, which proved the soil's fecundity. But agriculture was a long time coming to Peace River: it had to wait, primarily, for the wheat with a shorter growing season. So the region remained wild while homesteaders were streaming into the prairies farther south. Métis, attracted by the wildness, came to the region after 1885 to live as hunters, traders, trappers or off-and-on farmers. Their settlements focused on Lesser Slave Lake and on Grande Prairie. In the 1880s a small N.W.M.P. post was set up, the police as usual serving as an advance guard to clear the way for settlers. Some clearing was necessary: even as late as 1897 the Mounties were having trouble with the Indians, who resented the new incursions of strangers into an area where at the best of times game was scarce and survival difficult. Indeed, the Indians had made outright threats, telling a N.W.M.P. inspector in 1897 that 'we may as well die by the white man's bullets as of starvation'. But the pacifying influence of the Mounties and missionaries prevented an outbreak, and permanently forestalled the danger.

By 1899 more preparations had been made for settlers: the trails from the south had been improved, and most of Peace River's lands had been surveyed. But only a few pioneers – the more restless kind, who disliked the thought of the prairies' being filled and civilized – came north to take advantage of these benefits. They found what A. M. Bezanson, a pioneer in the 1900s, called 'the paradise of the Northwest'. To an American readership, he eulogized:

> Imagine a West with no hostile Indians, no sun-scorched desert of burning sands, no alkaline plains devoid of vegetation . . . but a West of broad prairies and timbered hills, where both water and feed for horses can be found in abundance. . . .

With admirers like Bezanson to publicize it, the Peace River soon drew more homesteaders. At first, though, like their counterparts on the prairies, they stayed close to the low lands of the river valley: on the plateau, frost struck early. And this fear of the open land (mitigated later by Marquis wheat and its offspring) kept the population down: according to J. G. MacGregor, northern Alberta's historian, in 1907 only 240 newcomers lived above the river. Not until 1914, when the Canadian Northern built a spur line across the muskeg from Edmonton, did the area open fully and the population begin to swell.

But, long before the railway, Peace River's frontier tranquillity had been upset by a different kind of invasion from the south. Into the bleak and dangerous north, in the late 1890s, stormed an unbelievable stampede of people, inflamed to near-madness with the smell of gold. They were heading for the Klondike, on the last great gold rush – and it made Cariboo look like a Sunday-school outing. The impact of the Klondikers on Peace River (and on other areas that they passed through on their way to the Yukon Territory) was merely a side-effect: Klondike's beginnings shook the continent, and sent tremors around the world.

Gold had been found and mined in the far north for some years before Klondike: mainly in Alaska, along the 'Panhandle' (the strip of U.S. territory that extends down the Pacific coastline almost to Prince Rupert) and along the Yukon river and its tributaries. But these finds had produced only minor rushes – enough gold-seekers to populate a few shack towns (Forty Mile, Circle City) but not enough to stir a continent. Then prospectors, as is their wont, spread restlessly up and down the various waterways near the river – not only in American-owned Alaska but in the British-owned[1] territory named after the river. And, in Yukon, in 1896, George Carmack found a creek of the river where the gravel was so thick with gold that a shovelful might be worth four dollars. (Prospectors considered a claim valuable if that amount of gravel produced ten cents worth of gold.)

His news spread slowly, restricted to the local miners. But the success of other prospectors, following Carmack's lead, and finding even richer creeks, soon emptied the mining camps of Alaska. Their inhabitants built the first few shacks of the Klondike capital, Dawson City, and spent the winter digging. In the spring of 1897 the citizens of Dawson sent out or took out to civilization their earnings from the winter's work. When the rough and ragged miners, carrying hundreds of thousands of dollars' worth of gold, arrived at the coastal ports (principally Seattle and San Francisco), the gold madness began to spread like a plague. It quickly infected the coast and reached the western states and western Canada, and then the cities of the east. It spread abroad, to Britain and Europe, to Asia and Australia. And, wherever it was carried, it sparked off a lemming-like rush to the Yukon – a suicidal assault on some of the most murderously impassable landscapes in the world.

[1] The fur traders had been there first: H.B.C. had built Fort Selkirk in the Yukon, and Fort Yukon within the bounds of Alaska (then Russian-owned).

Few Klondikers had any conception of the nature of the land they were rushing to; few remained calm enough to find out beforehand, to plan and prepare for the journey. Instead of plans, they had dreams – gold-seekers' mad visions of wealth. Others saw riches to be found in different ways: all along the coast, from San Francisco to Victoria, enterprising boat-owners cashed in on the rush. They dragged out all their vessels, some only half-afloat, throwing up crude partitions to make passenger boats out of freighters, and charging fortunes for fares. All summer and autumn the overloaded boats, clogged with people and animals and baggage, staggered up the coast to their Alaskan landing-places – on the Bering Sea, or in the Gulf of Alaska, or (mostly) at the top of the Panhandle, where the shanty town of Skagway stood as one of the nearest ports to the Yukon goldfields.

There, among the lawless and violent men who ruled the town under the corrupt leadership of J. R. 'Soapy' Smith, the gold-seekers felt the first tendrils of despair begin to interrupt their hysteria. Newcomers with money were tricked, defrauded or simply robbed – and beaten or murdered if they complained. Those without money faced starvation in the face of Skagway's cruel prices and limited supplies. Some turned back; but the gold fever drove most on, as long as they could move.

They fought their way north to the White Pass through the mountains, along a treacherous uphill path called the Dead Horse Trail – because thousands of pack-horses and mules died along it, from the impossibly heavy packs and the frantic pace imposed by the Klondikers. Men, too, collapsed and died, or turned back under the double onslaught of mountains and winter. But, for the survivors, turning back seemed even more fearful than going on. So the stream of agonized men and animals continued up White Pass, over the summit, down to the Yukon river – to wait for the spring break-up of the ice, when they could travel the rest of the way by water. In those winter camps scores of people died, as their provisions ran out, or as disease (above all scurvy) took hold in the midst of their filth and exhaustion and malnutrition.

Those who had started in time reached Dawson before freeze-up. But the 'city' was far from prepared for the arrival of new hordes. By autumn, the limited stocks of food were dangerously reduced, for the small boats on the river could not transport enough to meet the demand. In early winter Dawsonites were hurrying out of the Yukon, away from the spectre of a winter's starvation after the river froze and prevented the importation of more supplies. As they left, the survivors of White Pass were beginning to straggle in. Some joined the panicky exodus; others stayed, to take their chances with famine and disease. They had come to dig for gold, and they did so. Gold was about as abundant as snow in Dawson that winter, and about as valuable: new millionaires, hacking a fortune out of the permafrost, counted themselves lucky if they could buy a plate of half-rotten beans.

Spring brought some alleviation of the hardship, as a few boats puffed up the river, hardly able to haul supplies fast enough for the still increasing throngs of miners. No let-up appeared in the gold-finds; Klondike had not yet reached its peak. No let-up, again, came in the stampede of gold-seekers, who were scattered over the myriad of tortuous routes in Alaska and the Yukon. The onrush by boat continued unabated; and by 1898 a number of trails, entirely overland, had been attempted.

Pierre Berton, in his history of Klondike, states that some 1,500 men ventured north through British Columbia – from the Cariboo region through nearly one thousand miles of black muskeg and fir forest. Only a handful of them got through: many turned back, many more died in the forest, or in the torrential rivers; some, apparently despairing of finding a way out of the dank and tangled woods, killed themselves. Similarly ill-fated parties set out from Edmonton, encouraged by local businessmen who wanted a share of the boom, and who spoke vaguely of 'excellent' northern trails that were open all winter long. In fact, there were no trails at all. Even Indians starved and died in the swampy badlands of the north. Yet hundreds of men set naïvely off into the forest, hoping to ride peacefully all the way to the gold. Almost none of these innocents achieved his goal.

But for them, at least, there was a way-station: the semi-settled country of Peace River. And the Klondike contributed enormously to the opening of the Peace. Men who turned back from the sub-Arctic hardships of the Yukon retreated to the Peace, and found a haven. Men who had made their fortunes in Klondike came to the Peace to settle. And, of course, the region was enriched by the boom times which the swarms of Klondikers produced wherever they gathered or passed.

Klondike did the same service for most of the far west – where no settled centre wholly escaped the effects of the gold madness, or the fantastic economic expansion that accompanied it. As two examples, Berton notes that Vancouver's population nearly doubled during the few years of Klondike, while on the other side of the mountains Edmonton (calling itself the 'back door to the Klondike') saw its population expand from 800 to more than 4,000. But British Columbia as a whole owed an especially large debt to Klondike.

After the completion of the C.P.R. in 1885, the province had found itself on the crest of a wave of good times. By 1887 Vancouver's amazing growth potential had given the city 8,000 inhabitants, who were comforted by such small amenities as extensive graded streets, sewage disposal and two daily newspapers – all occurring in a place which had been, two years before, a virginal stand of giant trees. By then, too, British Columbia's character as an industrial province had become fully apparent. On the Fraser river and other waterways, where the salmon rushed upstream in an annual agony of reproduction, fisheries and canneries proliferated, manned by immigrants from the fishing shores of the Maritimes, Britain and New England. Scandinavians poured in to take part in the booming lumber industry, which battened on the inexhaustible forests and jammed Vancouver's docks with exports. Immigrant miners flocked to dig silver and other metals from the Kootenays, or coal from Nanaimo on the Island. New towns were born and thrived along the railway line, and elsewhere: for one example, a worldwide rush on silver in the 1890s brought more work to the Kootenay miners, and pumped up the village of Nelson into a good-sized and handsome town. Agriculture, too, found places to progress in British Columbia's multifarious territory: above all, the Okanagan valley came to be discovered as the magnificent fruit-growing area which it remains today.

But in 1893 the wave had collapsed, the good times ended. British Columbian industry depended to a large extent on American capital: and depression struck the U.S.A. that year. Investment was cut off. Stagnation, unemployment and misery swept the urban centres of the province. (To add to the misery, the Fraser river rose in flood after a severe winter's snowfall: it washed out the C.P.R. tracks, cutting the coast off from the rest of Canada for over a month; it inundated the farmland of the delta, leaving behind a destructive silt that prevented all seeding that year; and it disrupted the salmon fisheries.) For five years the economic pall hung over the province. Then, as the depression was beginning to lift, in 1897, the news from Klondike exploded throughout North America and dissipated the gloom. Like Seattle and San Francisco, the coastal towns of British Columbia felt the benefit of the stampede: business boomed again as the Klondikers passed through, buying outfits and equipment, and as the mercantile hangers-on, coming to capitalize on the rush, brought new money into the province.

With the new boom times came, again, the old problems: Asians continued to come in to take advantage of the money-making opportunities – in spite of the fact that the $50 head tax[1] on Chinese imposed in 1885 was raised, in 1900, to $100. Annually, many hundreds of Chinese simply paid the tax and entered. In 1903 the tax was raised to $500, and the flow was finally blocked.[2] But before the province could express its relief, a similar problem arose: Japanese began immigrating in force. And the Japanese were not self-effacing labourers, as most of the Chinese had seemed to be, but assertive and competitive. Their presence in the industries of the province awoke new fears of yellow-peril takeover. But the province's attitude upset Ottawa, which (in conjunction with Britain) had just concluded a highly satisfactory trade agreement with Japan.[3] As the province passed discriminatory legislation to ban the Japanese, Ottawa replied, as before, with counter legislation. The routine continued for some years. Then an exceptional influx of Japanese in 1907 – when more than 8,000 arrived – brought the province to the boil. The citizens of Vancouver formed an Asiatic Exclusion League (aimed also at a few hundred Sikhs and Hindus

[1] See p. 212.
[2] The tax remained at that figure until 1923, when the general immigration of Chinese was forbidden entirely by federal legislation.
[3] The Japanese Government had agreed to limit the amount of immigration, by insisting on passports for entrance to Canada and then holding the number of passports at a fixed figure. But the Japanese simply took out passports to Hawaii, on which there was no limit, and went on to B.C. from there.

who had by then found their way into British Columbia) and began lobbying and demonstrating.

In September of that year a League demonstration climaxed in destructive rioting. A series of wild race-hate speeches inflamed the crowd, and transformed it into a mob. Uncontrollable, the rioters streamed into Vancouver's populous Chinatown. The Chinese hid behind locked doors, while the whites stormed up and down the streets, bellowing insults, smashing windows and store fronts (they did over $30,000 worth of damage), pursuing and beating any unfortunate Chinese they came across. Then the mob made the error of trying to repeat their orgy in the Japanese section. As they swept into those streets, expecting more windows to break and more individuals to injure, the Japanese came out to meet them. They had armed themselves with anything that could serve as weapons – bottles, knives, clubs and stones. They formed a compact force and charged the whites. It was a short, sharp battle: within minutes the mob had become a disorganized rabble in headlong retreat.

But the Japanese victory, though a satisfying turn-about, did their cause little good. Under pressure from British Columbia, Canada decided to risk antagonizing Japan – and a diplomatic mission secured Japanese approval of a new plan to enforce a limit on annual immigration, maintaining it at 400. The province relaxed: government discrimination had done the job. The Sikhs and other East Indians (as Canada calls them) were barred by later legislation, which led in 1914 to the appalling scene of a shipload of Sikhs stranded for *eight weeks* in Vancouver harbour, forbidden to land. Eventually they lost a court case against the immigration authorities, and were forced to put to sea.

Though the racialism may taint (in our eyes) British Columbia's advance to prosperity and civilization, it had no such effect on the British Columbians. For them, their province was a wholehearted success. When the advance to the coast of the Canadian Northern and the Grand Trunk Pacific had been completed, that success had been given an extra stimulus and security. The province's potential was clear, and it was visibly equipped to realize it.

Manitoba, too, experienced a resurgence in the late 1890s that was to carry it to expansive heights in the new century.

Previously, the first western province had recovered slowly from the disastrous bursting of the land-speculation bubble during the 1880s – a deflation that was followed by the general continental slump of 1893. But the depression began to dissipate, as has been seen, within four or five years; and the Klondike rush, pouring money into circulation, swept away its last vestiges. Manitoba was injected with new life by the positive effects of the new boom.

Industry began to multiply in the province, bringing wealth especially to the happy citizens of Winnipeg. In the ten years following 1901, the city added more than 100,000 people to its population, and expanded its area to embrace neighbouring towns (such as St Boniface) in the form of those metropolitan appendages called suburbs. In the new era, immigrants continued to search the unoccupied Manitoban lands for suitable homes – and proved that rich land could be found without travelling to the Territories. Settlers occupied the area of Lake Dauphin, where Mackenzie and Mann's railway enterprise would shortly follow: others penetrated farther north, to the beautiful valley of the Swan river. Portage la Prairie shook off the effects of a catastrophic fire (and of the oppressive nearness of the metropolis) and developed into a thriving, self-possessed little city; Brandon gained its unshakeable position as the unofficial capital of western Manitoba. Years would elapse before Manitoba could extend its boundaries northwards – during which time it would challenge and defeat Ontario over the ownership of York Factory, Churchill and the other Hudson's Bay ports. But now, in the first years of the twentieth century, Manitoba had left far behind its character as an insecure clutch of backwoods communities bounded on three sides by wilderness. Like British Columbia, it had achieved its maturity.

The Northwest Territories were fast approaching the same hallowed state. The general mood of expansion, development and success permeated the great lone land: and as the new era progressed, the loneliness and emptiness looked as if they could soon be legends of the past. No drawbacks now remained to hinder the full occupation of the land: the floodgates were open. Sifton's publicity sent out its siren call, and land-hungry immigrants in their thousands swarmed in reply, clogging Canada's ports of entry. The railways were stretching out to transport them; the up-to-date agriculture was waiting to help them prosper. Wheat prices rose in the 1900s, and rain fell: no dry years like those of the '90s marred the impressions of the newcomers. As more homesteaders settled in and thrived, their glowing reports drew others, and settlement snowballed. Settlers spilled out over the dry and treeless southern plains, over land which even five years earlier had been considered worthless, and reaped huge harvests of wheat. The last best west came into its own.

To indicate the fantastic influx of people, two sets of figures: in 1901 the area that became Saskatchewan held about 90,000 people; ten years later, there were more than 490,000. Alberta contained 73,000 in 1901; in 1911, 374,000. As a more specific statistical instance, the city of Edmonton, which had held 4,000 people in 1898, held about 11,000 people seven years later. When J. G. MacGregor's family arrived to homestead in the early 1900s, immigrants were pouring into the city at the rate of 500 a day, and most of the quarter-sections within a forty-mile radius had been taken up. As MacGregor relates in his account of those homesteading days, his father selected land four days away from Edmonton – which turned out to be in the heart of the north woods, many miles from the prairie.

(Apparently in the land booms that each prairie town experienced in its turn, immigrants often chose quarter-sections from maps, sight unseen. But in this way many farmers found themselves owning extremely unlikely properties. One man's quarter-section might be mostly under water; another's might be entirely muskeg and scrub brush; or, as often happened in the foothill country of Alberta, the homestead might be on the side of a steep hill. The last situation is said to have driven one disgruntled farmer to leave the country: as he moved out, a friend asked him if he had improved his land. 'No,' the farmer grumbled, 'but I leaned on it some.')

In these early years of the century, final proof was provided to Canada that its west had been fully opened. *American* farmers began to swell the flood of incoming homesteaders. Sifton had noted earlier that the U.S.A.'s supply of top-quality homestead land was rapidly running out: his high-powered advertising campaign (which included a pamphlet proclaiming western Canada as the last best west) had been perfectly timed. American land values began to skyrocket as the free homesteads dwindled: for latecomers, only poor and/or expensive acreages remained. So the latecomers turned northwards to Canada because, as a Winnipeg newspaper put it, 'there is no other place to go'. Settled American farmers joined the exodus as well, hoping perhaps to find room for expansion, or profits from land speculation, or simply better land. European immigrants who had grown dissatisfied with the U.S.A. sought a fresh start in Canada. The American invasion began in 1898, when about 9,000 crossed the border: and 1911 saw its peak – when 120,000 Americans left home. In all, according to Paul F. Sharp, one and a quarter million people deserted the U.S.A. for the Canadian west.

Some came, admittedly, to take advantage of the country – coming as 'wheat miners', to plant and harvest as large crops as possible and then return home with the proceeds. Others perhaps came with thoughts of resurrecting the days of manifest destiny, using the same techniques of 'peaceful penetration' by which the U.S. had justified its claims to Texas and Oregon. But many arrived in Canada willing to become Canadians for the sake of the land. And they were made welcome, for they gave their adopted home good service. Americans, for example, led the venture on to the open prairie south of Saskatoon, which had been written off as not arable. The experienced dry farmers of the American mid-west knew better, and their successful example set the pace for Canadians. Also, the Americans brought with them quantities of badly needed capital – not only cash, but investments such as machinery or livestock – which injected new strength into the west's economy. Faced with this outflow, the U.S.A. mounted an anti-Canadian publicity campaign to keep its farmers at home, dwelling on the horrors of Canadian winters and the oddities of British rule. Nor can the U.S. be blamed, from its viewpoint, for this attitude – when in 1908 alone, Paul Sharp says, cash and possessions worth more than $50 million crossed over the border.

British immigration as well had felt the effects of the newly magnetic west, and, together with the continuing flow of eastern Canadians, maintained Anglo-Saxon overtones in the prairie population. Britain also at this time provided several famous – or at least widely publicized – passages in the story of the immigration explosion. One of these unique passages grew from the idea, begun in the 1880s,[1] of immigration sponsored by charitable organizations. The idea was utilized by the British children's charity, Dr Barnardo's Homes, established to care for orphaned or deserted boys from among London's poor.

A plan was devised to place boys on farms in settled areas of western Canada, in foster homes, where they could work as labourers and perhaps receive a better start in the land of opportunity than in the crowded back streets of London. Other organizations took up the idea: and soon a steady stream of juveniles, boys and girls, was on its way to Canada. In 1894, according to E. Heaton (in a pamphlet written in 1895) about 2,700 London children were taken into western homes, one-third of them from Barnardo's. They provided a badly needed labour force for many hard-pressed homesteaders, who could not afford adult help at regular wages. Not that the boys were exploited, even when they were not paid the going rate for hired hands. Their employers had first to guarantee that they would be maintained properly, schooled, and treated as members of the family. (Older boys, however, were found jobs as farm labourers and did receive the normal wage.) To ensure against exploitation, Canadian agents for Barnardo's sometimes made spot checks, dropping in suddenly on a homestead and checking on the children's welfare.

The Barnardo Home's concern for the children is indicated by a story of one boy in his early 'teens who found himself cast by his adoptive 'family' in the role of a semi-slave. He was ill fed and poorly clothed, overworked and generally maltreated. Also, he was forbidden to leave the area of the farmhouse – and had he tried to escape he would easily have been caught on the open prairie. So he endured these hardships, for two full years. But during that time he wrote a letter, describing how he had been treated, and addressed it simply to 'The Barnardo Home, London, England'. He carried the letter around with him at all times, hoping to find someone to mail it for him. Eventually he did: a Mountie dropped in at the farm, on other business, and the boy was able secretly to give him the letter. Somehow the crumpled, dirty bit of paper found its way through the postal services. And – to its everlasting credit – the Home responded by sending from London to Saskatchewan

[1] See p. 177.

a special emissary who investigated the conditions on the farm, found that the boy's complaints were not exaggerated, and whisked him away into a more congenial home on a farm elsewhere.

Another unique British contribution to the developing west followed in the footsteps of such colonization enterprises as the Bell Farm or Cannington Manor, but it gained far more notoriety, internationally, than both of those episodes together. The world knew it under the title of the Barr Colony.

In the early days of the new century, in Britain, a Church of England minister named G. E. Lloyd had made the acquaintance of a fellow cleric, Rev. I. M. Barr. They had something in common: Lloyd had spent some time in the Canadian west, had fought with the militia in the Riel Rebellion and had been wounded on Cut Knife Hill. Barr, too, said that he knew the west, that he had farmed there for fifteen years. He then confided in Lloyd that he was planning a large-scale colonization project, and invited Lloyd to go along as chaplain (since he, Barr, intended to return to the west as a farmer, not a preacher). Lloyd agreed, and in the following months did what he could to help Barr's project get going.

Soon, in response to a pamphlet that Barr had circulated, applications began to mount. Lloyd had moments of misgiving when he found that some of the anxious applicants had sent money with their letters – though they had not been asked to – paying in advance for homestead fees, or land purchases, or their travel expenses. Lloyd noted that Barr seemed careless about how he used the money. But, as yet, Lloyd did not remain troubled for long.

He might have done so had he heard the doubts being expressed in Canada about the project. Barr's flamboyant promises – that a site had been chosen, and vast preparations made to equip and provision the colonists – were exaggerations. The Saskatchewan *Herald*, especially, complained about the dangerous lack of arrangements made in advance to receive the arrivals. But these worries were apparently not broadcast sufficiently far.

In the event, exactly 2,684 colonists (according to C. Wetton's history of the episode) boarded the ship for the promised land. And at that point doubts and misgivings gave way to outright mistrust. The ship was found to be a former troop carrier,

263

hastily and crudely converted, and was judged to be able to carry no more than *900* people in safety. Furthermore, Barr had proved very reluctant to spend money: the supplies of food were totally inadequate for the number of passengers. Crammed into their fetid quarters, the colonists' outrage flared. Lloyd tried desperately to calm them, to organize a means of rationing the food, and to recapture some of the optimism that had pervaded the initial departure. He succeeded, to some extent: at least, as one account of the crossing put it (quoted by Wetton),

> it speaks well for British love of law and order that only eleven fights, seven incipient mutinies, three riots and twenty-two violent interviews with Barr occurred during the voyage.

When the ship finally docked at St John, New Brunswick, Barr (whose intentions concerning his own profit were now fully clear) enraged the colonists further by taking possession of the remaining stocks of flour, having bread made from it, and offering it to them for sale. Again Lloyd rose to the occasion, and prevented retribution descending on Barr.

Lloyd's stock was rising as Barr's plummeted; it rose further when a crisis over the train journey arose. Barr managed to disappear just when the last hope collapsed that some planning had preceded the ship's arrival. No concrete arrangements had been made with the railway to convey the colonists westward, nor to convey the enormous mounds of baggage that lay at the docks. Eventually Lloyd reached an agreement with the railway. The colonists would travel in four trains; their baggage would follow on a fifth. (In fact, the railway was to load the baggage on three trains.)

Finally, after a hectic journey, in April 1903 the colonists' trains rolled into the tiny village of Saskatoon. (By now they numbered only about 1,500, since many had despaired of Barr's plans for the Territories, and had left the train in Manitoba to make their own way.) There they were to disembark, collect their baggage, gather the equipment and other pioneer necessities that were waiting for them, and trek across the prairie to the colony's site. Except that the necessities were *not* waiting. The *Herald*'s worries had been fully justified. However, some hope appeared: the merchants of Saskatoon, with estimable foresight, had laid in extra stocks against just such an emergency. And it is said that, in spite of the dire need of the colonists – for farm implements, wagons, oxen or horses and the like – only a few of the merchants raised their prices and profiteered.

Then the group suffered another shock. Trains came and went at the village, but only a minuscule fraction of the baggage arrived. The settlers panicked. At this point Barr returned, which precipitated a hysterical riot among the colonists. But the baggage did not appear. And it never did emerge from whatever limbo the railway had consigned it to.

Having come so far, the settlers had little choice but to push on. And eventually an uneven cavalcade of wagons – groaning with their loads, so much so that the colonists walked most of the way – straggled out on to the prairie. Of course it was still April, an especially cruel month (because unpredictable) in western Canada. The procession was caught by a sudden late squall of snow, enough to mix with the soil into a particularly gluey mud. Wagon after wagon became mired to the tops of its wheels: oxen stopped and refused to budge. The settlers then would have to unload, carry their equipment piece by piece to a dry spot, and return for the oxen and wagon. Some settlers, having slipped entirely off the trail, had to dismantle their wagons and carry the pieces ahead to get out of a mudhole. And of course the delays made dangerous inroads into the provisions, so that once again the colonists went on short rations.

Most of the colonists were true greenhorns. Inexpert hunters, they were balked completely by the scarcity of game in a prairie April; inexpert travellers, they doubled their hardship and delay through ignorance. Many, for instance, knew nothing of tending or driving oxen, or even of the complexities of harness. Tom Rackham, the son of a Barr colonist, writes of one man who left the harness on his oxen throughout the entire journey (some weeks) for fear that, once it was off, he could never put it on again.

In the end – after more horrors of hunger and exhaustion, cold and mud and muskeg, rolling prairie that tipped wagons over, swollen creeks that smashed them in the currents – the cavalcade reached their colony, the promised land. Barr could not have chosen a more isolated site: on the Fourth Meridian, days away from either railway or towns. The colonists could take no more. They had fought through hardship, lack of preparation, outright confidence trickery,[1] in order to reach this bleak and empty prospect. In their distress the colony turned to Rev. Lloyd and asked him to take over the leadership. Lloyd agreed, with the proviso that a committee of colonists assist him, and so Barr was deposed. The originator of the idea – presumably much richer, and apparently unchastened by the chaos of his project – vanished eastwards, and was never heard of again.

Under Lloyd's energetic direction, the colony's spirits picked up immediately. The settlers put up their tents, collected themselves, and went to work. A town site was laid out, and proper buildings begun. Ground was broken for the first crop. And Lloyd proved his leadership by obtaining some security for the colonists: he talked a Battleford bank into backing the settlers with a loan (for by this time most of the colonists had spent whatever capital they had brought). Lloyd argued that if the colony failed it would have a disastrous effect on further British immigration. The bank produced the loan – against the security, as Lloyd said, of 'only my name and my boots'. Lloyd then exerted himself elsewhere: he talked Mackenzie and Mann into altering the route of the Canadian Northern sufficiently to bring it through the colony. Securing their agreement, he promptly bought land that would gain in value as railway land, planning to sell it later and pay off the bank loan with the profit.

Finally, Lloyd sent word back to Britain that the colony, without Barr, was very much alive and anticipating a flourishing future. He also informed Britons that the colony itself should now be known, in terms of postal address, as 'Britannia, N.W.T.' – and that the colonists had done him the honour of naming the town site 'Lloydminster'.

This favourable report cleared the air of some of the rumours that had been circulating through the east, Britain and Europe since the colonists' troublous arrival in Canada. More Britons came out to the colony to homestead, and it seemed as if all

[1] Barr had bought up provisions at Battleford for resale to the colonists at enormous profits – for instance, paying 25 cents a bushel for oats and offering them at $1.50. Similarly, when he finally disappeared from the colony he left a memento: he had sold a box of medical supplies to the colonists for $350 – but the box contained only a cot, a mattress and a pillow.

troubles were over – except the usual pioneer strugglings. For instance, Tom Rackham states that the colony's first crop, which seemed bountiful, was flattened to the ground by a fierce autumn hailstorm. Afterwards, he says, the hail left a fearsome sight: a strip of glittering ice, two *miles* wide, extending over the horizon. But, in the flush of better times under Rev. (later Bishop) Lloyd, the colonists recovered even from this setback, and proceeded on towards prosperity.

The whole of the Northwest Territories, with the geometrically multiplying onrush of settlement, proceeded along the same path. (Indeed, the Barr colony might not have survived had not the isolation of its site ended shortly after its arrival.) And, as more thousands of newcomers put more thousands of acres under the plough, an element of self-awareness crept into the minds of the Territories' inhabitants. They began to look past the confines of their own quarter-sections, and to realize that they were citizens of a separable region which – for all its youth and rawness – must shortly come to terms with the civilized world outside.

This regional consciousness led to a series of movements towards self-assertion. The first, naturally, concerned agriculture, the Territories' only livelihood.

It will be remembered from Chapter 9 that, in the days of the pre-Riel agitation, the farmers banded themselves together into the Manitoba and Northwest Farmers' Union. They protested that

> . . . the prices we obtain are not sufficient to cover the cost of production, and . . . that notwithstanding all our labour and outlay we can barely subsist.

Their complaints had been aimed at the C.P.R., for its 'excessive charges' in the days of the monopoly clause, and Ottawa, for the 'oppressive' tariffs it had imposed.

As a forum for protest, the Farmers' Union provided a base and a precedent for similar movements. One such began in 1891, modelled on an Ontario group called the 'Patrons of Industry'. It had trade union intentions:

> . . . to protect both farmer and employee against the overpowering influence of the financial and commercial classes. . . .

267

Like the Farmers' Union, it demanded the local right to build grain storage facilities, the end of duty on farm machinery, and the placement of farmers on the federal board which fixed the standards of grain. It achieved this last goal, by some intensive lobbying – but when it sought to enter politics directly, placing candidates in an election, it collapsed in a spate of internecine wrangling.

For some years the farmers were left without a defender, at a time when one was badly needed. In the 1890s the storage, shipment and sale of farm produce seemed designed to benefit the railways and the eastern dealers – never the farmers. As regards storage, for instance: because the C.P.R. could not, at first, provide facilities at every station along the line, farmers often loaded directly from their wagons on to the freight cars. Or, sometimes, they hauled their grain to privately owned storage facilities – where they might sell to the owner, or simply store the grain and make arrangements with a Winnipeg grain dealer. It was, undeniably, a slow and wasteful method, whether the wheat was loaded on to the cars from wagons or from bins in a storage warehouse. The railway preferred elevators – those tall wooden, slope-shouldered towers that loom over the prairies as man-made landmarks – which loaded the grain swiftly by simple gravitation.

Elevators were scattered fairly widely in the west by the mid-1890s. But only a small handful of companies owned the majority of the elevators. (A few had been built by small groups of farmers, co-operatively owned; but they could not compete.) Soon the elevator owners became the dominant buyers of the farmers' wheat, the middlemen. And then the C.P.R. dropped a bombshell in 1897, with an order that no more wheat would be loaded *except* from elevators. The farmers protested – and the protests grew louder as suspicions rose concerning price-fixing between the elevator companies, and fraudulent practice regarding wheat grades and weights.

In 1899 a Royal Commission investigated, and reported:

. . . the elevator owners have had it in their power to depress prices below what in our opinion farmers should realize for their grain.

The agitation resulted in the Manitoba Grain Act of 1900 (which applied as well to the Territories), providing inspectors, allowing farmers to oversee the weighing of wheat, and restoring the right to load directly on to railway cars. H. S. Patton, the economic historian, calls the Act the Magna Carta of the western farmers. Even so, the farmers still needed protection, as the next years proved.

The good growing years (and the abundance of growers) produced bumper crops in the early 1900s – and the existing facilities were not able to handle them. Elevators and warehouses were jammed with wheat; the railways were frantic with the strain on their limited quantities of rolling stock. The danger grew that winter's onset would destroy the vast quantities of harvested grain which had not by then been stored or shipped. In the face of the danger, the farmers closed their ranks. In 1902 they formed the Territorial Grain Growers' Association, to 'press persistently for an improvement in marketing conditions'. Pressure had its effect. Ottawa amended the Grain Act to include provisions that demanded equitable distribution of storage facilities and of greater numbers of freight cars. (The C.P.R. challenged the amendments by ignoring them, but in 1902 a farmer took the railway to court and won a test case.)

After 1905 the Association divided into separate provincial organizations. Later still (past the range of this book, but worth looking at briefly) the Associations entered the commercial field, setting up their own co-operative elevator companies. And eventually, well into the twentieth century, the farmers' co-operatives spawned their own sales organizations. The original of these, the Grain Growers' Grain Company, had been launched on a small scale in 1906, and had sought to sell its members' wheat on the great speculative clearing house of the Grain Exchange. But the established grain dealers of Winnipeg and the east (who were frequently accused of being a 'combine' and a 'conspiracy') blocked its path.

After the First World War, Ottawa sought to get agriculture on its feet again by setting up a Wheat Board to regulate prices at which wheat would be sold for domestic consumption or export. But the Board was only a temporary structure: when it disbanded the prices fell. Farmers demanded the restoration of the Board: Ottawa, always more anxious to please the east (where the votes and the funds were), refused. So the farmers went about improving matters for themselves. By then the co-operative elevator companies had formed a federation – the United Grain Growers – and this body developed a plan for a voluntary marketing *pool*. It would not compete on the Exchange, however: it was intended to circumvent the speculative open market with a farmer-controlled collective marketing system.

The campaign progressed, and semi-experimental provincial pools were set up in 1924. They did so well, thanks to the solidarity of the members, that they were able to amalgamate into the Canadian Co-operative Wheat Producers Ltd – which was naturally called the Wheat Pool. Soon the Pool and the co-operative elevator companies found it to their interests to join forces, and the prairie provinces finally became mastesr of their own productivity.

Earlier, after an extensive struggle, they had also become masters in their own political houses.

The Territories' first government arose from the Manitoba Act of 1870: the new province's Lieutenant-Governor also ruled (on behalf of Ottawa) the unsettled areas. By 1875 Ottawa saw fit to pass the Northwest Territories Act, establishing a separate Lieutenant-Governorship for the Territories, in the person of David Laird. He was the sole legislative and administrative power; though he had an advisory council of three, appointed by him, it was only a consultative body. (Laird's decisions, of course, could be overruled by the federal Parliament.)

A later amendment to the Act of 1875 allowed for *elected* members of council: as soon as any area of 1,000 square miles held 1,000 white male British subjects, elections were to be held for a councillor. The plan anticipated a gradual evolution of an elected Legislative Assembly, as the Territories were settled. It anticipated no further advance: certainly not any takeover of executive power by the settlers' elected representatives. The Lieutenant-Governor would still be in control (like any colonial governor), and responsible only to Ottawa.

The 1880s brought far-reaching changes to Territorial politics as to every other aspect of life. For one thing, the Territories were divided (for postal and administrative manageability) into four districts: Assiniboia, Saskatchewan, Alberta and

Athabasca.[1] For another thing, the influx of homesteaders and the growing towns along the C.P.R. main line led to the birth of a movement towards responsible government in the Territories – sponsored by a growing resentment of their status as titular colonies of Ottawa. Newspapers sprang up to give voice to the movement; more elected councillors made the people's feelings clear to the Governor.

But Edgar Dewdney had now taken over the gubernatorial seat, in the new capital of Regina, and his response was frustrating. Ottawa believed any adoption of executive power by Territorial representatives would be premature: Dewdney, wholly in John A. Macdonald's pocket, agreed. So a political unrest built up, among the people and the elected members, adding to the bitterness spreading throughout the west. Political strife was submerged in the general fury of the 1885 rebellion; but afterwards, as Ottawa recovered from the shock, it was more prone to listen.

So in 1886 (after a delegation had travelled east to argue the Territories' case) the districts acquired federal representation – Members of Parliament in Ottawa. But in spite of this sop, the Territories (echoing the Prince Albert *Times'* opinion of the advisory council as a 'wretched farce') continued to demand their long-overdue Assembly. By 1888 the Dominion gave way, and a new Act created a Territorial Legislature.

The citizenry then found that they had achieved nothing. The Assembly, now meeting separately from the Governor, still had no real powers: it was a debating society, where resolutions might be discussed, but where any legislation still had to pass the scrutiny of the Governor and of Ottawa. The Governor retained an advisory council, appointed from Assembly members, but it had no executive powers.

In the same year Dewdney's term ended, and Joseph Royal – a Québecois who had founded the French newspaper *Le Métis* in Manitoba[2] – became Lieutenant-Governor. Royal personally favoured the movement towards responsible government; he nevertheless found himself forced to do his (Ottawa-directed)

[1] To describe them broadly: Assiniboia occupied the south of the present province of Saskatchewan; the district of Saskatchewan lay to the north. The district of Alberta was the southernmost of the remaining two; Athabasca stretched across the north.

[2] See p. 90.

duty, and so to attract the wrath of a now highly-articulate reform group in the Assembly. Within a year the crisis broke over him. His advisory council – dominated by the reform leader F. W. G. Haultain – resigned, complaining that 'our most important powers are granted to us only in the form of concessions'. Haultain took charge of full-scale obstructionism and harassment – mostly directed at poor Royal – to force Ottawa's consideration of the movement's wishes.

Finally, after Haultain's tactics split the Assembly and balked the accomplishment of any work, Ottawa once more gave way. A few general powers were delegated to the Assembly – for instance, regulating the sale of liquor – but, as well, the Assembly had gained some control over the Territorial expenditure of public funds, including the federal subsidy. The Governor's decision regarding expenditure had now to be taken on the advice of the Assembly.

Haultain seized his opportunity. Cunningly, he caused the Assembly to appoint an Executive *Committee* – which was rather more broadly defined than a mere finance committee. The Committee, appointed by the Assembly, was of course not entirely legal: for it intended to take over executive powers. (An official Executive *Council* would have had to be appointed by the Governor, with Ottawa's approval.) But Royal, preferring to avoid a complete breakdown of his administration, allowed it to remain. Ottawa followed his lead. From then Haultain and Royal jockeyed for position, each trying to control specific executive powers – especially the purse strings.

The conflict still continued when in 1893 Royal gave way to another new governor, an ex-mayor of Ottawa named C. H. Mackintosh, than whom few people were more ignorant of western matters. Against such opposition the fury of Haultain and the radical assemblymen gained mightily in strength. Finally – to shorten the story somewhat – the stagnant federal government of the Tories was replaced in 1896 by the shiny new government of the Laurier Liberals. In the new era, the Territories gained hope. 'The time had come,' they proclaimed, 'when the Dominion Parliament must deal with the Territories in a more liberal spirit.' They had used the correct catch-word. Clifford Sifton took up their cause, presented and fought for a Bill in Parliament, and won his victory. The Bill became law: it permitted the formation in the Territories of a *true* Executive

Council, appointed by the Lieutenant-Governor, controlling administrative matters. Deservedly, the first chairman of this newly achieved representative government was Haultain.

So Ottawa lost direct control over its western colony. But the final steps towards full autonomy within the Confederation remained to be taken. The Territories had previously been indifferent to the prospect of becoming a province, or provinces. For one thing, the people would have had to pay more taxes. For another, the comfortable expropriations of federal money would be reduced, and the provinces would have to make their own way. So, for some time, they remained content with their new-found responsible government, and demanded no further political progress.

But Haultain, now in fact the Premier of the Territories, refused to rest content with half-measures. The Territories still could not (for instance) charter their own badly needed railways; nor could they control their own resources. Above all, they grew financially troubled by the pressure on the public funds of the huge settler influx. 'Our limitations,' Haultain complained, 'preclude our doing for ourselves the things that ought to be done, and, on the other hand, Parliament makes no effort to assist us.' Parliament, in fact, had expected the Territories to be satisfied. Instead, it was faced with a Haultain-inspired clamour for full provincial status.

In the early 1900s the new agitation gathered momentum. But it ran into the brick wall of Ottawa complacency. Haultain visited the east and presented his proposals, in 1901, to Laurier. His pressure was backed by the Territorial M.P.s, and by Clifford Sifton. But Laurier hedged. Almost a year passed before the answer came: provincehood would have to wait until the Territories contained more people, and until its legislators had decided how *many* provinces should come into existence.

The latter question had produced a wide argument in the west. A few Albertans (mostly in Calgary) wanted to split their district and become a province whether or not the rest of the Territories attained provincehood. Others felt that the Territories should become two provinces, one in the north and the other in the south. Still others felt, with Haultain, that they should become one giant province. And there was a faction (finding a home in Prince Albert) which plumped for three provinces: north, southeast, and southwest.

In 1903, after months of hectic exchanges, Ottawa tried to placate the Territories with an increase in the annual cash grant. And, though Haultain would not be quietened, Ottawa refused to budge an inch further. Laurier was facing a general election the following year, and had no intention of making any rash moves that might alienate voters. Above all, he feared stirring up the old demon of the 'separate schools' question. His fears, as will be seen shortly, were justified.

But nevertheless Laurier had apparently come to the conclusion that the demands for provincial autonomy could no longer be postponed. After he had decisively won the election of 1904, he proclaimed (by means of the Speech from the Throne in the new session of Parliament) that the 'rapid growth in the population' of the Territories 'justifies the wisdom of conferring on these Territories provincial autonomy'. The Opposition sardonically expressed their pleasure that Laurier had come suddenly to see the 'wisdom' of a course he had rejected less than two years earlier. But in the west, pleasure was genuine. After a series of conferences in 1905, Laurier personally presented a bill to create two provinces, Saskatchewan and Alberta, out of the Northwest Territories.

Then, as the bill's other provisions were made public, the Dominion was rocked by a mighty storm. Laurier (true to his French-Catholic origins) had stipulated that the provinces must provide for the establishment of separate denominational schools.

The problem of separate schools is too complex to be dealt with extensively here. It may be enough to say that the British North America Act of 1867, which gave provinces control over education, also stated that the provinces must not 'prejudicially affect' the rights of denominational schools to exist. Obviously, the clause in the 1867 Act grew from Quebec's anxiety to retain its language, religion, and religious instruction in education. Ontario Protestants, however, resented this intrusion into provincial rights, and fought it wherever possible. (It had, in the 1890s, been fought in Manitoba – by Clifford Sifton.) It had always awakened the flaming racial and religious hatreds that unceasingly threatened (and still threaten) the bonds of Confederation. Now Laurier had inflamed that hatred again.

The conflict was continent-wide. The English-speaking

population complained, in the words of a Montreal (English-language) newspaper, that '. . . the state . . . should not itself furnish sectional education at the public expense'. The French Catholics pointed to the British North America Act as the existing law. Laurier remained adamant – though Haultain raged, and Clifford Sifton threw up his career and resigned from the cabinet in protest.

Finally, however, the crisis ran out of steam, and the public grew bored with the furore. Laurier made a slight amendment, almost a formality, that permitted some of his opponents to give up a battle they had grown weary of. Meanwhile, the separate schools question had nearly drowned a more vital problem: Laurier's bill had provided for the Dominion Government's keeping control of all public (unoccupied) lands in the new provinces. Haultain objected strenuously to this passage as he had to the educational provision, but with as little effect. (In fact the public lands remained under Dominion control until 1930.) Finally the Territories resigned themselves and accepted the bill. By this time they were unable to work up much interest even in the dual-province idea – though Lloydminster was startled when the Alberta–Saskatchewan border, along the Fourth Meridian, sliced through the heart of the town site. And Edmonton was delighted at becoming a capital, in the face of Calgary's ambitions.

With the prelude, then, of conflict, recrimination and factional interest, the bill became law, which transformed the Northwest Territories into fully-fledged provinces. In September 1905 Saskatchewan and Alberta were formally inaugurated in their separate capital cities.

This ceremonial occasion provides a climax and a conclusion to one process – the opening of the west – and a beginning to another, which may be called the developing or utilizing of the west. In the 1900s the emptiness was occupied; but another generation was needed to see it filled. During the ensuing years, when the First World War and its aftermath brought the twentieth century into the backwoods, immigrant farmers in their hundreds of thousands descended on the remaining homestead lands, claimed them, fenced them, cropped them and cultivated them. Shanty towns grew into modern cities, and gathered the amenities of civilization to themselves.

Railways and highways crisscrossed the land, and the term 'pioneer' – still applicable to newcomers in 1914 – was relegated to history.

So, indeed, was all of the old west, as the new west hurried to catch up with the rest of the world. Today the fur trade remains, even thrives, but as an enterprise entirely of the far north. Today the Indians, for the most part, sit in their reservations, second-class citizens on second-rate land. Some resist their position, such as the Indian horse-breeders in Alberta and B.C.; the others live how they can, resigned, poor, depressed. The métis, too, find little room for themselves in today's west, and eke out their living on the fringes of society. A rare few have succeeded in breaking down the barriers against assimilation; a great many live (often in the northern forests) in a half-world between old and new, earning their way as trappers, hunters and tourist guides. Generally, these leftovers from the nineteenth-century wilderness take their places along with the true museum-pieces: the Red River carts, the early C.P.R. locomotives, the old farming and mining implements. Canadians of my generation tend to view these as relics of a long-dead past – forgetting that they were a normal part of life in their grandfathers' or even fathers' time, the time when the west was being opened.

Canada (as wiser Canadians than I have often said) has always been too future-oriented to spend much time contemplating her history. As the oldest emergent nation of the century, she has grown up far too rapidly, has been far too anxious to put her primitive beginnings behind her and prove herself mature. For this reason, perhaps, her beginnings are seldom properly appreciated, in that they have never been translated into the near-mythology of 'living' history, the true basis of viable national traditions. This book may serve as a reminder that Canada is yet young, but that in her brief lifetime a great many remarkable, dramatic and even sometimes admirable events have taken place, the memory of which is well worth keeping alive.

Selected Bibliography

The following list is offered as suggestions for further reading, not as a complete bibliography of materials consulted for this history. For reasons of space, many titles of only limited value have not been included; nor have magazine articles, newspaper reports, and most pamphlets. But many of the books listed below will be found to contain valuable and extensive bibliographical material, as will many historical periodicals, especially *Canadian Historical Review, Saskatchewan History, Historical and Scientific Society of Manitoba Transactions, Alberta Historical Review,* and *British Columbia Historical Quarterly.* And finally, for an abundant store of further reading on the west, the reader should consult Bruce B. Peel's *Bibliography of the Prairie Provinces* (Toronto, 1956).

T. Adney, *The Klondike Stampede of 1897–98*; New York, 1900.

H. F. Angus, *et. al., British Columbia and the United States*; Toronto, New Haven, 1942.

H. H. Bancroft, *History of the Pacific States of North America*; vol. xxvii, 'British Columbia 1792–1887'; San Francisco, 1887.

Alexander Begg, *The Creation of Manitoba*; Toronto, 1871.

—— *Ten Years in Winnipeg*; Winnipeg, 1879.

—— *History of the North-West*; Toronto, 1894–5.

Alexander Begg, C.C., *History of British Columbia*; Toronto, 1894.

G. L. Berry, *The Whoop-Up Trail*; Edmonton, 1953.

Pierre Berton, *Klondike*; Toronto, 1958.

A. M. Bezanson, *Sodbusters Invade the Peace*; New York, 1954.

John Blue, *Alberta Past and Present*; Chicago, 1924.

T. C. B. Boon, *The Anglican Church from the Bay to the Rockies*; Toronto, 1962.

G. E. Bowes, ed., *Peace River Chronicles*; Vancouver, 1963.

G. E. Britnell, *The Wheat Economy*; Toronto, 1939.

George Bryce, *Manitoba: Its Infancy, Growth, and Present Condition*; London, 1882.

—— *The Remarkable History of the Hudson's Bay Company*; Toronto, 1900.

—— *A History of Manitoba*; Toronto, 1906.

—— *The Romantic Settlement of Lord Selkirk's Colonists*; Toronto, 1909.

L. J. Burpee, *Sandford Fleming. Empire Builder*; London, 1915.

W. F. Butler, *The Great Lone Land*; London, 1872.

M. W. Campbell, *The Saskatchewan*; New York, 1950.

—— *The North West Company*; Toronto, 1957.

J. M. S. Careless, *Brown of the Globe*; Toronto, 1959–63.

A. A. Chiel, *The Jews in Manitoba*; Toronto, 1961.

D. G. Creighton, *Road to Confederation*; Toronto, 1964.

—— *John A. Macdonald*; Toronto, 1956.

J. W. Dafoe, *Clifford Sifton*; Toronto, 1931.

G. C. Davidson, *The North-West Company*; Berkeley, 1918.

W. M. Davidson, *Louis Riel*; Calgary, 1955.

C. A. Dawson, *The Settlement of the Peace River Country*; vol. vi of *Canadian Frontiers of Settlement*; Toronto, 1934.

—— *Group Settlement: Ethnic Communities in Western Canada*; vol. vii of *Canadian Frontiers of Settlement*, Toronto, 1936.

C. A. Dawson and E. R. Younge, *Pioneering in the Prairie Provinces*; vol. viii of *Canadian Frontiers of Settlement*; Toronto, 1940.

E. G. Drake, *Regina*; Regina, 1955.

W. E. Edmonds, *Edmonton Past and Present*; Edmonton, 1943.

E. W. Elkington, *Canada, The Land of Hope*; London, 1910.

Robert England, *The Colonization of Western Canada*; London, 1936.

J. C. Ewers, *The Blackfeet*; Norman, Oklahoma, 1958.

Epitome of Parliamentary Documents in connection with the North-West Rebellion, 1885; Ottawa, 1886.

G. A. Fast, *To Find the Daily Bread*; Saskatoon, 1954.

E. Fawcett, *Some Reminiscences of Old Victoria*; Toronto, 1912.

R. C. Fetherstonhaugh, *The Royal Canadian Mounted Police*; New York, 1938.

E. K. Francis, *In Search of Utopia*; Altona, Manitoba, 1955.

J. S. Galbraith, *The Hudson's Bay Company as an Imperial Factor, 1821–69*; Berkeley, 1957.

J. M. Gibbon, *Steel of Empire*; New York, 1935.

—— *Canadian Mosaic*; Toronto, 1938.

Heather Gilbert, *Awakening Continent: The Life of Lord Mount Stephen*; Toronto, 1965.

Marcel Giraud, *Le métis canadien*; Paris, 1945.

G. P. de T. Glazebrook, *A History of Transportation in Canada*; Toronto, 1938.

A. C. Gluek, Jr., *Minnesota and the Manifest Destiny of the Canadian Northwest*; Toronto, 1965.

G. M. Grant, *Ocean to Ocean*; London, 1873.

J. M. Gray, *Lord Selkirk of Red River*; Toronto, 1963.

L. E. Gruchy, *The Doukhobors in Canada*; Toronto, n.d.

M. L. Hansen and J. B. Brebner, *The Mingling of the Canadian and American Peoples*; New Haven, 1940.

J. J. Hargrave, *Red River*; Montreal, 1871.

J. Hawkes, *Saskatchewan and its People*; Chicago, Regina, 1924.

J. B. Hedges, *Building the Canadian West*; New York, 1939.

J. D. Higinbotham, *When the West Was Young*; Toronto, 1933.

R. B. Hill, *Manitoba*; Toronto, 1890.

C. Hoffer and F. H. Kahan, *Land of Hope*; Saskatoon, 1960.

J. W. Horan, *West Nor'West*; Edmonton, 1945.

F. W. Howay, *British Columbia, The Making of a Province*; Toronto, 1928.

Katherine Hughes, *Father Lacombe*; Toronto, 1911.

H. A. Innis, *A History of the Canadian Pacific Railway*; Toronto, London, 1923.

—— *The Fur Trade in Canada*; Toronto, 1956.

Diamond Jenness, *The Indians of Canada*; Ottawa, 1958.

Martin Kavanagh, *The Assiniboine Basin*; Winnipeg, 1946.

V. J. Kaye, *Early Ukrainian Settlement in Canada*; Toronto, 1964.

J. Kosa, *Hungarians in Canada*; Toronto, 1957.

A. C. Laut, *The Cariboo Trail*; Toronto, 1916.

W. L. Lindal, *The Saskatchewan Icelanders*; Winnipeg, 1955.

C. C. Lingard, *Territorial Government in Canada*; Toronto, 1946.

A. R. M. Lower, *Colony to Nation, a History of Canada*; Toronto, 1964.

Vera Lysenko, *Men in Sheepskin Coats*; Toronto, 1947.

P. McAra, *Sixty-Two Years on the Saskatchewan Prairies*; Regina, 1945.

R. G. MacBeth, *The Selkirk Settlers in Real Life*; Toronto, 1897.

—— *The Making of the Canadian West*; Toronto, 1898.

J. H. McCormick, *Lloydminster*; London, 1924.

John McDougall, *George Millward McDougall*; Toronto, 1888.
—— *On Western Trails in the Early Seventies*; Toronto, 1911.
Grant MacEwan, *Between the Red and the Rockies*; Toronto, 1952.
M. Macfie, *Vancouver Island and British Columbia*; London, 1865.
J. G. MacGregor, *The Land of Twelve-Foot Davis*; Edmonton, 1952.
—— *North-West of 16*; London, 1959.
C. M. MacInnes, *In the Shadow of the Rockies*; London, 1930.
Edgar McInnis, *Canada: A Political and Social History*; New York, Toronto, 1947.
Douglas MacKay, *The Honourable Company*; Indianapolis, 1937.
Hugh McKellar, *Presbyterian Pioneer Missionaries*; Toronto 1924.
B. A. McKelvie, *The Early History of British Columbia*; London, Toronto, 1926.
W. A. Mackintosh, *Agricultural Co-operation in Western Canada*; Toronto, 1924.
—— *Prairie Settlement: The Geographical Setting*; vol. 1 of *Canadian Frontiers of Settlement*; Toronto, 1934.
John Maclean, *McDougall of Alberta*; Toronto, 1927.
M. McNaughton, *Overland to Cariboo*; Toronto, 1896.
John Macoun, *Manitoba and the Great North-West*; Guelph, Ontario, 1882.
A. O. MacRae, *History of Alberta*; Calgary, 1912.
Chester Martin, *Lord Selkirk's Work in Canada*; Oxford, 1916.
J. H. Metcalfe, *Tread of the Pioneers*; Toronto, 1932.
W. F. Milton and W. B. Cheadle, *North-West Passage by Land*; London, 1888.
A. G. Morice, *History of the Northern Interior of British Columbia*; Toronto, 1904.
—— *History of the Catholic Church in Western Canada*; Toronto, 1910.
Alexander Morris, *The Treaties of Canada with the Indians of Manitoba and the Northwest*; Toronto, 1880.
A. S. Morton and Chester Martin, *History of Prairie Settlement and Dominion Lands Policy*; vol. ii of *Canadian Frontiers of Settlement*; Toronto, 1938.
—— *A History of the Canadian West to 1870–71*; London, New York, Toronto, 1939.
W. L. Morton, ed., *Alexander Begg's Red River Journal*; Toronto, 1956.
—— *The West and Confederation*; Ottawa, 1958.
—— *Manitoba, a History*; Toronto, 1961.
—— *Manitoba, the Birth of a Province*; Altona, Manitoba, 1965.

R. W. Murchie, *Agricultural Progress on the Prairie Frontier*; vol. v of *Canadian Frontiers of Settlement*; Toronto, 1936.

G. H. Needler, *Louis Riel*; Toronto, 1957.

J. E. Nix, *Mission among the Buffalo*; Toronto, 1960.

M. A. Ormsby, *British Columbia, a History*; Vancouver, 1958.

E. B. Osler, *The Man Who Had To Hang*; Toronto, 1961.

H. S. Patton, *Grain Growers' Co-operation in Western Canada*; Harvard, 1928.

B. B. Peel and E. Knowles, *The Saskatoon Story*; Saskatoon, 1955.

J. D. Pemberton, *Facts and Figures Relating to Vancouver Island and British Columbia*; London, 1860.

W. C. Pollard, *Pioneering in the Prairie West*; Toronto, 1926.

Joseph Pope, ed., *Confederation Documents*; Toronto, 1895.

W. T. R. Preston, *The Life and Times of Lord Strathcona*; London, 1914.

J. P. Pritchett, *The Red River Valley 1811–1849*; New Haven, Toronto, 1942.

The Queen vs. Louis Riel, Report of the Trial at Regina; Ottawa, 1886.

E. E. Rich, *The History of the Hudson's Bay Company 1670–1870*; London, 1958.

J. H. Riddell, *Methodism in the Middle West*; Toronto, 1946.

Morley Roberts, *The Western Avernus*; London, 1896.

Alexander Ross, *The Red River Settlement*; London, 1856.

R. C. Russell, *The Carlton Trail*; Saskatoon, 1955.

B. G. Sack, *History of the Jews in Canada*; Montreal, 1965.

E. O. S. Scholefield and F. W. Howay, *British Columbia from the Earliest Times to the Present*; Chicago, Vancouver, 1914.

Joseph Schull, *Laurier: The First Canadian*; Toronto, 1965.

J. H. E. Secretan, *Canada's Great Highway*; London, 1924.

Lord Selkirk, *A Sketch of the British Fur Trade in North America*; London, 1816.

Paul Sharp, *Agrarian Revolt in Western Canada*; Minneapolis, 1948.

—— *When Our West Moved North*; *American Historical Review* publication, 1950.

—— *Whoop-Up Country*; Minneapolis, 1955.

George Shepherd, *West of Yesterday*; Toronto, 1964.

Irene Spry, *The Palliser Expedition*; Toronto, 1963.

G. F. G. Stanley, *The Birth of Western Canada*; Toronto, 1960.

—— *Louis Riel*; Toronto, 1963.

Wallace Stegner, *Wolf Willow*; New York, 1962.

G. R. Stevens, *Canadian National Railways*; Toronto, Vancouver, 1962.

L. H. Thomas, *The Struggle for Responsible Government in the North-West Territories*; Toronto, 1926.

L. N. Tucker, *Western Canada*; London, New York, 1908.

J. P. Turner, *The North-West Mounted Police*; Ottawa, 1950.

P. Turner Bone, *When the Steel Went Through*; London, 1947.

Walter Vaughan, *Sir William Van Horne*; vol. x of *Makers of Canada*; London, Toronto, 1926.

M. S. Wade, *The Overlanders of '62*; Victoria, 1931.

P. B. Waite, *The Life and Times of Confederation*; Toronto, 1962.

W. W. Walkem, *Stories of Early British Columbia*; Vancouver, 1914.

W. S. Wallace, ed., *Documents relating to the North-West Company*; Toronto, 1934.

John Warkentin, ed., *The Western Interior of Canada*; Toronto, 1964.

E. West, *Homesteading*; London, 1918.

C. Wetton, *The Promised Land*; Lloydminster, 1953.

—— *Historic Battleford*; 1955.

W. M. Whitelaw, *The Maritimes and Canada Before Confederation*; Toronto, 1934.

S. W. Wilk, *One Day's Journey*; Calgary, 1963.

Gerald Willoughby, *Retracing the Old Trail*; Saskatoon, n.d.

Beckles Willson, *The Great Company*; Toronto, 1899.

—— *Life of Lord Strathcona*; London, New York, Toronto, 1915.

R. W. Winks, *Canada and the United States: the Civil War Years*; Baltimore, 1960.

C. J. Woodsworth, *Canada and the Orient*; Toronto, 1941.

J. F. C. Wright, *Saskatchewan*; Toronto, 1955.

C. H. Young and H. R. Y. Reid, *The Japanese Canadians*; 1938.

George Young, *Manitoba Memories*; Toronto, 1897.

E. R. Young, *Apostle of the North, Rev. James Evans*; Toronto, 1900.

Paul Yusyk, *The Ukrainians in Manitoba*; Toronto, 1953.

J. P. Zubek and P. A. Solberg, *Doukhobors at War*; Toronto, 1952.

Index

286

287

290